THE LONG *and* SHORT OF IT

FROM MASTER STORYTELLER

TED FINK

THE LONG AND SHORT OF IT

Edited by Kim Grenfell
Cover Design and Formatting by The Book Khaleesi

CONTENTS

ALSO BY TED FINK

The Tales I've Told
Descent Into Darkness
Pebbles in the Fire
The Incident at Parkside
Game of the Gods
In Search of Joel Gomez

To all the artists out there
who are compelled to create.

Forward

About this collection of stories...

In 1983 I made an enormous mistake. I stuffed three novels, thirty short stories, twenty songs, and dozens of poems into an overnight bag and checked it onto a plane that my family and I were taking to Puerto Rico. That suitcase weighed fifty-five pounds. It was everything I had written over the past twenty years. Back then I used a typewriter, but I was a lousy typist. I could never get a clean-copy. And I had no back-up copies. My plan was to spend my three-week vacation sorting that work out, and to start sending out the ones I thought had merit to publishing houses, editors, agents and literary magazines. During that time I did sell three stories from a book I had written about the Philadelphia School System to The Philadelphia Inquirer. So as I sat on that flight to Puerto Rico I was excited to analyze what I had written. I was ready, ready to breakout and become the writer I dreamed of becoming.

BUT! ... the freakin' bag with all my freakin' stuff never came off the plane. GONE! Twenty years of work, fifty-five pounds of paper: the novels, the stories, songs, poems, screenplays never came off the freakin' plane. The only thing I got out of it was a great story called "Where's The Bag?" which I told for years as part of my storytelling repertoire at theaters, clubs, bars, festivals, and street corners. The story "Where's the Bag?", also called "It's Policy", can be found in my first published book, *The Tales I've Told.* An audio version can be heard on my website: tedfink.com

The loss of that bag had momentarily stopped me from writing, but fortunately, I'm a persistent cuss, and I'm a storyteller. And that's why I love writing. It's the telling of the tale. Actually, the computer is what saved me and got me started again. With my Mac,

I could get a clean copy and I could safely save what I had written. For me, it was an enormous gift. In my later years, starting in 2012, I was able to complete six books: five novels and a collection of my performance stories and narratives.

To my delight, these six books received many, many excellent (five star) reviews, which, for me, validated the work I had put in over the years to create them. And validation is what makes the artist. Each review generates the energy to keep telling the latest tale, or putting paint on the latest canvas. Personally I smile each time someone tells me they enjoyed one of my books.

When I finished my last novel, Descent Into Darkness, I felt I had reached the goal I had set for myself. A weird kind of contentment captivated me, and I was almost ready to call it a day in terms of writing—after all, I'm eighty-four and had considered myself retired—but that idea vanished when I found, scattered on my desktop computer, thirty-seven stories I'd written and had forgotten about. Over eleven hundred pages! All kinds of stuff in various genres: screenplays, poems, essays, etc. Most of these stories had been written after I lost the bag, created between 1984 and 2010. Tales for one reason or another I had never told in performance. I started reading through them, and got excited. It was like reading them anew. And just like that, I was back into the flow, and putting together my next book. So here is *The Long and Short of it:* Tales too short to be novels, and too long to be considered short stories. I hope you find them as interesting as I do.

This collection starts with a film script: *A Dog's Story*. If you've never read a film script, you are in for a treat. It's just another way to tell a story. It's easy to read and it's fun, because you, the reader, get to really use your imagination. In your head, you become the director, the set designer, the casting director; you see the sets, the background, and the actors.

Enjoy!

THE LONG OF IT

A Dog's Story

Registered with Writer's Guild

EXT. PHILADELPHIA - DAY - ESTABLISHING

We begin in Fairmount Park, one of the largest city parks in the world. The camera takes us through heavy woods and fields, down a hill, across an old set of railroad tracks, and down another hill to the West River Drive. The river is on our left as we head for the city. Across the Schuylkill River is Boat House Row, the waterworks, and the art museum. We head down Benjamin Franklin Boulevard and see City Hall and the statue of William Penn sitting on top.

Right from the beginning, we hear the voice of an elderly African American man.

VOICE OVER

I don't rightly know how to tell
this story, 'cause this here story
is a hard one to tell. And I would
only be willin' to tell it if you
let me tell it correctly, and to do
that, you gotta believe that animals
can communicate with each other.
Yes, that's right, they talk, just
like you and me. No, they don't
move their lips; it's more like
mental telepathy. How do I know?
Because I got the gift. I can hear
what dogs are thinking, and I think
they can hear me as well. Hell, I
been talking to and listening to
animals for years. And I got this

here story right from the dog it
happened to.

We go around City Hall and back up Franklin Boulevard, past the art museum and the Rocky Statue, and onto East River Drive. The river is now on our left.

EXT. PARKING LOT - DAY

RON DAVIS pulls into the parking lot of a little league baseball field, driving his pickup. The game has just ended. He grits his teeth, mildly upset that he missed it.

Kids and parents are walking to their cars.

He sees his son CLIFFORD (CLIFF) dejectedly walking from the field, and BEEPS his horn. Cliff looks up, nods without smiling, and walks to the car.

INT. CAR - DAY

RON

How's it going?

CLIFF

Aw. All right.

RON

What's the matter?

CLIFF

I don't know.

RON

No hits?

CLIFF
No. I went three for four. Got a stinkin' double.

RON
I told you I couldn't be there. I wish I—

CLIFF
It's not that.

RON
No? Then…

CLIFF
I don't know.

Ron pulls over to the side of the road. He turns off the engine and turns toward his son.

RON
Listen, maybe I never said this before, but I got your back. You can tell me anything. I'll always be in your corner, no matter what.

CLIFF
Well…

RON
Come on. Tell me.

CLIFF
Well, here's what happened.

FLASHBACK

EXT. BASEBALL FIELD - DAY

Cliff is at the plate. He smacks the ball in the gap between center and right. The center fielder chases it down. Cliff rounds the bases. ALVIE JONES, the second baseman, is waiting for the ball.

RON (V.O.)
I'm listening.

CLIFF (V.O.)
It was on the double. I slide into
second. This kid, Alvie Jones, is
playing second base.

Cliff slides into second. He is clearly safe. Moments later, the ball is caught by Alvie, who turns and, with the ball in his glove, bangs Cliff viciously on the side of the head.

CLIFF (V.O.) (CONT'D)
I slide in, and I'm clearly safe, and
as I'm getting up, he gets the ball
and he bangs me on the side of the head.

END FLASHBACK

RON
What?

CLIFF
Yeah, it's not like he was putting
on the tag, he just whacks me with
the ball—hard.

RON
Are you okay?

CLIFF
Yeah.

RON
What did Mr. Jacobs do?

CLIFF
He said something, but Alvie just said he was trying to tag me. But I know it was more.

Ron stares at his son.

RON
Do you want me to talk to his father? I don't particularly like the guy, but I know him.

CLIFF
No. But I feel that I should have done something.

RON
Are you afraid of him?

CLIFF
No. Well, I don't know. Maybe? Alvie's kind of crazy.

RON
Has this happened before?

CLIFF
No. Not really. I don't know. I just stay out of his way, do you

know what I mean?

RON
Listen, let's chalk this one up to
an accident, but understand this:
I don't want you to ever let
someone hurt you. Do you understand?
Don't go looking for trouble,
but don't let anyone ever hurt you.

Ron starts the car.

CLIFF
But—

RON
No buts.

Ron maneuvers the car back onto the road.

RON (CONT'D)
Now, I got a surprise for you. First,
we're gonna pick up Mom and Sis.

CLIFF
What is it?

RON
It's a drive, but I think you're
gonna like this.

EXT. A COUNTY ROAD - DAY

Ron is driving the family car. His wife, CLEO, is in the front passenger seat. Cliff and his older sister, MISSY, are in the back.

CLEO
What a day! Glorious.

CLIFF
Yo, Dad, what's the story? Where are we going? How long is—?

MISSY
Can't you just ever sit back and relax?

CLIFF
I have a report due tomorrow, and my favorite show is on tonight.

RON
Dude, it won't be much longer.

Missy laughs, then her mouth drops open.

MISSY
You're calling him "dude" now?

RON
What's wrong with that?

MISSY
That is a total oxymoron.

CLIFF
That is exactly what you are, less the "oxy."

CLEO
Can we have a little less hostility here?

MISSY
I was just kidding.

CLIFF
Yeah, me too.

CLEO
I wasn't.

RON
We're here.

He makes a right onto a large, fenced-in piece of property, drives down a road leading to an Amish farmhouse.

CLEO
What a beautiful farm. Whose place is this?

RON
His name is Jonathan Hartman. He and his sons are fantastic carpenters. I use them to frame out a lot of my stuff.

CLIFF
We're going to a farm? Dad, I don't want to milk a cow.

MISSY
It might be a rewarding experience.

EXT. THE HARTMAN FARM - DAY

Sitting on the front porch is JONATHAN HARTMAN, tall, slim, bearded, dressed in Amish-style clothes. He is seated in a rocking chair, but when he sees the car, he stands, waves, and walks to meet them. The Davis family exits the car.

HARTMAN
It is good to see you, Ronald.

RON
And you, Jonathan.

Hartman formally shakes hands with everyone. Cliff is the last.

HARTMAN
Have you ever seen a litter of Curlies, Clifford?

CLIFF
Huh?

HARTMAN
Not many people have. They're a rare breed.

He begins walking to the picket fence, an area behind the main house.

HARTMAN (CONT'D)
But they are an old breed. Goes back to 1805.
Bred for the aristocracy of England.

CLIFF
What are they, some kind of cow?

Hartman laughs out loud, and opens the gate of the picket fence. Once everyone is inside the area, he whistles. Within seconds, two adult, solid black CURLY-COATED RETRIEVERS come running out of a shed located in the back part of the yard. They are followed by NINE eight-week-old PUPPIES. Everyone laughs in delight.

Cliff's mouth drops open.

CLIFF (CONT'D)
They're dogs!

Suddenly, the group is surrounded by Curlies. Each puppy weighs about 20 lbs. and has a different colored collar to tell them apart. Cliff bends down to pet one, but they knock him over, and then jump on him, taking turns at licking his face. He laughs with delight. Missy laughs.

MISSY
I'm jealous!

She lies down on the ground and the dogs playfully jump on her.

Ron looks at the dogs. One stands out from all the others.

RON
Look at that one. The one with the red collar.
He's enormous.

HARTMAN
Yes, he's a giant. He's going to be a big boy.

Hartman bends down and picks up the big, red-collared puppy, who has pushed the others out of the way and is kissing Cliff. Hartman holds the pup at arm's length.

HARTMAN (CONT'D)
Ronald, this is the dog I think is for you. He's
a tall boy, a big boy. He'll grow to be at least 120 lbs.

Missy and Cliff get up and shout in unison

MISSY/CLIFF
Are you getting him, Dad?

Ron holds the puppy at arm's length and looks into his eyes.

RON
Yeah, I think this is our boy.

MISSY/CLIFF
YES!

HARTMAN
You treat that boy right and he'll never stop lovin' you. Of all the pups, that one is a lover.

INT. CAR - DAY

On the ride home from the Hartman farm. The pup is in the back seat, sleeping between Missy and Cliff.

MISSY
What are you going to name him, Dad?

RON
I don't know. Got any ideas?

MISSY
Well, Mr. Hartman said his sire was from Australia. If it was a girl, we could name her Barbie. You know, put—

CLIFF
A burger on the "barbie."

RON
That was very good.

CLIFF
But he's not a girl.

CLEO
I like the idea of using an Australian… Hey, what about Wallaby?

CLIFF
I kinda like that.

MISSY
What about Wally? Just plain old Wally?

CLIFF
Yeah, Sis! That's it. It's perfect. Red Wally. What do you think, Dad?

SERIES OF SHOTS

EXT. REAR DECK OF THE DAVIS HOME - DAY

One week later. Ron is sleeping in a lounge chair and WALLY, bigger than before, is lying on his chest, sleeping as well.

INT. RON'S PICKUP - DAY
Ron is driving. Wally is sitting in the passenger seat, looking out the window. Radio blaring. Wally has grown.

EXT. GRAVEL TRAIL - DAY

Ron and Wally are walking down the trail through the woods.

They come to a narrow stream where DUCKS are basking in the sun and swimming. Wally sees them and goes charging down the bank and jumps into the water. The ducks swim away from him. He goes after them. When he is in deep water, the drakes turn on him and start pecking his head. Confused, he starts to go under. Laughingly, Ron has to go in and pull him out.

EXT. REAR DECK OF THE DAVIS HOME - DAY

The deck is twenty feet off the ground and looks out onto the woods, a hundred yards in the distance. Wally is staring out into the woods. There is a deer in the clearing. Ron approaches.

RON

Yeah, boy, someday all this is gonna be yours.

EXT. A CONSTRUCTION SITE – DAY

Ron is at a makeshift workbench, studying blueprints. Wally is sitting at his side. GEORGE, head carpenter, approaches. Wally stands. He puts his snout in the man's crotch. George laughs and tries to get him away. Wally is persistent. George holds up his hands as if to say "What?"

RON

He's not a watchdog, he's a crotch dog.

George laughs.

GEORGE

I'm glad he just didn't come out of a puddle of water.

RON

Actually, he just had his snout in

some gopher hole.

George jumps back and looks down at his pants.

RON (CONT'D)

Gotcha!

INT. CLIFF'S BEDROOM - NIGHT

Ron opens the door and peeks in. Cliff is asleep. Wally is sleeping next to his bed. Ron motions for Wally to come. Wally doesn't move. Ron smiles, nods, and shuts the door.

INT. CLIFF'S BEDROOM - DAY

Ron opens the door. He is dressed for work. Wally and Cliff are still sleeping. Wally opens his eyes. Ron whispers.

RON

Let's go to work.

Wally immediately jumps up and leaves the room.

EXT. OLGA'S DINER - DAY

Ron pulls up in front of the diner. Wally is standing in the truck bed. MIKE NEMAN approaches.

MIKE

Hey, Ron, how you doin'?

They shake hands. Mike pats Wally's head. George comes out of Olga's, holding a paper cup of coffee.

MIKE (CONT'D)
What a great looking dog.

GEORGE
Yeah, real great, and you should see the way he says hello.

MIKE
What is he?

RON
He's a full-blooded curly-coated retriever.

George gets in his car.

GEORGE
I'll see you at the site.

Ron and Mike walk into the restaurant.

INT. OLGA'S DINER - DAY

Ron and Mike are seated at a table, looking out onto the parking lot. Ron sees Alvie Jones standing by the truck, teasing Wally. Ron knocks on the window, and Alvie looks around and sees him. Ron motions for him to stop. Alvie stares at him, then sullenly walks away.

MIKE
Boy, that kid is something else.

RON
Who is he?

MIKE
Alvie. I think he's Sam Jones' kid. Sam's not a bad guy, but the kid is just plain mean.

Ron just nods.

EXT. FAIRMOUNT PARK - DAY

A large, grassy field. Wally is seated, staring intently, anxious, almost shaking in anticipation as Ron rears back and throws a Frisbee. Cliff is at his side. Wally immediately runs after it. His strides are magnificent. Suddenly he leaps high, at least seven feet in the air, and catches it.

CLIFF
Oh my God! Did you see that?

RON
Unbelievable.

Wally comes to them and drops the Frisbee at their feet.
Cliff pats his head.

CLIFF
He's amazing.

Ron pats his head.

RON
He's my boy.

CLIFF
Hey, I thought I was your boy?

Ron laughs, puts his arm around Cliff's shoulder, and they begin to walk back to the truck.

RON
That is correct. And you are my son, my best son, my number one son.

CLIFF
I'm your only son.

RON
That is correct. And you are my boy, my best boy, my number one boy. Wally's number two.

Ron looks down, but Wally's not at his side. He looks back, and Wally is still sitting where they had been, with the Frisbee in his mouth. Ron laughs.

RON (CONT'D)
Hey, number two, the game's over. Let's go!

Wally reluctantly trots after them. At that moment, a MAN and WOMAN appear in the clearing. When they see Wally, they freeze, frightened by his size.

RON (CONT'D)
Not to worry. This dog loves everybody. He wouldn't hurt a fly.

The couple relaxes as Wally ambles to them and sticks his snout in the man's crotch.

CLIFF
Yeah, he's not a watchdog, he's a crotch dog.

The couple laugh. Ron smiles down at Cliff.

CLIFF (CONT'D)
I thought I'd beat you to it.

EXT. OLGA'S DINER - PARKING LOT - DAY

Ron pulls in. Wally is in the flatbed. This morning, the lot is full. Ron circles the diner, looking for a spot, and finds one on the side of building. He exits the vehicle and walks to the entrance. He takes a seat at the counter.

EXT. STREET LEADING TO OLGA'S DINER - DAY

Alvie Jones and ERNEST HAWES are walking past the diner. Alvie sees Ron's pickup and Wally. They are pulling a red wagon.

ALVIE
Want to have some fun?

ERNEST
Yeah.

They go to the truck. Alvie has a rope in the wagon. Wally greets the boys affectionately. They tie the rope to Wally's collar, put down the back flatbed flap, and pull Wally off. Wally is confused but follows the boys as they pull him into the woods behind the diner.

EXT. THE WOODS - DAY

They take a path through the woods that leads to a deserted paved lane. An old work road. They begin to run, Alvie leading Wally, Ernest pulling the wagon.

ERNEST

Where we goin'?

ALVIE

To Bucky's Hill

ERNEST

We better get this dog back.

ALVIE

Don't you want to see him fly?

Alvie stops.

Alvie's P.O.V. The lane descends steeply and narrows.

ALVIE (CONT'D)

Bring me that wagon.

ERNEST

What are you gonna do?

Alvie takes the wagon and tugs on the rope holding Wally.

ALVIE

Get in.

Wally is confused.

ALVIE (CONT'D)

Get in, stupid.

Still holding the rope he lifts Wally's front paws into the wagon. Wally gets in the wagon. Alvie ties his end of the rope to the handle of the wagon, then pushes the wagon down the hill.

With Wally sitting in the wagon, the thing careens down the hill, picking up speed as it goes.

WALLY

Aaaaaaaaaaaah!

The wagon flies down the road and finally rams into a telegraph pole. Wally is flung forward and slams, head-first, into the pole. The force of the collision snaps the rope that is holding him and he is thrown to the ground. He manages to get to his feet and, in a daze, staggers into the woods. After a few moments, he drops to the ground.

EXT. THE WOODS - NIGHT

The moon shines on the spot where Wally has fallen. He has not moved. His eyes open, then quickly shut.

EXT. THE WOODS - DAY

Wally has still not moved, but sounds and movement in the forest alert him. His eyes open and he moves his head slightly in the direction of the movement. His front legs begin to shake with fear, but he cannot stand.

Out of the woods appears an old dog. She is of medium size. She has some shepherd in her. There is a white dot over each eye. This dog is known as KIT.

Kit immediately stops and points toward Wally.

KIT

There.

Out of the woods come five more dogs. They approach with

caution. A spotted dog called Monte growls and sniffs Wally. Monte has a bit of a British accent.

MONTE
What do you think happened to him?

A short, deep-brown male with a pushed-in face, broken bottom jaw, and an under bite that touches his snout, wheezes. He sits on his haunches and sniffs the air. His name is EDDIE G.

EDDIE G
Probably hit by a car.

MONTE
Poor kid. He's just a bloomin' puppy, is all.

Kit moves closer and sniffs his head.

KIT
He's alive, but barely. What do
you think we should do with him?

EDDIE G
Now listen here, we have no time
for this, see. Don't go feelin'
sorry for him. He's a goner, see.
We gotta think of ourselves.

There is a mean growl and the pack moves aside to make room for BUTCH, a huge pit bull, to examine the situation. He takes one look at Wally and begins to walk away.

BUTCH
Eddie's right. He's done for. Let's go.

KIT
It's not right. He's huge. Look
at those legs. I bet he can run.

BUTCH
That dog will never run again. Let's go!
It'll be full daylight soon.

KIT
He's just stunned, is all. Look at his chest. He's
breathing without strain.

The pack begins to follow Butch. But Kit doesn't move.

KIT (CONT'D)
I'm going to stay with him. You guys go on ahead.
I'll catch up. I just can't leave him here.

Kit sits down next to Wally and watches the pack as they disappear into the forest.

VOICE OVER
Wally didn't know why at the time,
but he would always be grateful
that Kit stayed with him. Maybe
he reminded her of a dog she knew a
long time ago. He couldn't ask,
but it didn't matter.

Kit begins to lick his wounds.

VOICE OVER (CONT'D)
All he knew was she took care of
him, licking his wounds and making
him feel safe and somewhat secure

through the day and when night fell.

EXT. THE WOODS - NIGHT

The moon is full and bright. The sky is starlit and bright. The night shimmers. Kit is still next to Wally, guarding him. He drifts in and out of consciousness, mumbling.

WALLY

Fr…is…bee. Fr…is…bee.

Kit looks at him.

KIT

Is that your name, dear? Is Frisbee what they call you?

Wally opens his eyes and tries to answer.

VOICE OVER

But he couldn't remember what he had been called. He couldn't remember anything and was too hurt to try. He was just grateful she was still there, and once again, he closed his eyes and fell back to sleep.

EXT. THE WOODS - DAY

Early morning. Wally opens his eyes and sees Kit standing close by. He struggles to his feet.

VOICE OVER

His legs were shaking when he got to his feet and his head still hurt, but at that moment, something hurt worse. It was his stomach. He hadn't eaten or drank anything for over three days. He was starving and needed water.

Wally, on shaky legs, follows Kit, who leads him to a clear running brook. He enters the stream and lies down in the shallows. Kit watches as Wally submerges and then drinks heavily.

VOICE OVER (CONT'D)
Yeah, old Kit knew what he needed. The water was glorious, and it was miraculous, for it invigorated him.

Wally leaves the pool, shakes off the water, and sees Kit is waiting at the edge with a morsel of food. He eats it quickly, then follows her as she leads him to a grassy glen where he once again lies down and falls asleep.

INT. RON'S OFFICE - DAY

Ron is standing by a computer watching as it kicks out copies.

INSERT: Printed poster. LOST DOG in caps and a picture of Wally.

INT. KITCHEN - DAVIS HOME - DAY

Ron enters. Cliff is at the table. He looks up.

CLIFF
Did you make them, Dad?

RON
Yeah. Here they are. We'll put

these up tomorrow.

CLIFF
Do you think there's a chance? It's been almost a week.

RON
We're gonna find him.

EXT. THE WOODS - DAY

It is late in the day. Kit is standing over Wally as he opens his eyes.

KIT
It's time to go.

WALLY
Where?

KIT
To join the pack. Follow me.

Wally gets to his feet and follows her into the woods.

EXT. THE CAMP - DAY

Just as morning comes, Wally and Kit approach a rocky ridge and the mouth of a cave. Kit stops and turns to Wally.

KIT
Be careful of Butch. He's one mean dog. Stand still and let him do his thing. The others are all right, I can handle them. But Butch is bad. He's ninety percent pit bull and ten percent snake.

As they climb the ridge, a sentry dog stands and growls. Other dogs come to the precipice and stare down. Kit barks and they come down to greet her.

VOICE OVER
The pack wasn't in a very pleasant mood that day and it was easy to see why. Plain and simple: they were starving. Not a single one of them had an extra pound on them, and there wasn't a single dog whose rib cage couldn't be seen.

Angrily, the pack circles Wally. SERGIO, a spotted, pointy-nosed dog, approaches.

SERGIO
Who's dis? What's his name?

KIT
I think he calls himself Frisbee.

They look at Wally with sullen, angry eyes.

VOICE OVER
Yeah, they looked at him mean, and they looked at his size and they thought about how much they'd have to give up if he stayed. But his stayin' wasn't up to them. It was up to the leader of the pack, and that dog was Butch.

Butch comes out of the cave and looks down at the pack and Wally. Growling, he immediately races down the crest, his back hairs

stiffened. Wally stands still, submissive. Butch circles the big dog. Now he shows his teeth and is about
to attack.

KIT
Easy, Butch.

BUTCH
He ain't nothin'! What'd you bring him here for?

KIT
We need him.

EDDIE G
He's just a puppy, see. All he's gonna do is chase the falling leaves. What do we need a puppy for?

BUTCH
I don't like him.

EDDIE G
How we gonna feed him?

MONTE
We can barely feed ourselves.

KIT
I got a plan.

BUTCH
I don't like him.

MONTE
What's the plan?

BUTCH
It better be good.

The pack gathers around Kit.

KIT
As soon as he's well, we're gonna get those ducks...

VOICE OVER
While the pack was planning their attack, across town, another dog's life was about to change.

ESTABLISHING

EXT. PHILADELPHIA CONVENTION HALL - DAY

INT. CENTER RING OF THE PHILADELPHIA DOG SHOW - DAY

It is the final round of the show and the dogs and their handlers are prancing around the ring. BELLA DONNA MARIE, a light brown Basenji with a white chest is being led by JACK WOTHERS.

Suddenly, Bella stops and sits.

INT. T.V. BOOTH - DAY

RONALD WELLINGTON, the T.V. announcer, is calling the event for NBC.

T.V. ANNOUNCER
Oh no. That's bad. A dog is absolutely not allowed to sit on the floor.

INT. CENTER RING OF THE PHILADELPHIA DOG SHOW - DAY

This absolute no-no is reflected in the faces of the judges. A trace of anger shoots across Jack Wothers' face. He tries to recover by coaxing her, and reluctantly she proceeds.

INT. GROOMING TABLES. DOG SHOW - DAY

Wothers is steaming. He is approached by HENRY BITTLE, Bella's owner.

BITTLE
What the hell happened?

WOTHERS
Did you see what she did?

BITTLE
That's why I'm standing here.

WOTHERS
We had it won, and she just stops dead. I've had it with her.

Bittle bends down and lifts up Bella. The dog licks his face.

BITTLE
Bella, my beauty, what's wrong girl? Are you unhappy, little dumpling? What am I going to do with you?

Wothers is still fuming.

WOTHERS
I'll tell you what I'm gonna do with her!

Bittle turns and stares at Wothers.

BITTLE
You're gonna treat her with love and affection. Maybe that's what's wrong.

Bittle stares at Wothers.

BITTLE (CONT'D)
I'm going to get the car.

Bittle begins to walk away. Wothers waits until he is gone and sneers at Bella.

WOTHERS
Are you unhappy, little dumpling? Hm? I hope so, because I'm unhappy!

EXT. THE WOODS - DAY

It is late in the day. The pack begins to stir.

VOICE OVER
This pack was not united by blood. There was no common ancestry that ran through their veins. Throwaways, runaways, lost an' lonelies had somehow found each other and were now united in an attempt to stay alive. And they were not doing well.

Monte, the Old English sheepdog stands and limps over to nudge Eddie G. Huffing and puffing, Eddie gets to his feet. He sounds as if he's always tired.

VOICE OVER (CONT'D)
They were long on gray and short on young legs. They had come together by chance and stayed together out of necessity.

MONTE
You okay, old bean?

EDDIE G
I was just thinking about the good old days. I gave up the best years of my life for my guy, see, only to be kicked unceremoniously out of the house by his new wife who said I slobbered, was ugly, and would pass wind whenever she came into the room.

MONTE
Yeah, old bean, our best years are behind us.

Sergio is listening.

SERGIO
Hey, amigo, did you really fart when she came in?

EDDIE G
Absolutely. But I'm always fartin', see. It's my nature, see. It's

part of my charm.

Eddie shakes his head and lets fly a billow of white saliva. Then, to the delight of all, he followed up with a boisterous, obnoxious, malodorous puff of anal wind.

SERGIO
How'd they get rid of you?

EDDIE G
One day, he asks her to take me for a walk, see. So she puts me in the car, see—the new one that he got for her—and she drives me to the woods and walks me down a trail. Then she takes off the leash, and kicks me in the ass, and runs off.

SERGIO
And you couldn't catch her?

EDDIE G
Sure, I coulda caught her. But at that point in my life, I didn't want to.

Eddie clamps his jaw together so that his protruding tooth touches his nose.

EDDIE G (CONT'D)
I had paid my dues, see. I was there six years before she ever came on the scene. We were good friends. I was sure he'd come back for me. Waited there till nightfall,

thinkin' he would come and then when I knew he wasn't comin', I just wandered, see, wandered away.

SERGIO
With me, they just threw me out of a speeding car. They were high on something. I was in the back with one of my master's friends and he just threw me out the window.

MONTE
Really?

SERGIO
They didn't even slow down. My master was in the front. He must have been real mad when he found out.

BUTCH
Master! Master! Are we their slaves? Are we? When are you punks gonna learn? They knew what they were doin' when they tossed you.

Butch leans down and growls in Sergio's face.

BUTCH (CONT'D)
They got rid of you 'cause you're a wimp! (Beat) Masters!

SERGIO
That's not right, amigo.

BUTCH
Yeah, well, let's see... You come from Spanish town, isn't that right, Ser-gee-ooo? That's one tough section of the city. My guess is they didn't want a dog that would back down; a dog like you, that wouldn't fight.

SERGIO
I'll fight, Butch.

Butch backs up two steps and snarls.

BUTCH
Are you challenging me? You dirty, stinkin' son of a flea-bitten taco!

SERGIO
No, amigo, I don't want to fight you.

Butch immediately stops.

BUTCH
See? See what I mean? They threw you out the window because you were a chicken. You backed off when you were challenged. Admit it, isn't that what happened?

SERGIO
You're right, amigo, that's probably what happened.

BUTCH
Not probably.

Butch sits down and relaxes.

BUTCH (CONT'D)
Yeah, I know about Spanish town. It's a tough town. I once fought a fight there that lasted fifteen minutes.

Kit turns to Wally.

KIT
Butch used to be a professional fighter.

BUTCH
Yeah, that's right kid. Eddie G spent the best year of his life fartin', and I spent the best years of my life fightin'. I hit every town where big money fights were held. Tucson, Memphis. Fought in all the shit-sheds from Brick Town to the big arenas in New York City. Do you know how many dogs I've killed?

WALLY
Why'd they let you go?

BUTCH
They didn't let me go, pup. I ran. One day, I lost a fight. Got tore up pretty bad. The only one I ever lost. Could barely walk. And my

"M A S T E R" comes in after the fight and beats me up some more for losin'. I crawled out the window that very night and left that son of an Adam's apple on his own.

KIT

It's time.

In single file, the pack follows Kit as she leads them into the woods. They move slowly and quietly through the brush until they come to the Wissahickon Creek. Then she goes to Wally and motions him to swim across the water to the other side. Wally goes into the water and begins to swim across.

KIT (CONT'D)

Look at that boy swim.

The pack watches Wally until he reaches the other side, and then they move off along the bank. Both Wally and the pack are moving in the same direction on opposite sides of the creek.

Ahead of them, a flush of ducks is resting along the same side of the river Wally is on. Some are in the water, but most are on the shore.

Suddenly, Wally rushes down the bank. The startled birds race to the water. Wally plunges in after them. They begin to swim to the other side of the creek, where the pack is waiting.

EXT. THE WOODS - DAY

It is FALL. Leaves are turning and beginning to drop.

EXT. A HUGE STONE MANSION IN CHESTNUT HILL, PHILA. - DAY

The house has many acres that foot into Fairmount Park. The grounds are vast. The sun is beginning to set. A limo pulls up into the circular driveway, and Bittle steps out, carrying an empty dog crate. Bella is walking on a leash beside him. They walk to the house.

INT. BITTLE MANSION - NIGHT

The house is magnificent—marble floors, expensive rugs and furniture. A huge staircase leads to the second floor. Bittle is at his desk in his study. On the floor, sleeping peacefully, is Bella. Bittle yawns, then looks down at Bella and smiles.

BITTLE
Okay, Bella. Time to go to sleep.
Get in your crate.

Bella looks at him.

BITTLE (CONT'D)
Come on. Get in. We can't have
you messing up the place.

Reluctantly, Bella gets up and enters the crate.

EXT. THE BITTLE ESTATE - DAY

Wothers is carrying the crate with Bella in it out to the grooming table behind the house. Bella is sullen. He leaves, then returns to Bella's cage with a plate of food. He stares at Bella in disgust. He opens the cage door and puts the dish inside.

WOTHERS
Don't think I've forgiven what you did.

Bella, whose head is resting on her paws, hears him and stares disinterestedly at the food. She doesn't move. Wothers shuts the door to the cage, but it doesn't lock and remains slightly ajar. He reaches forward to shut the door when at that moment his cell phone RINGS. He answers it and turns away. When he turns back, Bella is gone. He whirls around, looking for her, but she is nowhere to be seen.

WOTHERS (CONT'D)
Bellllaaa! Damn you!

EXT. REAR FENCE OF THE BITTLE ESTATE - DAY

Bella is digging a hole under the fence. She crawls under the fence and heads for the woods.

EXT. THE WOODS - DAY

The pack is lying around contentedly, well fed for the first time in weeks. Feathers and bones are scattered as the dogs sleep.

Wally lifts an eyebrow and sniffs the air. Sergio, ever on the alert, also looks up. Kit stands and stares as Bella struts into the camp. Butch comes down from his mound of rocks and gently sniffs her.

BUTCH
Now, what the hell are we gonna do with you?

Bella silently looks at him with her big brown eyes.

BUTCH (CONT'D)
Sorry, sister, you can't stay here.

WALLY
How come, Butch?

Butch stares at Wally, but remains calm.

BUTCH

Why? Well, pup, open your eyes and learn. Because she got a pretty little ribbon in her fur, she has tags, she's been combed out for a parade, a stroll down the Champs Elysees. This is one little girl that they'll come looking for. Unlike you and me, this little baby cost some change. She'll lead the authorities right to us.

WALLY

What authorities? What's "authorities"?

EDDIE G

Now listen to me Fris, Butch is right, see. They'll follow her scent right here, see. They're the men in the white coats. They get you in their nets and haul you away to a holding pen and lock you up in a cage. It's a horrible place, see, a terrible place. Every dog screamin' to be let out, see, pleadin' to be free.

MONTE

That's right, Fris. I spent some time there. Pulled two short stretches for pissin' on the sidewalk, so to speak. Got caught

with my snout in the wrong trash
cans, if you can imagine that.
But it's not as bad as Eddie makes
it sound, especially if you're
young and got a chance to get
adopted. They give you three
squares a day, they do. The only
problem is the accommodations are
cold and damp, and it's always the
same four walls you're lookin' at.
It's the lack of freedom that
drives you crazy.

BELLA
I know. I know exactly what you
mean.

All the dogs stare at her.

KIT
She looks fast, Butch, and things
have been good.

BUTCH
She can't hunt with them tags
a-jingling.

KIT
I could chew them right off, Butch,
quick as spit. It's only a leather
collar.

BUTCH
She's too dainty. Look at her,
will you? What do you think she's

gonna bite?

MONTE
What was your breed bred for, little darlin'?

BUTCH
Could you use those little teeth to bite something if you had to, little darlin'?

Bella stares at him and snarls.

BELLA
Yes, I believe I could bite something if I had to.

VOICE OVER
It was amazing how calm Butch was on a full stomach.

BELLA
And sir, if you took this collar off, I bet I could catch more squirrels and mice than you could shake a bone at.

Every dog thinks this incredibly amusing.

KIT
I like her spunk, Butch.

Butch is dumbfounded. His mouth drops open.

BUTCH
You mean you want to stay ... with us?

BELLA
Yes. I believe I do.

BUTCH
It's no easy life. No buttons and bows.

BELLA
I can see that.

BUTCH
Okay, I believe it's a mistake, but ... we'll chew off that collar tonight, and tomorrow, we'll see what you can do. If you can catch us dinner, you can stay. I'll send a couple of boys out to cover your trail, and hope for the best. But if you don't make it, then you won't have a collar, no means of ID, and you'll be put out on the road.

BELLA
How many for dinner?

INT. THE BITTLE MANSION STUDY - DAY

Bittle is at his desk. Wothers has his head down. Bittle is furious.

BITTLE
What? You've lost Bella? How the hell did you do that?

WOTHERS
I don't know. I'll put up fliers. We'll search the woods. She can't be far.

EXT. THE CAMP - NIGHT

Bella is sitting calmly as Kit gnaws off her collar. The collar drops to the ground.

EXT. THE CAMP - DAY

VOICE OVER

The next morning, Bella left the pack silently and, with an air of confidence, she headed into the woods. She wasn't gone more than a half-hour before she returned and, to everyone's delight, she had a white-bellied field mouse in her jaws. She strutted into the camp and dropped it at Butch's paws. Without saying a word, she turned and went back to her hunting. She kept bringing in the mice and dropping them at the feet of different dogs. Well before noon, she had caught enough little critters to feed everyone, except Wally.

It is late in the day when Bella next returns, and this time she has, not an itsy-bitsy mouse, but a big fat rabbit. This incredible, delectable meal she drops at the paws of Wally.

Butch sees the prize and strolls over to snatch the rabbit, when the rest of the pack stands in defiance. To the surprise of all, he turns and walks away.

SERIES OF SHOTS

EXT. THE WOODS - DAY

Wothers and several men are walking through the woods, searching. Their search is futile.

EXT. GERMANTOWN AVE - SHOPPING DISTRICT - DAY

Wothers is taping Bella's picture on a storefront. He walks up the street and pins another flyer on a billboard by the train station.

EXT. CHESTNUT HILL AVE - ENTRANCE TO PARK - DAY

Wothers is posting another picture of Bella. This time, he pins it over an existing but fading picture of Wally.

EXT. THE CAMP - DAY

The pack is resting contentedly. Bella looks at Wally, who is snoozing with his head on his paws. She gets up, goes over, and lies down next to him. He opens his eyes. He sees her near him and, thinking nothing of it, goes back to sleep. But Butch sees it, and from his perch, stares down at them.

VOICE OVER

What I have learned in my life is that food makes you content. The hunting was good. The duck and geese raids always reaped rewards. Bella taught the other ladies, Spot and Kit, the art of trapping field mice. The rib cages that were so prominent just weeks before seemed to be vanishing. Times were so good that they even started playing a game. Monte taught it to them.

It was called "stick."

Monte goes into the woods and returns holding a STICK in his mouth the size of a policeman's billy. He carries it into camp and drops it in the middle of the ring.

MONTE
Ladies and gentlemen, can I interest you in a game of "stick"?

VOICE OVER
To his astonishment, no one had ever heard of it.

MONTE
You might know it as "tug."

VOICE OVER
It seemed incredulous to him that not a single dog in the pack knew of this game.

SERGIO
How's it played?

MONTE
It's very simple, my friend. One dog takes one end of the stick and another dog takes the other. First one who lets go, loses.

EDDIE G
That's no fair. I can't hold on to no stick. Not with my bad bite.

MONTE

Then you, my friend, shall be the referee.

EDDIE G

What are the rules?

MONTE

Well, this is a game, so there can't be any real anger. No biting. Sportsmanship is key. And no hard feelings afterward.

Monte picks up the stick.

MONTE (CONT'D)

Anybody game?

Sergio grabs the other end of the stick, and the game is on.

VOICE OVER

It was a tug of war, and although there was plenty of growling, it was all good-natured stuff. They pulled and tugged and ran, trying to get the other dog to relinquish the stick. It was quite a match, which Sergio eventually won, and quite a sight to see, with Eddie G running around between the two as the referee. Everyone had a good time.

Kit and Spot are next to have a go at it, and although the match didn't last as long, it was still good sport.

Then Butch saunters down to the center of the circle from his perch on the high rocks and picks up the stick. He looks around the pack, then goes over to Wally and puts the stick in his face.

BUTCH
Don't worry, pup, it's only a game.

VOICE OVER
So Wally grabs it. And as soon as
he does, Butch pulls hard and drags
him into the center of the ring,
growling, but Wally ignored the
growl, because he knew Butch
couldn't bite, not unless he wanted
to lose, and Butch wanted to win.

Butch drags Wally left and right. Wally can't get his feet planted. It's as if Butch is toying with him.

But then, using all his strength, Wally anchors himself and slowly but surely begins pulling Butch into the center of the circle. Eddie G is right with them, barking and farting and huffing and puffing and having a grand old time. He cautions them not to show anger.

EDDIE G
You bite him, you lose!

Then Butch starts shaking his head violently, and suddenly the stick breaks. Each of them are holding a piece in their mouths.

EDDIE G (CONT'D)
It's a tie!

VOICE OVER
Everyone agreed it was a tie.

Butch dropped his stick and walked slowly away. He stopped once before he reached his perch and looked back at Wally with a strange light in his eye.

EXT. THE CAMP - NIGHT

Just as the sun goes down, Monte comes to Wally and sits by him.

MONTE
I like you, Fris, and I hope you won't mind if I offer you some words of wisdom. A game is a game, and that's all well and good, but you've got to be careful when you're dealing with a dog like Butch. You've got to be smart. You've got to always be thinking.

WALLY
What do you mean, Monte?

MONTE
Well, at the end of the game between you and Butch, he dropped his stick, but you held on to yours. If he attacked you, you wouldn't have been able to defend yourself. You can't defend yourself when you got a stick in your mouth, see what I mean?

WALLY
But it was a game.

MONTE
Kid, use your head. I like your spunk and I don't want to see you get hurt. If we play the game again, don't you play with Butch, and if you do have to play with him, let him win.

WALLY
But—

MONTE
No buts. And remember this: if you ever get in a fight with him—

WALLY
But I don't want to fight him.

Monte becomes impatient.

MONTE
Will you listen to me, please! Pay attention. Someday you may have to fight Butch. It's ... well, it may be inevitable, and when that happens—and I pray it won't—don't expect any mercy. And remember this: if you ever get in a fight with him, don't let him get to your neck. That neck grip of his is a killer.

EXT. CENTER CITY, PHILADELPHIA - CITY HALL - ESTABLISHING

INT. MAYOR'S OFFICE - DAY

Mayor JOHN REYNOLDS is at his desk. In front of him is HARDY COLLINS, city commissioner. The intercom on the mayor's desk buzzes, and he flicks the switch.

REYNOLDS
Marge, I told you no calls.

MARGE
I know, sir. But this is important. Henry Bittle is in your office and needs a moment of your time.

Reynolds raises his eyebrows and is a little more than surprised.

REYNOLDS
Really? In the office? Send him in.

Both men stand as Bittle enters the office. They shake hands. Reynolds offers Bittle a seat, but he declines.

BITTLE
No, thank you, John. I know you're busy so I won't take much of your time. This may sound trivial, but I've lost my dog.

REYNOLDS
Oh, I'm sorry. Where? When?

BITTLE
Somewhere in the park, a little more than a week ago.

COLLINS
The park? That's several thousand acres.

BITTLE
I know. But I want her back.

COLLINS
Have you posted a reward?

BITTLE
I have, to no avail.

REYNOLDS
Is it that cute little dog I met at that reception you held at your estate several months ago?

BITTLE
It is.

Reynolds frowns, concerned.

REYNOLDS
Henry, I don't want to bring you down, but the park could be a dangerous place for a small dog. In certain areas it is extremely wild. Fox, coyote.

BITTLE
John, I'm aware of that. But if you find my Bella, you won't have to worry about that school financing problem you're up against.

Reynolds studies him.

REYNOLDS
I'll do what I can.

Bittle sadly nods. They shake hands. He leaves. He picks up his phone as soon as Bittle leaves.

REYNOLDS
Henderson. I need you to find a freakin' dog!

INT. OFFICE OF THE DIRECTOR SPCA - DAY

At his desk, on the PHONE is LAWRENCE HENDERSON, director.

He is listening to Collins and taking notes.

HENDERSON
She's female. She's small. Weighs about fifteen pounds. In the park. (Beat) Do you have any idea how many acres we're taking about? (Beat) It's that important? (Beat) A big feather in my cap. I'll put my best man on it. If she's alive, he'll find her.

Henderson hangs up. He flicks the intercom.

HENDERSON (CONT'D)
Connie, get me Slade.

EXT. THE WOODS - DAY.

Leaves are falling.

Wally and Bella are strolling through the woods playfully.

VOICE OVER
These were glorious days for the pack. The food was plentiful. The

weather, perfect. The cool nights
and bright, shiny, sun-filled days
sent the colors glimmerin'.
And for Wally, everything would have
been absolutely wonderful, if there
wasn't this constant gnawing in his
stomach that couldn't be explained.
Something was missing; something he just
couldn't put his paw on, just couldn't remember.

They come down a slope and onto a gigantic rock that overlooks a deep pool of water, and they marvel at the beauty. Wally stands tall on the rock and looks over the edge.

WALLY
This is my favorite spot in the whole wide world.

BELLA
I can see why.

VOICE OVER
To Philadelphians, this place was
known as Devil's Pool. In the
summer kids jump off the rock, high
diving to the water below. But now,
with the leaves falling and the
weather changing, it was deserted.

Wally and Bella lie down on the rock and bask in the sun.

EXT. CHESTNUT HILL AVE - ENTRANCE TO PARK - DAY

An SUV pulls into the lot, and STANLEY SLADE exits. He is tall and slender, wearing a khaki safari vest and an Australian bush hat. He takes a backpack out of the vehicle and begins to walk down the gravel trail. Then, turning right, he disappears into the woods.

EXT. GROVE IN WOODS - DAY

Slade enters a secluded grove in the woods. He studies the place, then kneels down and examines something on the ground. He takes out a small container to sample the specimen.

EXT. WOODS - DAY

Wally sees a falling leaf floating in the air. He runs after it, tries to bite it. Then he sees another falling leaf and goes after that. He is suddenly mesmerized by the falling leaves.

Butch sees him and turns to Sergio.

BUTCH
What did I tell you?

Eddie G goes over to Wally.

EDDIE G
Hey, dummy. What are you doin'?
They're leaves, see. Just leaves.
It happens every year.

EXT. THE CAMP - DAY

As the leaves continue to fall, the canopy of the woods continues to disappear, and almost overnight the forest seems stark and bare. Butch is in a foul mood. All of the dogs are walking on eggshells. Wally and Bella enter the camp and feel the tension. Wally turns to Monte.

WALLY
What's going on?

MONTE
Butch is worried and nervous.

WALLY
Why?

MONTE
With the falling leaves, this camp is much more visible. We're gonna have to move.

WALLY
Where to?

MONTE
That's the problem.

INT. A LABORATORY - DAY

Slade is looking through a microscope. Sample specimen jars are on the counter where he works.

EXT. THE CAMP - DAY

Wally is gnawing on an old deer bone. Butch comes out on his rock and looks around. Butch growls, and all the dogs look up and stand. As Wally stands, a brief flash of light catches his eye. He stares in the direction from which the light emanated. Bella comes and stands beside him.

EXT. A RIDGE IN THE WOODS - DAY

Stanley Slade is on the ridge looking through a pair of binoculars. He is scanning the woods in the distance. Suddenly, he stops. He sees the pack.

SLADE'S P.O.V.: Wally, Bella, and the rest of the pack.

Slade smiles and takes out a map. He studies his position.

INT. DIRECTOR'S OFFICE - SPCA - DAY

Henderson is at his desk, where Slade has rolled out a map. Also in the room are two men wearing white coats, JOHN D. BERKS and LEROY LOMAN. Slade points to the map.

SLADE
There. Right there. There's a pack of them. Maybe six or seven.

HENDERSON
Is Bittle's dog there?

SLADE
Yes, she is.

HENDERSON
Can you get her? I don't care about the other dogs.

Slade looks at the two men standing next to him, and they smile and nod.

SLADE
Listen boss, I hear you, but I think we have to get them all. It's important, if you know what I mean...

Without turning his head, Slade subtly signals to Henderson with his eyes that he doesn't want to reveal too much.

SLADE (CONT'D)
These dogs are hard and wild. You can't have a pack of mean, wild dogs running around the woods.

For a brief moment, Henderson stares at him.

HENDERSON
Oh ... yeah ... I get you. But that's gonna be tough.

SLADE
Yeah, I know. And there's a big black male up there that looks like he could pull a freight train.

Slade turns to Berks and Loman.

SLADE (CONT'D)
John, how many men will you need to do this?

BERKS
We only got six, but I think that'll be enough.

SLADE
Okay, we'll do it tomorrow at noon when the sun is high. Now, this is what we'll do...

The men gather around and study the map.

SLADE (CONT'D)
I want you to come in from this trail and...

EXT. THE CAMP - DAY

Wally is sleeping, but suddenly his head snaps up. He begins to sniff the air. He stands, still sniffing. Kit comes over to him.

KIT

I have two pieces of advice for you: first, run if you see the men in white suits coming. Run as fast as you can. Don't think of any dog but yourself.

WALLY

Not even you, Kit?

KIT

Not even me. And listen, Frisbee, when you fight Butch—

WALLY

Fight him. Fight him! Why do I have to fight him? I don't want to fight him.

KIT

No, not now you don't.

WALLY

Not now, not ever.

Kit shakes her head at Wally's naïveté.

KIT

Wake up and smell the biscuits, pup.

Kit looks over at Bella, who is approaching and looking at Wally.

KIT (CONT'D)
The forces of that good lady
called "nature" are strong, Fris.
Stronger than any dog. Stronger
than you. Stronger than Butch.

WALLY
What do you mean by nature?

VOICE OVER
But she didn't answer; she just
scratched her ear and walked off to
complain to Monte or Eddie G. And
Wally really wasn't listening. It
seemed that, for some strange reason,
all of his attention was on Bella.

Wally, as if in a trance, begins to follow Bella as she leads him away from the camp. Butch suddenly comes out of his cave and begins to alertly sniff the air.

Bella, dancing playfully, leads Wally away.

VOICE OVER (CONT'D)
Certain things were happening that
Wally didn't quite understand. The
scent of Bella intoxicated him with
strange feelings. He was drawn to
it as if it was a drug, and it
dominated his thoughts. He was
both excited and nervous.

Bella leads Wally to his favorite spot, the rock above Devil's Pool.

VOICE OVER (CONT'D)
Up until that moment, he had been secretly in love with Bella but thought she considered him just a good friend or younger brother. Now, things seemed strangely different. Now, all he wanted to do was touch her and be with her, and tell her how much she meant to him.

Bella looks at Wally and starts to do this little dog-dance, sort of jumping and nipping. Suddenly, behind them, there is a furious GROWL.

It's Butch, and he's in a foul mood. The hairs on the back of his neck are standing straight up. He is leaning forward, but stands at the foot of the huge rock. Behind him is the rest of the pack. Wally looks back at Bella, and as he does, Butch charges, aiming for Wally's throat.

Wally sees the charge out of the corner of his eye and jumps straight in the air.

VOICE OVER (CONT'D)
That jump kept Butch from getting that deadly lock on Wally's neck, but Butch didn't miss him completely. He caught a piece of the big dog's chest, which made Wally howl in pain.

Butch hangs on to Wally, trying to pull him down. At that point, he is under Wally.

VOICE OVER (CONT'D)
If Butch pulled Wally down to his knees, the big dog would be a goner but then Wally did something instinctively smart.

With Butch still hanging on, Wally leaps off the rock, and together, as if one, they plunge into the dark pool below. Butch hits the water first, with Wally on top of him, and they both go down to the bottom. It's at that moment Butch releases his grip.

They both struggle to reach the top.

VOICE OVER (CONT'D)
Wally had the advantage because he was a water dog. His chest was killing him, but it was tempered by anger, an anger he'd never experienced before.

Wally follows Butch to the top, takes a quick breath and dives again. While Butch is gasping for air, Wally dives again, comes up under him, grabs his leg, and pulls him down.

Once again, Butch struggles to the top, and this time, Wally grabs the back of his neck and makes him scream in pain, forcing him under.

Butch comes up again, gasping, choking, and exerting all of his energy. He flounders on the surface. Wally swims ashore. He looks back at Butch and growls.

WALLY
Come on! Come on! You started this. Come on!

But it is obvious that Butch is not going to make it ashore.

He is floundering badly, gasping for air and going down.

VOICE OVER

Wally never knew why he saved Butch. Old Butch had put him through a lot, but he had also taught him a lot, and although it went against everything that every dog had ever told him, he jumped back in the water and pulled Butch out of there.

Wally goes back into the water and pulls Butch ashore.

VOICE OVER (CONT'D)

The rest of the pack had gone downstream, crossed at the shallows, and was now waiting for some sign from Wally, their new leader.

Butch mournfully groans and struggles to stand. Wally bares his teeth, but he is still shaking from the confrontation.

VOICE OVER (CONT'D)

Butch stared at Wally with new respect, and then looked at the rest of the pack. He was very vulnerable at that point; the fall from the rock had knocked the fight out of him. He had swallowed a lot of water, and it was he who'd suffered the most from the full impact of the fall. Somehow, he had badly injured his front left leg. He hung his head low and limped away.

Wally and the pack watch as Butch limps away and heads for the camp.

VOICE OVER (CONT'D)
At that moment, all the hatred he had felt for Butch was gone. At that time, there was only love in his heart. What did he know? He was young; barely old enough not to chase the falling autumn leaves.

The pack turns and looks at Wally, but he is not concerned with them. He turns and walks away from them, and they turn and follow Butch back to the camp.

EXT. CHESTNUT HILL AVENUE ENTRANCE TO THE PARK - DAY

Three SPCA trucks pull up and park on the grass bordering the woods. Two men, wearing long white coats, emerge from each vehicle, and remove dog control-poles and chains from the vans. Silently, they carry the equipment into the woods.

EXT. A SMALL GROVE – DAY

Wally wanders alone and lies down in a small grove.

VOICE OVER
At that moment, Wally needed to be alone. He needed to think. He was totally confused. He was now, he knew, the leader of the pack, but there was still something wrong, something he couldn't explain or remember.

EXT. THE CAMP - DAY

The pack follows Butch into their camp and, just as they settle down, the men in white coats rush in. There is growling and barking and yelling and confusion as the men try to take control of the dogs. The volume of noise echoes through the woods.

EXT. A SMALL GROVE - DAY

Wally hears the noise and becomes attentive.

EXT. THE CAMP - DAY

One by one, the dogs of the pack are subdued. Using a net, Slade corners and captures Bella. He picks her up and begins to carry her away.

SLADE
I got what we came for. But I want
them all. Hey, where's the big black?

But the men aren't really listening. They are still trying to capture and harness the rest of the pack. Using control poles, the other dogs are collared. Despite his injuries, Butch is the only one who really puts up any kind of fight. Butch is finally harnessed and, along with Monte, Eddie G, and Kit, is chained to a tree while the other dogs are taken out of the woods to the vehicles a couple of miles away.

EXT. THE WOODS - DAY

Wally is running at full speed through the woods.

EXT. THE CAMP - DAY

Just as the men in white coats have left the camp, Wally comes racing in.

VOICE OVER
All of those dogs restrained to trees were happy to see Wally. But he had no magical powers to free them, and suddenly their excitement faded. Sadly, they all told him to run, to save himself.

MONTE
Don't be sad old bean. Fly, Frisbee, fly!

EDDIE G
Now see here, Fris, don't you worry about us, see, we'll be fine, we're okay, see.

BUTCH
Fris, come here, I want to tell you somethin'. There's nothing you can do for us, pup. Take off. Be free. Birds are free and chipmunks and squirrels and even bees, but dogs can't be free. It's just the way things are. Take off. Be free … and listen, kid, I know I gave you a bad time, but I just want to tell you, fella, you got heart. You know what I mean? You know what I'm trying to say?

WALLY
Yeah, Butch, I think so.

Wally sadly turns to Kit and walks to her with his head down. She had been waiting for him patiently.

KIT
Oh, Frisbee, what am I going to do with you? Didn't I tell you what to do if you saw the men in white coats? Well, didn't I? I said "run," didn't I? Once you're tied up like this, you can't be saved. Why are you so stubborn? Now get out of here, and don't you dare look back.

WALLY
What did they do to Bella?

KIT
Now, don't you worry about her. She'll be taken care of just fine.

Then the sound of the men in white coats returning is heard, and all the dogs start barking. Wally slips into the bushes.

When the MEN reach the camp, Loman decides to take a breather. He sits down on the stone where Butch used to lie, pulls out a pack of cigarettes, and lights up. John Berks is annoyed.

BERKS
Do you have to light up right now?

LOMAN
I need a break. I'm tired.

BERKS
If we don't leave soon, it'll be dark before we get back.

LOMAN
We'll be fine. I just never figured on so many dogs, is all.

BERKS
The more the merrier, as far as I'm concerned. Slade told you—

Berks' cell phone rings. He looks at it.

BERKS (CONT'D)
That's him now. (Beat). Yeah. No, the black ain't here. Are you crazy? We're not gonna go looking for him now. I don't care how big he is, today ain't the day. We got the princess, and the pack, and that's the important thing.

He angrily ends the call and jams the phone into his pocket.

BERKS (CONT'D)
Okay, kill that smoke and lets get goin'. I don't want to be in these woods after dark.

EXT. PARKING LOT - NIGHT

The men in white coats finish loading the dogs onto the truck just as night falls. They are exhausted. Wally has followed them and watches from afar as they load the vehicle. The men get into the cab of the truck and start to drive away. Wally follows the truck. As the truck picks up speed, he begins to run, but soon, the truck leaves him far behind, and he stops in the middle of the road and watches it disappear.

The park is on his right, and finally, he disappears into it.

VOICE OVER
I guess at that point Wally just wandered. He had no idea where he was, and he really didn't care. He was lost, both spiritually and emotionally.

SERIES OF SHOTS

EXT. WOODS - NIGHT

The moon is bright as Wally walks sadly through the woods until he finds himself on the Wissahickon Creek. He walks along the edge of the water and follows the creek until it merges into the Schuylkill River.

EXT. THE SCHUYLKILL RIVER - NIGHT

Wally looks out at the river and climbs the bank leading to Kelly Drive. Ignoring the traffic, he crosses East Falls Bridge and then disappears again into the park.

EXT. BELMONT PLATEAU - NIGHT

With the moon still high and the stars ablaze, he finds himself on the slopes of Belmont Plateau. He sits and studies the spectacular view of the far away city lights. He looks to his right and sees for the first time the green dome of Memorial Hall and, for no particular reason, heads toward it.

EXT. WEST RIVER DRIVE - NIGHT

He walks along the West River Drive and up Parkside Road, which leads under the old freight railroad bridge, and just before morning merges at Whispering Walls. He enters Horse Chestnut Island and falls asleep, exhausted, in the nearby woods.

EXT. DESERTED SIDE STREET - NIGHT

It's raining. Berks exits his car and looks around. The street is deserted and is made up of mostly old factories. Berks walks down an alley, where he meets a HUGE MAN who is standing in front of a metal door. We can hear muddled NOISE coming from behind the door. The man looks at Berks, smiles
and opens the door. Suddenly, the noise is loud and intense.

INT. WAREHOUSE - NIGHT

Berks enters. There is a large number of men shouting and yelling. Dogs are growling and snarling.

Berks ignores the crowd and walks directly to an office and KNOCKS. The door opens and he enters.

INT. WAREHOUSE - OFFICE

Berks walks by another HUGE MAN, who is guarding the door. Sitting behind the only furniture in the room, counting
money, is RUSSELL "BANG BANG" RUSSO.

RUSSO
What you got for me?

BERKS
We got a couple of good prospects.

RUSSO
Good prospects? I need some fighters.

BERKS
I got one today. He's older, but he looks like he's been in a couple of tussles. Right now, he's got a bad leg. I'll get him healthy, and then I'll make him mean.

RUSSO
Boy, I'd hate to be in his shoes. Don't make him too mean; I don't want my boys hurt by a set-up.

BERKS
Don't worry. Your guys will tear him apart … but who cares?

Russo laughs and shakes his head.

RUSSO
How'd a guy like you ever get to work for the SPCA? You don't even like dogs.

Berks laughs.

BERKS
No. Actually, I hate them. And what the good people at the SPCA don't know, won't hurt them. Actually, I'm doing them a favor by getting rid of their easy-kills. They think those old non-fighters are being adopted by sweet old ladies.

Russo chuckles.

RUSSO
How long before the one with the bad leg is ready?

BERKS
About a month.

RUSSO
A month? I need something now. I need a star.

BERKS
I'm gonna get one for you. It won't take too long. He's big, and huge, and black. And when I get done with him, he'll be a fighter.

Russo smiles viciously and hands Berks a fistful of money.

INT. DAVIS KITCHEN - DAY

Ron Davis is at the kitchen table, having his morning coffee. Cliff disgustedly enters and sits down to join him. Ron looks at him and sees he's depressed.

RON
What's the matter, pal?

CLIFF
I don't know.

RON
Tell me.

CLIFF
Well, I know this sounds crazy, but

I had a dream about Wally, and he was in trouble.

Ron sighs heavily.

RON

Listen, boy, it's been months. I guess we've got to face facts. He's gone. We'll get another dog.

CLIFF

There'll never be another dog for me.

Ron stares at him, then sadly nods.

CLIFF (CONT'D)

I'm gonna put up some more fliers.

Ron nods.

EXT. A STREET – DAY

Cliff is thumb-tacking a flier of Wally onto a telegraph pole. Kids are walking to school. Alvie and Ernest are passing-by and see him putting up the "lost dog" poster. Alvie viciously smiles and pokes Ernest in the ribs.

ALVIE

Watch this. Hey, Cliff, you still looking for that stupid dog?

Cliff turns and stares at the two of them. Alvie laughs and pokes Ernest in the ribs, but Ernest looks sad and walks away. Alvie follows him.

ERNEST

What you do that for?

ALVIE

What's wrong with you?

ERNEST

Did you ever have a dog?

ALVIE

No.

ERNEST

Then you wouldn't understand.

INT. THE GYM LOCKER ROOM - DAY

Cliff is sitting on a bench in front of his locker, changing into his gym clothes. He is approached by Ernest, whose head is down.

ERNEST

Hey, Cliff ... listen, I got something to tell you. It's about your dog. I ... I ...

INT. THE SCHOOL GYM - DAY

Kids are coming into the gym from the locker room. Cliff, with an angry look on his face, comes into the gym and looks around. He sees Alvie playing basketball with a group of other boys. He marches over, grabs the ball, and turns to Alvie.

CLIFF

My dad once told me not to let people hurt me. You hurt me.

ALVIE

Who the hell do you think—

Cliff angrily bounces the ball to him, and when Alvie instinctively reaches for it, Cliff hauls off and punches him in the mouth. Alvie goes down, then scrambles to his feet, but Cliff is on him and clobbers him with a right that sends him back down. The GYM TEACHER is there to stop him from hitting Alvie again.

INT. PRINCIPAL'S OFFICE - DAY

MR. STEGMAN, the principal, is sitting at his desk, hands folded in front of him, staring coldly at Alvie and Cliff.

ALVIE
He hauled off and hit me.

CLIFF
He did something mean and vicious
to my dog. He may have killed him.
Wally's been missing for two months.
I just found out it was him.

STEGMAN
Is that true?

ALVIE
Well … yeah, but I didn't mean to
hurt him. I … hell, it was just a
joke … he was just a stupid old
dog … I …

Stegman's mouth drops open. He looks down at his desk in disgust. Finally, his mouth hard and grim, he looks up at Alvie and sadly shakes his head.

SERIES OF SHOTS

EXT. WALLY'S ROCK - DAY

Wally has found a rocky crest overlooking the old freight train tracks.

INT. CAR - NIGHT

A BOY and a GIRL are parked along the river, necking. The girl looks up, sees Wally walk in front of the car, and SCREAMS.

EXT. PARK ROAD - NIGHT

A car is coming down the road as Wally crosses. The car swerves to avoid him and goes off the road.

EXT. THE WOODS - DAY

Wally sees a rabbit and chases it down.

EXT. SOCCER FIELD ON PARKSIDE AVE - DAY

There is a game being played. One KID looks beyond the goal post and sees Wally come out of the woods. The kid runs to his coach, pulls on his sleeve, and points to where he saw Wally.

INT. BARBER SHOP ON GIRARD AVE - DAY

Two twelve-year-old African American boys, JARAD JONES and DENIS WILLIAMS, are waiting to have their hair cut. The BARBER is working on a MAN in the chair. The man is SONNY "BIG DADDY" WISCOMB. Denis picks up on an ongoing conversation between the barber and Wiscomb.

WILLIAMS

The ghost? Hey, I saw that dog. We

was comin' out of Memorial Hall and he was standing right there. They said he was a bad ass, but I picked up a stone and hit him right in his bad ass.

The barber looks up over his glasses and raises an eyebrow. Jarad starts laughing.

JONES
Denis you lyyyyin'! Yeah, you throwed a stone, but it missed him by ten feet, and when he looked at you, you ran like a rabbit.

EXT. WHISPERING WALLS - NIGHT

Wally has knocked over a trash can and is rummaging for food. Suddenly, he stops and begins sniffing the air. The scent leads him to a bowl of dry dog food sitting on the stone bench. He looks around, then devours the food.

INT. DIRECTOR'S OFFICE SPCA - DAY

Slade enters. Henderson is behind the desk.

SLADE
I can't be sure, but I think the big black has been seen around Parkside Ave.

HENDERSON
Not sure?

SLADE
Well, there've been some crazy

reports. Nobody has actually seen
him long enough to take a picture.
I want to go check it out.

HENDERSON
Right now is not a good time to go
on a wild goose chase. Let's make
sure. Besides, we have to solve the
big problem. That's why you're here
and that's your most important job.

Slade shrugs and nods in agreement.

SLADE
Okay.

EXT. WHISPERING WALLS - NIGHT

The moon is full. Wally comes into the Whispering Walls complex. There is another bowl of food waiting for him. Once again, he devours the food.

EXT. THE WOODS - NIGHT

Wally comes out of the woods, crosses the road from Horse Chestnut Island to the Whispering Walls monument, but upon entering the marble complex, he stops dead in his tracks. Next to the bowl of food is an old Black man bundled up in heavy clothes with a cloth hat pulled down around his ears. This man is Sonny "Big Daddy" Wiscomb. It's his voice that we've been hearing in the voice-overs.

WISCOMB
Hey, there, Blackie.

Wally curls his lip, shows his teeth, and GROWLS. Sonny

seems unafraid and talks softly.

WISCOMB (CONT'D)
I just thought I'd wait for you
this time and say hello.
You like the chow? Yeah, it's good
stuff. Alpo.

Wally begins to back up.

WISCOMB (CONT'D)
Hey, big dog, you don't have to
leave. I ain't gonna hurt you.
I'll go. I just wanted to see if
you was real, is all. You have any
idea what they call you? Huh?

Wally just stares coldly.

WISCOMB (CONT'D)
People around here call you The
Ghost. You got quite a reputation,
you know. "First you sees 'em, and
now you don't" is how they go on.
They ask me how a dog as big as you
can hide in the park. I tells 'em
that it's easy because Fairmount
Park is the biggest city park in
the whole wide world, is why. It
just goes on and on for thousands
of acres. But I guess nobody knows
that like you.

Wiscomb gets to his feet. He is carrying a cane. Wally growls ferociously and readies himself to attack.

WISCOMB (CONT'D)
Okay, okay, I'm leavin', Blackie.
You don't have to worry about me.
I won't tell anybody I know you.
Just wanted to say hello, is all.
Nice meeting you. No hard
feelings. I hope to see you again,
if you don't mind.

Wiscomb begins to walk away like the old man he is: stoop-shouldered and slow. When he is gone, Wally goes to the bowl of food and devours it.

INT. WISCOMB APARTMENT - NIGHT

Two small rooms. The furniture is shabby. Sonny is in the kitchen putting dog food into a paper shopping bag. He puts on a heavy coat, picks up a small pillow, and walks out his front door.

EXT. 42ND AND PARKSIDE - NIGHT

Wiscomb crosses Parkside Avenue and enters the park.

EXT. WHISPERING WALLS - NIGHT

Wiscomb enters the complex, puts a pillow on the stone bench, and sits. He pours the dog food into the empty bowl. He puts the filled bowl a good distance from where he sits and begins to whistle a tune.

Bundled up from the cold, Wiscomb pours himself a cup of coffee from a thermos, then waits to see if the big dog will come.

Out of the shadows Wally appears, sees Wiscomb, and growls.

WISCOMB
Hello, Blackie. Now, now. No need to carry on. Just tryin' to be friendly, is all.

Wiscomb talks in an easy singsong voice as Wally devours the food. Wiscomb whistles a soft tune. Wally disappears.

EXT. WHISPERING WALL – NIGHT

The NEXT NIGHT. Wiscomb puts down the bowl of food but this time a little closer. He sits and pours himself a cup of coffee.

Wally appears and, without growling, he goes to the food.

WISCOMB
I can see my cooking is doing you some good. You beginning to put on a little weight.

Wally looks down at the bowl, then at Sonny.

WISCOMB (CONT'D)
What's that you say? (Beat) Oh, no need to thank me. Go ahead, get started. Enjoy.

Wally begins to eat the food.

WISCOMB (CONT'D)
Yeah, Blackie, I was a lot like you. I had me some fame, just like you. You ever hear of Big Daddy Wiscomb? No? Well, that's probably because I'm a lot older than you.

Wally stops eating and looks at Sonny.

WISCOMB (CONT'D)
Me? How old am I?

Sonny laughs, then gets lost in calculating.

WISCOMB (CONT'D)
Well, I'll be ninety next month. Although you and me are the only ones who will know it. Hell, I used to be one of the hottest trumpet players in this whole United States of America. Yeah, I was a lot like you, and you are a lot like I was. Sure, sure, we're both Black—black as the ace of spades—but it's more than that, big dog. I was a loner, just like you. And, Blackie, I'm here to tell you that it's no way to be. Sure, in my day, I traveled from town to town, ate the best food, lived in the best hotels, but then I got too old to play. Lost my lip.

Wally finishes the food and stares at Wiscomb.

WISCOMB (CONT'D)
And Blackie, you know what they say: No play, no pay. Now, I'm so old, all my friends are gone, and I keep asking myself why I keep hanging on. Everybody else has been dead for years. See what I

mean? It's no good, Blackie. No
good at all.

Wiscomb stands.

WISCOMB (CONT'D)
Well, I'll be moseying. Hope to
see you next time. And, Blackie,
maybe next time you'll tell me
about you. I'm a good listener, big
boy, and I know you must have a heck
of a story to tell.

EXT. ROW HOUSE - NIGHT

Wiscomb comes out of the front door of his house with his shopping bag and walks toward the park. Two MEN take notice as he crosses Parkside Ave. They begin to follow him. As he nears Whispering Walls, they catch up to him and stop him.

FIRST MAN
What you got in the bag, old man?

SECOND MAN
And what the hell you got in your pockets?

Wiscomb stares at them coldly.

WISCOMB
Dog food is in the bag, and my gun
is in my pocket!

SECOND MAN
Dog food?

FIRST MAN
You ain't got no gun, and by the time you put your hand in your pocket, I'd knock your brains in.

Wiscomb raises his cane, but the second man hits him and knocks him down. The first man is about to kick him, when Wally suddenly appears out of nowhere and viciously attacks him. He knocks the man down. The other man begins to run, but Wally jumps on his back, knocking him down. The man is screaming as Wally tears at him.

WISCOMB
No, Blackie! Don't do it, boy!

The first man gets up and begins running toward Parkside Ave.

Suddenly, there are cop cars heading toward them.

WISCOMB (CONT'D)
Get out of here, Blackie! Go ahead, boy!

As the cop cars approach, Wally disappears into the woods.

INT. HOSPITAL ROOM - DAY

Sonny Wiscomb is in bed. His left leg is up in a cast and there is a bandage around his head. Stanley Slade enters the room.

SLADE
Mr. Wiscomb, my name is Slade. I heard you were attacked by a dog.

WISCOMB
Can't those people get anything

right? I was attacked by two no-good dogs dressed up as humans.

SLADE

Wasn't there a big black dog?

WISCOMB

Yes. That dog saved my life.

SLADE

Well, the police say one guy was torn up pretty bad.

Wiscomb raises his eyebrows.

WISCOMB

Yes, that is correct, and he deserved it. And had I been a few years younger, he'd be in a lot worse shape. Broke my damned leg. Can't fall like I used to.

Slade smiles and nods.

SLADE

I want to know about this dog.

Wiscomb folds his arms.

WISCOMB

I ain't talking.

SLADE

Mr. Wiscomb, we can't have no wild dogs running around the park.

Wiscomb is adamant.

WISCOMB
What I say?

EXT. HORSE CHESTNUT ISLAND - DAY

An SPCA van pulls up, and Berks and Loman exit. They remove a huge cage from the rear of the vehicle and carry it into the woods. They bait the trap with meat and leave.

EXT. WALLY'S ROCK - NIGHT

The moon is almost full, and Wally gets up and sniffs the air. He begins to follow the scent, which takes him to where the men have set the trap. He is about to approach it, when he sees CRAZY-CRAZY, a raccoon just outside the entrance of the trap. Crazy-Crazy enters the trap and the door springs shut. Then the raccoon goes crazy. When he has exhausted himself, he sees Wally.

CRAZY-CRAZY
They got me. Do you believe it? They got me. They set a trap for you, and they got me! They set a trap for a nitwit, and they got me!

EXT. RAILROAD TRACKS - DAY

Wally is walking along the tracks, when he sees a train coming slowly down the line. He climbs the ridge and watches as it jerks to a stop. The train is pulling boxcars, and one boxcar has its door ajar. Riding inside is a dog, a Rhodesian Ridgeback named BEERY, who appears at the entrance.

Beery jumps out of the car and scrambles up the ridge but comes to an abrupt halt when he sees Wally staring down at him.

BEERY
I ain't looking for no fight, pard,
just a safe place to lay.

VOICE OVER
It had been a long time since Wally
had smelled the musk of another
dog. This dog looked mean. He
was a big Ridgeback. Wally had
seen one or two of them before but, of
course, he couldn't remember where.

WALLY
Barely enough food here for one, Bo.

BEERY
The name's Beery, friend, like in Wallace.

WALLY
What?

BEERY
Never mind. It's just something my
partner used to say. I have no idea what
it means. What's your name, friend?

WALLY
They call me Fris.

BEERY
Well, Fris, what's it gonna be? Can
I come aboard, or do we have to
bang heads? (Beat) You don't have

anything to worry about. I haven't been in a fight in years. These days, I'm more lover than fighter, and I'll be leaving in the morning.

VOICE OVER
But Beery stayed nearly two weeks, and the two of them became the best of friends. And friendship is what Wally missed the most. Beery also taught Wally things that kept him alive.

SERIES OF SHOTS

EXT. BELMONT PLATEAU - NIGHT

Wally and Beery are sitting on the high ridge, looking at the city.

EXT. GRASSY PATCH - DAY

Wally and Beery are hunting. A RABBIT darts by. They race after it.

EXT. WALLY'S LAIR - DAY

Beery and Wally are sparing playfully.

VOICE OVER
One morning, Beery tells Wally to stand up, and when he does, before you could say "boo," he nips Wally on the neck. Just a nip, mind you, but enough to tell Wally he wants to play.

WALLY
Okay, Mr. Beery, you asked for this.

VOICE OVER
Bing, bing, bing, Beery nips the other side of his neck. Wally can see a light in Beery's eye that bothers him. He swings his head back and forth and, biff, bam, boom, Beery nips him again. And for the next ten minutes, Wally can't make a move without Beery getting to his neck.

Beery stops and looks disgusted.

BEERY
Thanks for the workout, Fris, but it's no fun if I got all the moves.

Wally is upset that Beery wants to stop. Beery sees it.

BEERY (CONT'D)
Awright, here, let me show you something. It'll make it more fun. This is called the "sweet science," it's the art of the fight, and believe me, it's something that all animals do. Now watch me, I'm gonna do this in slow motion. Feint, feint, neck. Left, right, neck. Everything is done in threes. Paw, thigh, neck. Get it? And you're a big dog, so use your shoulder. Keep your neck out of reach until you're ready to attack.

Then they begin to work out.

BEERY (CONT'D)
You know, Fris, if you weren't the

kind of dog you are, you could have been put in the ring. In a way, you're lucky, 'cause you're big enough and strong enough, and you sure do learn fast, but being a—

WALLY
What do you mean by "the kind of dog I am"?

BEERY
Wait a minute, you mean to tell me you don't know what you are? Are you kidding me?

VOICE OVER
Wally started getting that feeling again. It was right there, on the tip of his nose, all fuzzy and ready to expose itself, but it vanished as quickly as it came.

BEERY
Well, Fris, you're some kind of retriever, that I can tell you, for sure. What your exact origin is, I couldn't say, but you are definitely retrieverish, and retrievers aren't mean dogs. To be a professional fighter, you've got to be mean.

WALLY
Were you a professional fighter, Beery?

BEERY

Nay, my pal didn't want me to get hurt for the sport of others. He always said "running away was the better part of valor," but we were always at the camps where the pros would fight, so I watched and I learned. It's important to be able to defend yourself.

WALLY

I once fought a professional fighter.

BEERY

Yeah, and Rin Tin Tin was a Dachshund.

WALLY

I'm serious.

BEERY

Okay, who'd you fight?

VOICE OVER

And when Wally told him…

BERRY

Wait a minute, was this Butch part pit bull? White, with a black tail and spot over his left eye?

WALLY

Yeah.

BEERY

And you lived to tell about it?

Man, I once saw him fight a junk
yard dog named Killer. Man, that
Butch was one mean dog! Tell me
everything. How did it happen...?

INT. KENNELS. SPCA - DAY

Loman and Berks are locking up a dog they just captured. Berks walks three stalls down. Monte, Eddie G., and Kit are sharing this large cage. Berks stares at Eddie G and tries to imitate him by jutting out his lower jaw.

LOMAN
Yeah, he's really funny lookin',
ain't he? And Berks, you do that real good.

BERKS
Real good, huh? Well, some real
dog is gonna tear him apart real
good, real fast. He'll be the
first to go. Maybe next week, huh,
little fella?

Eddie G blinks his eyes and begins to shake.

LOMAN
Hey, it won't be fair. He can't bite anything.

BERKS
Fair? No, it won't be fair, but
it'll be funny. They'll laugh like crazy.

Berks goes to the next stall where Butch is being housed with Sergio. Berks bangs his fist on the cage. Sergio cowers, but Butch stares at him, curls his lip and growls softly. Then Berks bangs his head against the chain link fencing and growls back at him.

BERKS (CONT'D)
It won't be long now, fella. And I can't wait for us to have a little one on one, a little tête-à-tête.

Loman joins him.

LOMAN
Hey, be cool. Look who's coming.

They see Slade approaching. Slade walks to them and nods, then looks in Butch's cage.

SLADE
How's he coming?

Berks smiles warmly.

BERKS
Well, sir, I'd say he's almost well enough to be adopted.

SLADE
I don't want him adopted right now.

Berks is taken aback.

BERKS
Really? There's a guy that's been coming around who's really interested in adopting him.

SLADE
He's not to be moved until I say so.

Slade looks at the other cage containing Kit, Eddie G, and Monte.

SLADE (CONT'D)
As a matter of fact, I don't want any of these dogs from the pack moved.

BERKS
I thought that's what the SPCA was all about? Providing homes for strays.

SLADE
Not 'til I say so.

Berks looks at him coldly.

BERKS
You're the boss, boss.

SLADE
Now, what about the black?

LOMAN
We pulled that trap. It caught everything but the big black.

SLADE
Damn. I want that darn dog. Get him!

Slade and Berks stare at each other.

BERKS
Dead or alive?

SLADE
Don't do anything stupid.

BERKS
Dead or alive?

Slade sighs heavily.

SLADE
Just get him.

Slade leaves. Loman looks at Berks and sees something crazy in his eyes.

LOMAN
What are you gonna do?

BERKS
You'll see.

LOMAN
Nah, don't do that. It's dangerous. Besides, I thought you wanted that dog alive.

BERKS
Not anymore. You heard Slade. Slade just wants him. And I want him, too. I want him bad. There's never been a dog I couldn't get, and this dog ain't gonna be the first.

LOMAN
But this ain't the way. Besides, I

thought you said he'd be worth a
lot of money.

Berks grabs Loman's shirt, pulls him to him, and whispers.

BERKS
This isn't about money anymore.

Then Berks releases him and brushes off Loman's wrinkled shirt. Loman looks at Berks and swallows hard.

EXT. THE WOODS - DAY

Wally and Beery are walking in the woods.

BEERY
So the white coats got old Butch.
Well, you got away, and now you know
the idea is not to get caught. I
learned from a guy who was the
greatest. He taught me everything
I know, and I'm gonna teach it to you.

VOICE OVER
And that very day he taught Wally
the greatest lesson of his life.

Suddenly, Wally stops. He sniffs the air. He leaves Beery and begins to follow an aroma down a path he'd not taken before. The scent gets stronger, and then he sees what it is. Hanging from a tree is a fresh piece of meat. He is just about to jump up and snatch it, when Beery charges him and knocks him into the bushes. Surprised, Wally gets up, ready to fight.

BEERY
Holy Toledo, you are stupid.

Beery sniffs the meat.

BEERY (CONT'D)
Don't you dare touch anything that smells like that, do you hear me, Fris? It's poison!

WALLY
Huh?

BEERY
Look at the ground.

At Beery's feet is a dead crow.

BEERY (CONT'D)
That bird just ate it.

Wally stares down at the bird.

BEERY (CONT'D)
These people must want you awful bad, boy, and if I know them, they're gonna keep trying until they get you. You gotta keep moving, Fris. You can't stay in one spot. You gotta have a way out. Don't let them trap you, Fris.

EXT. HORSE CHESTNUT ISLAND - DAY

Loman and Berks exit the truck and walk into the woods. They come to the spot where they hung the tainted meat. On the ground in addition to the crow is a dead squirrel.

LOMAN
This was stupid. We got everything but the damned dog.

BERKS
You're right. I agree. Cut it down.

LOMAN
Suppose a kid touched it?

BERKS
I said you're right, didn't I?

EXT. RAILROAD TRACKS - DAY

Wally and Beery are walking the tracks. Up ahead is a freight train that has stopped. Beery stops and looks at it for a long, long time. Then he looks at Wally.

BEERY
That one seems to be calling my name.

WALLY
Don't go, Beery.

BEERY
I got to, kid. I got to find my partner. He raised me. He got busted for vagrancy in a train yard

about a year ago and we got
separated. I've been looking for
him ever since. Someday I'll find
him. He'll be sittin' by some fire
and I'll walk up to him and he'll
say "Hey, Beery, where you been?"
And just like that, we'll be
partners again.

WALLY

Wow!

BEERY

Who raised you, Fris? Who's your partner?

WALLY

That's the problem, Beery. I can't remember.

BEERY

Geez, that's a tough one. I wish I
could help you. But remember this:
you didn't come from nowhere. Somebody
out there loved you. I can tell
that just by the way you are. And,
Fris, just like me, you gotta find
that person to be whole.

WALLY

I know, Beery. I know.

BEERY

You'll figure it out, kid. I know you will.

The train starts to move, and Wally and Beery run alongside, looking for an open freight car. Beery sees one and jumps on board.

Wally watches as the train pulls away. Beery looks back at him and lets out a parting YOWL.

EXT. THE WOODS - DAY

Wally is chasing a rabbit. The rabbit disappears into a thicket. Wally tries to circle around him and discovers a hole in the ground. He sticks his head in and sees that it is some sort of very old, man-made tunnel. He enters it briefly.

VOICE OVER

Wally had been looking for another
place to hide in case his present
hideout was discovered, and this
looked like the perfect spot,
hidden behind some bushes.

EXT. WALLY'S ROCK – DAY

Wally is lying down in his lair, but is suddenly alert. He hears the noise of approaching footsteps. He stands and looks out over the ledge and sees Berks and Loman coming up the train tracks toward his den. Suddenly, they see him.

LOMAN

There he is!

Loman and Berks start running up the ridge. Wally jumps to a higher ledge and dashes away. Fifty yards from his lair, he crawls under the brambles and into his tunnel hideout. The dogcatchers reach the top ledge, but Wally is nowhere to be seen.

BERKS

Where the hell did he go?

LOMAN
He's got another hideout.

Berks looks out over the vast area. He grinds his teeth in frustration.

INT. THE SPCA INDOOR KENNELS - NIGHT

The dogs are sleeping. A door SLAMS. FOOTSTEPS are heard. The dogs of the pack immediately become alert.

KIT
It's him.

MONTE
This is bad.

BUTCH
Stay cool.

SERGIO
What's he want?

BUTCH
Pretend to be sleeping.

The footsteps get closer. The BEAM OF A FLASHLIGHT approaches and stops in front of the cage holding Butch and Sergio. It's Berks.

Berks shines his light into Butch's eyes, and Butch growls.
He whispers to Butch.

BERKS
Not this time, but soon.

Then he goes to the adjoining pen, opens the gate and shuts it behind him. In his hand he is holding a dog-neck-pole. He secures it around Eddie G's neck and drags him out of the pen. Eddie G tries to resist, but Berks is too much for him. As he pulls him away, he whispers.

BERKS (CONT'D)
Time to play your part, little dog.

EXT. THE SPCA OUTDOOR KENNELS - DAY
It's the next morning and it's beginning to snow. Berks comes out of the building and looks up at the sky. He smiles and goes back inside.

INT. EMPLOYEE LOCKER ROOM, SPCA - DAY

Loman is changing into his work clothes and listening to the RADIO.

RADIO (V.O.)
This just in: The rains have been
so heavy upstate this month that
the Schuykill River for the first
time in seventy years has overflowed
its banks. And now, with this added four
inches of snow...

Berks enters.

BERKS
See what's going on out there?

LOMAN
Yeah, it's snowing.

BERKS
Put the chains on the truck.

LOMAN
What?

BERKS
This is supposed to stop around noon.

LOMAN
Hey, what's up? We never go out in the snow. It's like a day off.

BERKS
We're leavin' here as soon as this stops. Let's get ready.

LOMAN
This is bull!

BERKS
Trust me.

EXT. SPCA PARKING LOT - DAY

Slade pulls in just as the truck with Berks and Loman is leaving. He studies the truck as it pulls away, scratches his head, then enters the building.

INT. SPCA KENNELS - DAY

Slade walks through the area, stops in front of the pen holding the pack, and sees that Eddie G is missing.

EXT. HORSE CHESTNUT ISLAND - DAY

The snow has stopped but has left a fresh blanket of white on the ground. The SPCA truck pulls up, and Loman and Berks exit. They take the neck-poles out of the vehicle and start trudging through the snow.

LOMAN

I got to hand it to you, this is brilliant.

BERKS

Yeah, we're gonna see him and we're gonna be able to track him.

LOMAN

We're getting him today! And we're gonna get him alive! Even if he starts running, the snow will slow him down.

EXT. WALLY'S LAIR - DAY

Wally hears the men approaching. He looks out over the ridge and sees Berks and Loman laboriously coming up the trail. They look up and see him.

BERKS

There he is!

Wally GROWLS and then disappears.

LOMAN

And there he goes.

BERKS

He ain't getting away this time!

They continue to climb the ridge, and when they reach the top, Wally is nowhere to be seen. But his tracks are deep.

BERKS (CONT'D)
We got you now, Blackie!

They follow the tracks that lead them to the clump of bushes. They circle around the bushes, but the tracks disappear.

LOMAN
Where...?

And then they see the opening to the tunnel. Berks points.

BERKS
Look. He's one smart son of a bitch.

LOMAN
He's down in there.

BERKS
Yeah. This dog is driving me crazy.
But this time I think we got him.

LOMAN
What is this thing?

Berks studies the landscape, gauging his position.

BERKS
This thing, believe it or not, is a
hundred-and-fifty years old.
In the old days, when they were
building that freight line, they
would dig tunnels that would lead
to an underground room. They used

it to store things. Often, they would go under the tracks; led from one side to the other without crossing them. Sometimes they would go on for miles.

LOMAN
Do you think anyone's using it now?

BERKS
Who knows? Maybe hoboes.

LOMAN
Well, how we gonna get him?

BERKS
Well, I thought we could send you in after him.

LOMAN
Yeah, right! If you think I'm going in there after that big black thing, you must be crazy.

BERKS
Just kidding. Just kidding.

LOMAN
Don't make with the jokes. It scares me when you make with the jokes.

Berks looks into the hole and grins.

BERKS
No, you ain't goin' in and he ain't

getting out. Stay here, I'll be right back.

Berks goes into the woods and comes back dragging a large branch that had fallen. He lays it on top of the opening and goes back to get another. Soon, the opening of the tunnel is covered.

LOMAN
He'll die in there.

BERKS
Yeah.

LOMAN
Berks…

BERKS
Shut up!

INT. RAILROAD UNDERGROUND TUNNEL - DAY

Wally, crouching in the shadows of the tunnel, hears the CRUNCHING SNOW and knows the men in white coats are leaving. He stands and looks up at the debris covering the entrance preventing his escape, then he turns and looks into the blackness behind him. He begins to walk.

VOICE OVER
Was he scared? Who wouldn't be?
He knew he couldn't get out the
way he came in, so he did the only
thing he could: he began to walk
into the blackness. The tunnel led
down, down into who-knew-where. But
that's where he went, deep into the
old railroad underpass. He relied

on his sense of smell and hearing.
But then up ahead he saw a faint
glimmer of light.

A LIGHT appears, as if it's a distant star, so small, but it grows as he moves ahead. Then he hears very low SOUNDS. It's almost as if men in the distance are faintly talking.

INT. ELECTRIC COMPANY UNDERGROUND CONNECTION ROOM - DAY

Three MEN in yellow jackets, boots, and hard hats with lights are working on connecting two gigantic electric cables. ARON JACKMAN is in charge. LONNIE BRIGHT is working at his right. HENRY STUBS has just entered from the only entrance. The walls of the room are made of stone. The floor is damp. The walls are sweating.

JACKMAN

Come on! Let's do this and get the
hell out of here.

Bright and Stubs each have an end of the cable and are struggling to pull them together.

INT. RAILROAD UNDERGROUND TUNNEL - DAY

Wally is walking cautiously toward a growing light.

VOICE OVER

Wally thought that light was his way out, even
though the tunnel he was traveling through
continued to lead downward.

Suddenly there is an EXPLOSION.

INT. ELECTRIC UNDERGROUND CONNECTION ROOM - DAY

The men hear the explosion. The ground shakes.

JACKMAN
Did you hear that?

Stubs drops his end of the cable. Jackman takes out his cell phone and calls the ground crew working above ground. STEPHAN LEVERING, the foreman, answers.

JACKMAN (CONT'D)
What's going on up there?

LEVERING (O.S.)
Aron, get the hell out of there, now!

JACKMAN
What?

LEVERING (O.S.)
Do as I tell you. Get out—now!

JACKMAN
Okay.

Jackman turns to his men.

JACKMAN (CONT'D)
Let's go! Out! Now!

There is a roar, and suddenly water starts pouring into the room.

JACKMAN (CONT'D)
Steve! We can't get out. Water is

pouring in!

LEVERING
I know. The river has gone crazy.

JACKMAN
It's already up to our knees. How do we get out of here?

STUBS
Get us the fuck out of here!

LEVERING
Try to stay calm!

JACKMAN
Stay calm! Are you crazy?

INT. RAILROAD UNDERGROUND TUNNEL - DAY

Wally hears the explosion and, in a panic, runs for the light. The light is coming through the hole in the wall, and it's not what he hoped for. He sticks his head through the hole and sees the men, Jackman, Stubs, and Bright, eight feet below him. He can sense their panic. As the water rises, the men become frantic.

INT. ELECTRIC UNDERGROUND CONNECTION ROOM - DAY

JACKMAN
Steve! You've got to stop the water. It'll be over our heads in ten minutes!

LEVERING
We're working on it. I'm calling

in an extra crew.

JACKMAN
An extra crew! Are you crazy? By the time they get here, we'll be dead.

INT. RAILROAD UNDERGROUND TUNNEL - DAY

Wally backs away from the hole in the wall.

VOICE OVER
Yes, Wally turned away and started heading back the way he came, but then he stopped. As he stood watching them he knew what they were feeling. They saw no way out, and neither did he. Where was he going? Who could he trust? Most of the humans he had come across, or could remember meeting, did not seem worthy of helping.
But then maybe, just maybe, he thought of me ... heh, heh, heh ... the old man who left him food on the stone bench, the one who had been kind. Or maybe he thought of Beery, whose love for a human being was so strong, he was willing to spend the rest of his life riding the rails in an attempt to find his partner. And there was something else, something warm and sweet, something so important ... if ... if only he could remember.

Wally turns back toward the light.

INT. ELECTRIC UNDERGROUND CONNECTION ROOM - DAY

The three men are in a panic.

STUBS
Dear God, dear God!

BRIGHT
Shut up, for Christ's sake!

Jackman is still on the phone.

JACKMAN
Steve, for cryin' out loud, the water is up
to our waists! You have to turn
off the damned water.

Wally sticks his head into the area and lets out a tremendous HOWL.

BRIGHT
What the hell was that?

They look up, and the lights on their hard hats shine on the face of Wally.

JACKMAN
Holy shit, it's a dog!

STUBS
A damned dog! Where the hell…

JACKMAN
It means there's a way out.

STUBS
Oh, dear God; thank God!

JACKMAN
Lonnie, get on my shoulders and see what it is.

BRIGHT
But the dog…

JACKMAN
Would you rather drown? Come on!

The water is rising rapidly. It is almost up to their shoulders.

Stubs helps Bright onto Jackman's shoulders. Wally stares into his face and shows his teeth.

BRIGHT
Easy, big boy. Please.

Wally backs off.

BRIGHT (CONT'D)
It's a damned tunnel!

INT. RAILROAD UNDERGROUND TUNNEL - DAY

Bright and Stubs help Jackman out of the flooding room and into the tunnel. Jackman uses his cell phone.

JACKMAN
We're in some sort of old tunnel. I think it leads west. We need help. We're soaked and we're

freezing. How? A dog. Yeah,
that's what I said. A big,
beautiful black dog. We're heading
up the tunnel now.

EXT. THE WOODS ABOVE THE RR TRACKS - DAY

POLICE CARS and an AMBULANCE and a NEWSPAPER CAMERAMAN and a REPORTER are searching the woods. Suddenly, they hear Stubs, Bright, and Jackman yelling. Finally, they figure out where the entrance to the tunnel is located. They clear the debris, and the men and Wally exit. Jackman goes over and hugs Wally. He looks up at the cameraman.

REPORTER
How do you think that dog got down there?

JACKMAN
I don't know.

REPORTER
Looks to me like someone tried to kill him.

JACKMAN
Thank God they didn't succeed.

REPORTER
You guys were lucky, all right.

JACKMAN
It's a miracle.

A POLICEMAN comes over and points to Wally.

POLICEMAN
My captain says we should take him to the SPCA.

JACKMAN
No way! This boy is coming home with me.

POLICEMAN
But...

JACKMAN
Forget it.

INT. HOME OF ARON JACKMAN – NIGHT

Jackman enters the house. He has Wally with him. BETH, his wife, greets him with a hug.

JACKMAN
Put up a steak, baby. This guy is hungry.

Beth looks down at Wally. She gently, but tentatively, pats his head.

BETH
He ... he looks so sad. So concerned. He doesn't wag his tail.

JACKMAN
Yeah, like something is on his mind. He's probably starving.

BETH
He'll never go hungry again. The news said the SPCA wants him.

JACKMAN
What? Why?

BETH
They say he's dangerous.

JACKMAN
Dangerous? Look at him.

BETH
Will they let you keep him, Aron?

JACKMAN (CONT'D)
I don't know, but I'm not giving this dog up to the SPCA, not for one minute!

INT. APARTMENT OF SONNY WISCOMB - NIGHT

Sonny is watching the evening news on TV.

ANNOUNCER
It's an election year, folks, and once again Mayor Reynolds is stomping for ballots.... Today we learned he's trying to get the canine vote. Tomorrow at ten at City Hall, he's giving a party for a dog! No, actually, folks, this is quite a story. It seems Fido—no one knows his real name—seems he's an amazing hero...

Sonny pops up and listens intently.

EXT. DRIVEWAY TO THE DAVIS HOME – DAY

Ron comes out of the house and walks down the driveway. He picks up the morning newspaper, puts it under his arm, and brings it into the house.

INT. KITCHEN - DAVIS HOME - DAY

He drops the paper onto the kitchen table and pours himself a cup of coffee. He yells up to his son.

RON

Come on, Cliff, let's go. You'll be late for school.

He sits down and opens the paper. His mouth drops open.

INSERT: A picture of Wally. Aron Jackman is kissing him.
He runs to the foot of the stairs holding the paper.

RON (CONT'D)

Cliff!

INT. LOCKER ROOM OF THE SPCA - DAY

Berks and Loman are changing into their work clothes. Slade walks in. He drops a morning paper at their feet.

SLADE

Did you guys do something stupid?

SERIES OF SHOTS

EXT. THE ROW HOUSE OF ARON JACKMAN - DAY

He leaves the house. He is leading Wally, who is on a leash.

EXT. 42ND STREET - DAY

Sonny Wiscomb, limping with a cane, leaves his house and enters a cab that is waiting for him.

INT. RON'S PICKUP - DAY

Ron and Cliff are caught in a traffic jam on the Schuylkill Expressway.

INT. SLADE'S CAR - DAY

Slade looks in his rearview mirror and sees Berks and Loman following in the SPCA van.

EXT. CITY HALL COURTYARD - DAY

Aron and Wally walk across the courtyard and enter the building.

INT. CONFERENCE/ANNOUNCEMENT/MEETING ROOM – MAYOR'S OFFICE - DAY

Reporters and dignitaries are gathering for a press conference by the mayor.

EXT. NORTH MARKET STREET - DAY

Sonny Wiscomb's cab pulls up in front of the CLOTHESPIN STATUE. He limps across Market Street toward City Hall.

EXT. THE EXPRESSWAY - DAY
The expressway is jammed. Frustrated, Ron leans on his horn, even though he knows it will not help.

EXT. SOUTH MARKET STREET - CITY HALL ENTRANCE - DAY

Slade pulls up on the pavement at the south entrance to city hall. He is followed by Berks and Loman. The men exit their vehicles. Berks and Loman are in white coats, carrying canine neck braces.

INT. CONFERENCE/ANNOUNCEMENT ROOM - MAYOR'S OFFICE – DAY

The mayor walks in, smiling, and steps up to the podium.

REYNOLDS

Hello, everybody. Thank you for coming. I called this little reception today because sometime something extraordinary happens that we must take note of. In a way, it's a reaffirmation that we should never, ever give up. Recently, three lives were saved from drowning. Three of our own were trapped in a stone room far beneath the ground, with no apparent means of escape, when a dog…

The mayor turns and nods to Jackman, who is holding Wally. They walk to the mayor and take the podium. Wally sits calmly at Jackman's side.

REYNOLDS (CONT'D)

This dog appeared out of nowhere and showed them a way out.

A REPORTER shouts out.

REPORTER

How'd he get into that old tunnel, your honor?

REYNOLDS
Well, that remains a mystery.
Who would have done such a terrible
thing? We don't know. But the
gods must have been aligned in such
a way, for sometimes a cruel deed
works to the good of all, despite ...
well, suppose I let Aron Jackman, who
was saved by him, tell—

REPORTER
What's his name?

JACKMAN
We don't know.

REPORTER
What do you call him?

JACKMAN
Well, I've been thinking about
calling him "Rescue."

REPORTER
Are you planning on keeping him?

JACKMAN
Absolutely! I want to make sure—

REYNOLDS
Well, that seems only fitting...

Slade, who has just entered the room with Berks and Loman, raises his hand and begins walking forward.

SLADE

I don't think that will be possible, your honor.

The mayor turns. He is disturbed that someone has spoken out and stares at Slade as he walks forward.

REYNOLDS

And who, may I ask, are you? And exactly what do you mean?

SLADE

City code says that dog must be put in quarantine. He—

Wally stands when he sees the men in white coats and backs up. He growls and shows his teeth.

SLADE (CONT'D)

may be dangerous.

The mayor tenses, as does the crowd.

JACKMAN

Easy, big boy; easy, Rescue.

REYNOLDS

Is ... is he okay?

SLADE

We've been chasing that dog for six months. He may be a killer and may have to be put down.

JACKMAN

This dog is no killer, and no one

is putting him down!

The mayor looks at Slade.

REYNOLDS
Put him down? Sir, you must be a republican. No good deed goes unpunished! I'm here to give this dog a medal.

SLADE
A medal?

JACKMAN
This dog saved my life!

Suddenly, Sonny Wiscomb stands up and shouts.

WISCOMB
He saved my life, as well!

REPORTER
What? Who are you, sir?

WISCOMB
Wiscomb is the name. Sonny Wiscomb. And I was attacked by two hoodlums, and that big boy there saved my life—

SLADE
Your honor, I'm just trying to do my job.

WISCOMB
... and now you want to throw him in jail? Ain't that just the way?

SLADE
Your honor, this old man prevented us from capturing this animal and—

WISCOMB
And ain't that man up there holding him, happy I did? Why, had it not been for Blackie—

REPORTER
Blackie? Is that his name?

WISCOMB
That's what I call him.

Wally sits and blankly looks out at the crowd. The mayor holds up his hands.

REYNOLDS
Quiet!

VOICE OVER
It was at that time I looked at Blackie, and I knew what he was thinking. What's in a name? Fris, Frisbee, Blackie, the Ghost, Pard, Rescue ... The name didn't matter. Because at that moment, he felt no name could satisfy the emptiness from which he could not escape. At least that's what he thought. But he was wrong.

REYNOLDS
I came here to give this dog a

medal and—

VOICE OVER

And that's when everything changed, 'cause from the back of the room, we all heard it—heard it loud, and heard it clear.

RON

Waaallllleee!

VOICE OVER

And that big dog jumped up and started looking around the room. Bright-eyed, he was. Hearing his name, it was like everything cleared up all at once.

Wally jumps up, his eyes bright and alert. And then Ron lets out the WHISTLE—his call—loud and piercing, and Wally's tail begins to wag. The crowd parts, and Wally sees Ron and Cliff standing at the back of the room. With one mighty surge, he pulls the leash out of Aron's hands, leaps off of the platform, and runs to them. He runs through the crowd, past Slade and Berks and Loman, and he leaps onto Cliff, knocking him down, and starts licking his face. Cliff is laughing, Ron is crying.

VOICE OVER (CONT'D)

Yes sir, praise the Lord, it all came back to him in that split second. And that's the truth. I'm telling it to you like he told it to me; telling it to you like it was, and like it is, and like it always will be. It's called

love, folks. Unconditional and
free. Hey, now that is a rhyme.

DISSOLVE TO:

EXT. WHISPERING WALLS - DAY

Sonny "Big Daddy" Wiscomb is sitting on a pillow on one of the stone benches.

WISCOMB

Oh, I almost forgot. A lot of things happened
because of Wally. A lot of good things. First of all,
as you are probably aware, it became a national
news story. Every newspaper picked it up.

SERIES OF FLASHBACKS

EXT. THE DOG POUND – DAY

Berks and Loman are being arrested and escorted to police cars.

WISCOMB (V.O.)

It was discovered that Berks and
Loman were secretly involved in a
dog fighting ring. The police
busted that up right quick.

INT. THE DOG POUND - DAY

Slade is standing in the middle of a room filled with cages and angry dogs. He begins to open the cages.

WISCOMB (V.O.)

It was Slade who cracked the case.

He was really a federal undercover
agent who was working with the
SPCA, in an attempt to stop
that kind of vicious crime.

END FLASHBACK

EXT. WHISPERING WALLS - DAY

Sonny is still talking.

WISCOMB
And most importantly, with all that
publicity, a lot of people started
adopting dogs. For instance...

EXT. A CITY STREET - DAY

Monte is walking proudly with an elderly man. The man is dressed smartly, wearing a tweed hat and a monocle in his left eye. The man tips his hat as he passes a lady on the street.

WISCOMB (V.O.)
Monte was, of course, adopted by an
English gentleman.

INT. A BACKYARD - DAY

Sergio jumps into a wading pool with three little laughing KIDS.

WISCOMB (V.O.)
Sergio was adopted by a family with
a lot of kids and is now one happy amigo.

INT. LIVING ROOM OF HATTIE PIERCE - NIGHT

Kit is sleeping on a sofa, snuggled up against MRS. HATTIE PIERCE, who is prim and proper and knitting. Mrs. Pierce stops knitting, looks down at Kit, and pats her head.

WISCOMB (V.O.)
As is Kit. And then there is Butch … well…

EXT. PASSYUNK FOUNTAIN - DAY

Butch is sitting next to a group of young ladies. One girl has her arm around him. Butch looks at her affectionately and licks her face, then looks out onto the street.

WISCOMB (V.O.)
He might be the happiest of all.
It seems that nowadays every young
girl in Philly has to adopt a pit
bull, and a very pretty young lady
just fell head over heels in love
with him. I tell you, if a dog could
smile. … Well now, Butch, he's
smilin' all the time.

EXT. WHISPERING WALLS - DAY

WISCOMB
Oh, yeah, and Bella. Well, Mr. Bittle fired that
Wothers fella, and Bella went on to win the
Westminster Dog show.

FLASHBACK

INT. WESTMINSTER DOG SHOW - NIGHT
A judge is awarding Bella first prize. The crowd is applauding. Mr. Bittle, standing by her, picks her up and kisses her.

END FLASHBACK

EXT. GERMANTOWN AVE. SHOPPING DISTRICT - DAY

Ron's pickup truck is heading down Germantown Avenue. Wally is in the back. When the truck stops for a red light, Wally sees Bella. He becomes incredibly excited. She is on a leash, crossing the street with Mr. Bittle. He leaps out of the truck. Mr. Bittle is startled, but Bella is delighted. She playfully starts nipping Wally's ear. Wally's tail is wagging furiously.

EXT. PARK - DAY

Ron is tossing out a Frisbee. Standing on his right is Cliff. Standing on his left is Mr. Bittle, and at his side is Bella. They watch Wally as he chases down the Frisbee, then leaps high into the air to get it.

WISCOMB (V.O.)
And, of course, Wally is back where
he belongs: chasing Frisbees.

EXT. WHISPERING WALLS - DAY

Sonny Wiscomb stands.

WISCOMB
Well, I guess that's about it.

He picks up his pillow and looks around.

WISCOMB (CONT'D)
Now, come on, let's go. I'm ready to
get something to eat.

Eddie G comes running over and looks up at him.

WISCOMB (CONT'D)
You hungry, Eddie, or what?

Together, they start walking toward Sonny's home. We watch them as they walk away, and we hear Sonny.

WISCOMB (CONT'D)
Eddie, I got a feelin' this here is
gonna be a beautiful friendship…

FADE OUT

THE END

James

Based on true events...

James' rehab program was somewhat akin to being incarcerated in a medieval prison, or locked to an oar as a slave on a ship bent for Hell. The term of his sentence was totally dependent upon him.

The program was simple: break an addict down, expose his bare fiber, make him subservient to one and all, degrade and humiliate him beyond what he'd already done to himself, then allow him to rise and regain himself, not just as the man he once was, but as a spiritual quasi-monk of sorts, able to rise above the addiction.

He'd enrolled himself into the program, because the crack cocaine he'd lusted after had seeped into every fiber of his being and had ruined his life. It had robbed him of his job, his wife, and his five-year-old son, and in the end, even his father and mother.

Greek mothers don't easily turn their backs on their sons, but Mrs. Patrakis finally had when she caught James stealing from her and his father. The drug, whose power she could never understand, was killing her son. In Greek, she'd cursed the evil thing, and spat on it every time she thought about it, but she secretly never believed it had the power to make a man steal. She didn't know crack had the artillery to shatter a man's resolve to the point where, for one bloody hit, he'd sell his morality, not to mention his mother and anything she might have worth selling. She could never understand what had happened to her handsome young son, why he'd taken the drug in the first place, and why he had to take it again and again and again. She pleaded with James to do what the president's wife said: "Just say no."

"Just say no," she'd plead time and again. James could say the words, but he couldn't do what they meant.

The program was his last resort. All else had failed. For over eight years, his life had drifted downward, destroying everything and everyone in his path, interrupted intermittently by unsuccessful attempts to recapture his life. Only when he'd found himself locked up for vagrancy, with no one to bail him out, that he saw clearly for the first time in many years where and how far he'd fallen. James was smart enough to understand it was either the program or the Pen. The judge had made that dramatically clear.

"Do you have any family, Mr. Patrakis?"

"Not that I haven't hurt. None that would help."

"Children?"

"A boy. Six."

The judge had heard it all before. He gritted his teeth. "Find this man a program," he said with a bang of the gavel, and he sent James off with a guard into the next room to see a social worker whose job was to find an available program.

The social worker filled out a form, and she noted that James was six-foot-two, down to one hundred forty pounds, barely skin and bones, and was shaking. He was staring into his lap and had trouble making eye contact.

"Married?" she asked.

"She divorced me a year ago," he said. "Maybe a year and half."

"Education?" She already knew where he'd attended high school; she'd gone there, too. Cheltenham High. She was a freshman when he was a senior, and she'd watched him from the stands when he played football, saw him gain over a hundred yards against Amity. Although they were of different races, she'd secretly had a king-size crush on him.

God, she thought, *how the mighty have fallen.* Now he was just another crackhead.

"I graduated from Cheltenham High, and had a year of college."

"Where?"

"Temple."

The questions went on until she finally put down the papers and said, "James, I'm sure you've heard this before, but this is the truth: Boy, you are in trouble. Right now, you are at a crossroads."

He'd expected something like this earlier from the judge, but because of the caseload, the lecture had been passed down to the social worker.

"I want to kick this thing," he said. "I hate it. I know what it does to me, how debilitating it is. It's taken everything. I don't know what to do. My own parents won't even talk to me." He wasn't whining like some others did, just recounting the information in a flat, methodical tone.

"You've got to find a program, and you have to voluntarily agree to be part of it."

"I've been in two programs. They don't work."

"This isn't like the ones you've been in, and this is the only alternative you've got."

"I have no money. I—"

"This program will cost you one hundred and twenty dollars a month—whatever you get in food stamps. After a couple of months, you'll be expected to get a job."

James scratched his head. "A hundred and twenty dollars a month?" he said. "What kind of place only costs a hundred and twenty dollars a month?"

"Exactly," said the social worker. "But if you stay with it, you'll have to get a job, and then it will cost you more. It's a *whole* program."

The program, for Roger Price, was a business, an enterprise he'd bought from a former addict who, it was said, had relapsed back into addiction. Emil Bond, the originator of the idea, had been an old army sergeant and had written the basic principles of the program based on army discipline. What Price had bought was nothing more than seventeen beat up properties in rundown, predominately Black neighborhoods, along with an idea for a program. In these rundown properties, first Bond and then Price housed addicts—over 270 of them—and made money, with the business grossing over two million dollars a year.

Roger Price, a once-practicing karate black belt, had attempted to add a mystic quality to the regimented life.

"You been in the military, boy?" Price asked James.

"No," James answered, gritting his teeth.

Price was the color of fine, polished ebony. "That's a shame, 'cause then you'd have some understanding of what's in store for you." He scrutinized James, wondering if the kid could take what he was about to go through. The crack had given him that sunken, emaciated look.

"You got AIDS?" he snapped.

"Not that I know of."

"You got anything against Blacks?" At this, Price smiled. It hadn't been a malicious remark.

"No," James replied.

"That's good. Because of the two hundred seventy men and women in this program, you will be the first White man. Does that mean something to you?"

James showed no emotion, said nothing.

"Do you think Black is beautiful?"

James snickered. "Not especially."

"Hmm," said Price. "We'll see."

* * *

Two months later, Rocky Segal hired him as a schlep, but would later say, "Of all the dumb sons of bitches that came to me through that program, none worked as hard as James."

Segal hired guys in recovery because he knew those trying to recover needed to work to forget the drug. They needed to be so tired at the end of the day that sleep would be more important. Segal tapped into that need, and he worked them until they fell.

When he met James, Segal was rebuilding an eighty-four-square-foot roof on a historic mansion and he needed some grunt to carry shingles to the roof, five stories up. Segal, only five-foot-seven, took in the Greek over his reading glasses positioned on the tip of his nose.

"Can you climb?" he asked James.

"Yes, sir," James answered.

"Not afraid of heights?"

"No."

"You look strong."

"I've been working out."

"See those bundles?" Rocky pointed to the stacks of asphalt roofing tiles. "Each one of them weighs a hundred pounds. They go four stories up."

"Right now?" He sensed James's eagerness to get started.

Segal slowed him down. "One minute. Dave bring you?"

"Yes."

"What's your drug?"

"Nothing now."

"What was it?"

James gritted his teeth. "Crack."

"How long you been clean?"

"Two months."

"Okay, I'm gonna give you a shot, but I want you to know one thing. I catch you stealing, I'm gonna cut your fucking fingers off. I have no time for thieves."

James didn't respond, just smiled, and Segal watched as James easily hoisted a bag of shingles onto his shoulder and started to climb the ladder. He could tell within the first couple of minutes whether a man could make the ascent. James, he knew instantly, would have no trouble. He was an animal. He'd hired men out of the program before; they were all hungry to work. But no one had ever worked like James.

* * *

The two hundred seventy men and women who were a part of the program were housed in buildings built in the late 1900s, and of the seventeen buildings, sixteen were originally designed for large Victorian families. They were typical for their time of construction—many small rooms meant for servants and maiden aunts. The architect had originally conceived maybe ten, twelve family members, or people, at most ... never thirty, thirty-five men.

The largest of these facilities, the one to which James had been assigned, had actually been built as a small factory. It accommodated seventy-five people. This facility, called Bainbridge for the street it was on, was also the headquarters, the dining area, and the meeting hall for all of the men in the program.

Sparrow, a huge Black man with a clean-shaven head and sunglasses, took James to the seventy-bed dormitory—a long room with a twelve-foot ceiling and thirty-five cots on each side.

"Dis your bunk," Sparrow said. "Dat your footlocker. The rules is this: You is what's known as a Grub. If you stick, it takes three months for a Grub to become a Key. A Key is guy who's kicked, a guy who can be trusted. He's a person who's given a key to the house. No Grub can leave this house, for any reason, unless he's accompanied by a Key. You want a pack of smokes, you have to ask a Key to escort you. If you can't get no one who wants to do that, you shit out of luck. So make friends. Get along. Smoking's no good for you anyway. Everything else you need to know will be explained to you later on."

The dormitory was on the second floor; the beds made, army style. The room was devoid of personal possessions, pictures, and memorabilia. Stark. Reminiscent of a Roman garrison.

What James noticed immediately was that the place, painted bright white, was spotless, and he soon learned why. Essentially, it was cleaned and scrubbed from top to bottom no less than three times a day. If you didn't have a job that took you out of the house, you cleaned. The wake up was at 5:30 every morning. Breakfast was at 6:00. First cleaning was from 7:00 to 8:30, then a big meeting at nine. Second cleaning was from 11:00 to 12:30. Lunch was at 1:00. Meditation meeting was at 2:00. Third cleaning was from 3:30 to 5:00, then free time and dinner at 8:00. Night meeting was at 9:00. By 10:00 p.m., people were anxious to get to sleep. The Keys enforced the cleaning, but they also cleaned. The person who made sure everyone did their assignment was Sparrow, and Sparrow was not to be played with.

John "Easy" Easley, the Key in the bunk next to James, explained why he thought the program worked.

"This program don't give a shit for you, but you got to give a shit for the program. It works, 'cause if you fuck up, you out. You do drugs, you're out. You start a fight, you're out. You don't pay your food stamps, you're out. Boom! They just pick you up and kick you the fuck out, and they say go fuck yourself, cocksucker. Because this ain't no prison; they don't have to put up with your shit. This ain't no social services, dig? You don't want to kick, get the fuck out. Mr. Price don't care. He don't got to report to nobody. And he ain't worried about your shitty rent, 'cause as soon as you're gone, there's some other fool druggie just like you and me who gonna fill your bed, dig?"

"Hey, Mr. Easley…" James said, and smiled at the man's energy.

"Yeah?"

"Go easy."

"That's what they say."

* * *

James's ex-wife was blunt, and she had one thing to say about her ex-husband: "James can go fuck himself! The only thing I care about is my boy," she explained to the judge. "I don't want James to see him, because he's an addict. I don't want James to ever see him."

"I'm assigning James to a rehabilitation program," the judge said, never looking up. "If he cleans up and gets off the drugs, he'll be able to see his child. He is, after all, the boy's father."

She became distraught and angry. "Suppose he starts using again? Suppose he's driving and something happens? Once an addict, always an addict. Do you have any idea how many times he has tried to clean up, get off drugs?"

"James has asked to be assigned to a program," said the judge. "He seems to know he needs help. If he gets off drugs and is clean for two months, he'll be able to see his son."

"Over my dead body!" she cried.

The judge ignored her outburst. "If he has a relapse, we'll take that privilege away. That is all. Next case."

To her girlfriend, James's ex-wife said bitterly, "Fuck James. I hate him for what he did to me. Six years of humiliation; six years of being alone, of struggling. It's payback time. I'll bust his balls any way I can. After leaving Little Jimmy alone for years, now he wants to see him? No way. No fucking way!"

On a phone call to James's mother, his ex-wife said, "I don't think it's a good thing for any Patrakis to see Jimmy."

"But Elaina, he is my grandson."

"James will get to see him through you. I don't want that. Not since the accident, I don't want him near our—my son. He's an addict. I don't want that."

"I understand how you feel. But Elaina, I'm not on drugs." She'd wanted to say: My son wasn't on drugs before he got married to you. Could you be part of the blame? But she didn't say a word. She wanted to see her grandson.

"No."

"But Elaina—"

"No," Elaina yelled. "Don't call here anymore." And she hung up.

* * *

The meetings James attended three times a day were for neophytes. The Keys had their own meetings and were separate from the new men; AA had a meeting once a week. This program felt it was important to vent three times a day. Graduates of the program, men and women who'd been clean for a year and had left the housing part, led these meetings.

Rudy Robinson, a man who'd been clean for three years, listened to someone talk about how hard it was to be on the street and to run into an old friend who was still on, still dealing. A feeling suddenly comes over you. This man was from Jamaica, very Black with deep lines in his face.

"Right now," Rudy said, "you are suffering. You think about it all the time. Your mind needs it, your body needs it, but the longer you do without it, the fewer those moments will occur. And those moments won't require such a fight as they do now, you know what I mean? It'll be easier as time goes by, but for the rest of your life, you'll feel it, know it's danger, and wonder if you could take the drug just once more and survive....

"But you can't," he went on. "And don't dare think that once you become a Key you can get high and come back here, thinking you can hide it. You can't. We'll know. We'll know immediately, and it won't be good. I've been clean for over thirty-seven months. Shit, it's like I been reborn.

"You gotta rise above the common place. If your mother's gettin' high, you gotta be strong. If your sister's gettin' high, you gotta be strong. If your son's gettin' high, you gotta be strong. You can't help them if you get depressed and slip back to their level, and you yourself know that you can't help them unless they want to quit. You can't quit for someone else, and neither can they. You must quit for yourself."

Rocky Segal liked James better than any man who'd ever worked for him, and within months Segal was using him for all different kinds of jobs. Didn't take long for Segal to find out exactly what James could do, and he soon saw that the boy had many different skills: He could plumb, take apart a toilet, replace the seal, sweat a joint. James had what Segal called "soft hands." He didn't over tighten, and like Segal, he knew instinctively when it was right. In the beginning, Segal was always looking over James's shoulder, inspecting his work, until he gradually gained confidence in James' work. Not only in his plumbing, but also in his painting, roofing, and carpentry skills. Never before had he allowed an ex-addict to learn so much about his business, and this worried him. The longer he got to know James, though, the more he trusted him. He liked the fact that James was conscientious, always on time, eager to learn what he had to teach.

Beverly, Segal's wife, however, urged caution. "Don't bring him around the house. I don't want him working here."

"Why not?"

"You've never allowed any of your workmen to know where you live," she said, throwing his own rule back at him.

"This kid's different."

"Yeah, sure. Today he's straight, so he's okay. But what happens if he starts using again? What are you going to do then? If he sees this house, he'll think we're rich—even though we are not—and suppose he decides to rob us? Breaks in. Does something stupid."

"I'd kill him."

"That's what I'm afraid of."

* * *

Approximately twenty days into the program, Price scheduled a clean out. "Clean out" was a good name for it, because this was the line in the sand. Many an addict with twenty clean days dropped out of the program during and after a "clean out." It didn't matter to Price whether or not a man stayed. He'd been paid by the government for the month in advance and others were waiting to get in. More importantly, though, the city paid him an additional fee for every clean-out, and the program was, after all, a business. He told Sparrow to set his alarm for 5:15 in the morning, which would put the men at the clean-out site at 7:30. The cops were supposed to be there at 8:00.

James was one of the men assigned to the task.

Easy Easley told James that what he was about to do was no joke.

"What about breakfast?" one of the new men had asked as he and twenty others were shuffled out the door.

"There'll be no breakfast this mornin'. You won't want it. You won't be able to keep it down."

"What are we doin'?" James asked Sparrow as the Key issued him a cleaning implement.

"We're gonna clean out a crack house," the Key told him. "Move on and wait for me in the lobby."

The twenty men followed Sparrow's lead out the door and into the street. Then they marched in a disorderly line, each with a mop or a bucket or a broom, to an old abandoned house not eight blocks away. At one time it must have been something extraordinary, for the cut Philadelphia fieldstone that could not be destroyed still showed the masterful workmanship that such Victorians required. Everything else, though, was falling apart and in disrepair—the eaves had rotted away and squirrels were nesting (James noted one squirrel looked out to see what was going on); the windows were broken; the porch had caved in, one support post missing; the yard was overgrown, the black wrought iron fence surrounding the place kicked down.

The cops were already there when the men arrived. Four cars, sirens off but lights flashing. Some of the cops were drinking coffee, sitting on the cars, waiting. One of them, obviously the one in charge, told Sparrow he was late.

"Yeah, I didn't want to be early," Sparrow said. Then he checked his watch and declared, "I'm on time."

The cop raised his lip in contempt. "Okay, let's get this over with," he said to his men while glaring at Sparrow, as if Sparrow had assigned him to this task.

Half of the cops put on gas masks, took out rifles, and walked into the house, while the other four positioned themselves in the yard. The men from the program stood in the street and watched. Although James had been addicted to crack for over six years, he'd never visited a crack house. He usually found himself in motel rooms.

In short order, a straggly stream of addicts, hands shielding their eyes, squinting in the sun, were ferreted out of the stone shell. They were not arrested; rather, they silently scurried away.

Soon, the cops came out. They'd gone through the house and had declared that everyone was out. Then they took off their masks and shook their heads. One even said he'd never seen anything like that, and the others agreed.

Sparrow spoke up. "Okay, it's our job to sweep, mop, and clean that house. Another crew will be here in about five hours to board it up."

James had wondered about the gas masks, since the cops had not used tear gas to get the addicts out. He soon understood—the stench inside was nauseating, overwhelming to the point of giving you the dry heaves. He was glad he hadn't had breakfast. He surely would have lost it. The house reeked of urine and human feces; people had just defecated and urinated in corners. James knew, when you're on crack, you had no time to go to the bathroom or to even look for one. Someone had somehow deposited his dung in a bottle; others hadn't cared, and it was all over the place. And where foul excrement wasn't, there were instead vials, hundreds of them, covering the floor, crackling underfoot like broken seashells washed up on the shore.

Yet as disgusting as the place was, some of the men, sweeping up the tiny broken vials, had begun to be overwhelmed by the need to use. They began to joke about how high all those vials could get them. And those men, Sparrow knew, would not be part of the program tomorrow; they'd use before the night was over. Even in the stench of this pit from Hell, it evoked an overpowering need to have the drug, like a hand had reached up straight from Hell and dragged them down. Those, like James, who grimly did the work assigned and couldn't wait to escape the hovel would pass the test.

The program lost eight recruits that day. No one cared. No one tried to bring them back. The next day, when everyone knew they were gone, Sparrow said, "They weren't ready. They didn't want to kick."

* * *

With the exception of his wife and children, Segal didn't trust anybody. If he set up a man in a job, he'd tell him in detail what he wanted.

"Listen to me; pay attention," he'd say. "Get a bucket, put a capful of the chemical in the bucket—not two, just one—then use the brush and wash the wall. Make sure there's a tarp on the floor. Be careful of the floor. This is somebody's house. Once you got the floor covered, and once you're sure there is no water on the floor, warping those boards, that's when you begin to scrap."

"Boss, I've done this before."

"Yeah, I know. That's why I'm tellin' you again."

"I've done it at least five times."

"Do you mind?" he'd snap. "Are you crazy?" he'd shout. "Who's workin' for who here? I want this done right. I don't want any aggravation! I don't need the aggravation. Listen to what I say. I'll know when I don't have to tell you something. I know you better than you know yourself." Then he'd leave the room, cursing and "sonofabitchin'" everything.

"Who the fuck does he think he is?" the man said to James.

"He's the boss," James said. "All he was doin' was tellin' you how he wanted it done. Do it right and he won't bother you."

"Yeah, but how many times do you have to hear it?"

"That's just the way he is. What do you care?"

Didn't matter who you were, what you knew, or where you'd

come from, until you proved yourself, Segal treated you as if you were from outer space, as a total novice. He'd spent several years as an elementary school teacher and had learned the importance of repetition. If a man let him, Segal would teach him the right way to paint, to roof, to make repairs. Even guys who'd been in the trades listened and learned. But his forte, what made him money, was taking a man who knew absolutely nothing and, in just a couple of months, teaching him a useful piece of trade. In exchange, he'd work the man like a dog and pay him minimum wage. Sometimes he'd buy lunch. Segal could tolerate even the most inept man, provided he listened and at least tried. He'd learned over the years that a man who didn't listen and instead rushed right in, usually ended up making mistakes, costing him money, time, and aggravation. Most of all, Segal could not abide aggravation.

James did not give him aggravation; he'd listen and do exactly what Segal said.

One day, as they rode in Segal's truck to the next job, Segal talked and James listened.

"James," he said, "you're doin' good work." James thanked him. "How the hell did you get so fucked up as to end up in the mess that you're in?"

James had told him, only because Segal had insisted on knowing about his wife, his boy, and his addiction.

"And, you don't have to tell me," Segal said. "I've been there. For a couple of years, because it was the fashion, I was snortin' a lot of cocaine. Thank God I was able to stop. Hey, just like you, I got an addictive personality. Every time I see somebody smokin' a cigarette, I get that feelin'. There's nothin' harder than quittin' smokin' after you been smokin' twenty-five years. But I did it.

"You know what finally made me quit, other than the fact that I couldn't breathe? My uncle was dyin' from emphysema, and I went up to see him. He was walkin' around with an oxygen tank and still sneakin' cigarettes. When he saw me, he started cryin'. 'Rocky,' he told me, 'it's killin' me, and I can't stop.'"

Segal shook his head. "He knew it was killin' him, and he

couldn't stop. Jesus. So I stopped, just like you stopped. And you gotta stay stopped. So far, you got it together. This..." — he swept his arm, indicating the world — "is the good stuff. Because no matter how bad it gets, it's a hell of a lot better than what you've been through. Don't waste it. It goes by too quick; it flies by. Look at me. What the fuck?"

* * *

Anna Marie Silkwood had come to Philadelphia on a bus from a small town in Tennessee. She'd left her home, not really wanting to, because she'd gotten into a fight with her stepfather—a good man, really—over some silly thing, and being headstrong and wanting to teach him a lesson, caught a Red Rider bus to New York, but with only enough money to get her to the city of brotherly love.

She was spotted as a "lost and lonely" as soon as she'd stepped off the bus and was almost immediately picked up by Dion "the juice" Jones. Dion was a "finder"—a finder of flesh for pimps—and his territory was the 13th Street Reading Bus Terminal, his specialty young White girls, for they always brought a big buck.

Anna was not totally White but White enough, and Juice saw how beautiful she could be: her hair, her body, her poise all made her special. To Anna, Dion Jones looked totally harmless, appeared to be the perfect gentlemen. But behind the little boy charm lurked a total motherfucker. Didn't take long for the friendly, helpful procurer to drug, debauch, and enslave a girl, and with Anna Marie, it happened so fast, she never understood—one minute, he was kissing her hand; the next, he was beating her up and forcing her to have sex with whomever he bought home.

Kissing his feet, sucking his cock, being fucked up the ass, and begging him for crack cocaine were the activities around which her life soon revolved. Before The Juice had gotten her, she'd never even smoked cigarettes.

Then, one month after she'd arrived in Philadelphia, The Juice sold her to an associate, a Jamaican pimp, Clive Brown, in lieu of some nebulous debt plus five grand. Clive put her on the street immediately, but only after his obedience lecture. "Bitch," he said, "it be like this: The Juice, who brought you to me, is like an old-time ship captain who used to capture and run slaves to America. He sell them to a man like me. After all those years, nothing change—still the same thing. I buy you; you my slave, I your master. Only thing that change is the color of the skin. You probably say, 'How I get in this mess?' That what Juice's great-great-great granddaddy musta said. But don't you worry. You know, I not so bad, and better than most. You do what you told, I don't beat you, I feed you, and keep you in shit to get you high.

"Now go, Silky, and make your new daddy some money. Get your White ass on the street. It be a beautiful day." She started to say something, but Clive smacked her hard across the face and shook a finger. "What I say?"

It took several more blows for Silky to understand what he was saying. However, Clive, despite his lack of formal education, was an excellent instructor. That initial indoctrination lesson had ended with her on her knees, tears running down her face, kissing her master's bare feet and swearing her allegiance. At that moment, Clive smiled down at her, then rewarded her with a healthy smoke of the pipe.

It was a year before she knew she had to escape; that if she didn't get free, she'd die. The realization had occurred one day when she saw herself in a storefront window and didn't recognize the person staring back at her. The image that had glared back was something from a nightmare; she'd become a ghoulish ghost of herself. At that moment, she knew she had to escape. But how?

Seeing herself in that dark store window, she knew she'd been kidnapped, and now it was as if she had been marooned. She had no one. Where could she go to escape? Where could she run? She'd seen what Clive had done to another girl who'd tried to run: he'd caught her, cut her, beat her, and she was still his, working the fields, making their master rich, keeping their master happy. Silky was so depressed she walked in front of a bus and ended up, nearly dead, at Temple Hospital.

* * *

Stacy Spears had been in recovery for five months and was living at the Chew Street house, the smallest of the sites in the program. Under the best conditions, it could only accommodate seven girls, though nine were currently living there.

Stacy was tall, almost gangly, and lately people noticed she was holding herself straighter. Price said she was gaining pride, a good sign in anyone's recovery. Few women were in the program, and fewer women made it through. Most dropped out long before they ever became Keys. Stacy, however, having had the longest tenure at Chew Street was the only Key.

As a young girl, she'd wanted to be a blues singer, and when she reached the age of sixteen, she literally had something to sing the blues about: that's when she'd become addicted to heroin. For about seven years, she nodded into a depression that kept her from vocalizing. Just lately she starting to once again bring out the melodies. Another positive sign she was starting to feel good about herself. She could also see the humor in herself and would joke when someone heard her singing and told her she was good. She'd tell them that her best parts were her voice, her butt, and her boobs. "All the rest ain't worth diddly," she'd tell them. She was not the most attractive lady, but she had personality. She was there when Silky came into the program.

* * *

Rocky Segal awoke angry, aggravated, and gasping from what was now becoming a nuisance nightmare. He was angry because of this latest version of what he knew was an anxiety-performance-bad-dream kept him tossing and turning all night, and it was robbing him of his sleep. In this dream he was, as usual, back in college and, of course, the big exam was coming up for a course he needed to pass in order to graduate. In other versions of the dream, he never attended the classes, so of course he could never pass. But in this one, he did attend the classes, even studied for the test, but couldn't find the building to take the exam!

"Unfortunately," he said aloud, trying to wipe the exhaustion out of his eyes, "I know where the building is..."

Rocky Segal—nicknamed by his father after the legendary boxer and heavyweight champion, Rocky Marciano, because Rocky was built like him, low to the ground, and fought like him—was born Robert Lewis Segal. At thirteen, Robert confronted a sixteen-year-old who was stealing groceries out of his father's store, and beat him to a pulp. The elder Segal actually wanted to chase the little bastard down the block himself, beat the shit out of him, but that would have brought the little bastard's father around and possibly cause bad sentiment in the neighborhood.

It was hard for a Jew to own a store in a predominantly Polish neighborhood, and Rocky's father had to carefully walk the line between what was right and what was good for business. No one would complain if a thirteen-year-old whipped a sixteen-year-old ... or so he thought. Sure enough, the kid's father came around, but Rocky's father chased him out of the store with a butcher knife. The kid's old man, fat on beer, had come around, thinking the old Jew had beaten his boy, but the old Jew happily straightened him out.

"I'm gonna call you Rocky from now on," Rocky's father told him, delighted with the boy, "after the champ!" He'd never told him to take on the bully; he'd tried to never let Rocky see how upset the kid had made him. But Rocky had been sensitive enough to see it on his own, and this pleased his father. Rocky wondered if his father suffered from the same performance-anxiety nightmares that he did, and if he'd inherited it from him. He knew the nightmares meant that he was worried.

What had he forgotten to do?

Being a landlord was driving him crazy. Trying to make old buildings new was a never-ending ordeal; he had to get out. It took too much out of him to stay afloat, and he was sinking under the weight of it all. He needed to drift down some slow-moving river, to lie on the ground, to feel the heat of the earth. He was missing the fullness of life.

As a young man, he'd vowed he'd never allow himself to be caught in a web that binds and ties a man down. But he'd allowed it to happen, and now he was trying to wind down. His father had always wanted to go west and search for gold, to stick his feet in the Columbia River and pan for nuggets. But his father had never gone anywhere. Rocky had always had the dream of going deep into the woods of western Canada, living in the mountains, building his own place, finding peace, making new friends. That had been the lure.

Now, he knew that fantasy was out of the question. Ridiculous! He was too old to be building a log cabin, and people his age had great difficulty making friends. What made him testy and sad these days? He had no lure, nothing to capture his soul.

He needed to get away from the fix-it-for-you business of being a landlord, dealing with unappreciative tenants. Sure they paid, but it was depressing work, because it never ended and he was tired. He didn't know how much he needed someone to help him until James had come along.

* * *

One rule of the program was very restrictive; it forbade involvement with other addicted people. It read: "You (being the resident) cannot get involved with anyone but yourself, because if you can't take care of yourself, you can't take care of someone else."

When you are fighting off an addiction, you must be selfish, because you will need all the strength you can muster just to handle your own problems. You don't need anyone's troubles.

When James saw Silky for the first time, this is what went through his mind. He wasn't sure what attracted him to her. Possibly their both being White had something to do with it—they stood out like thumbs on a hand—and it might have been partly sympathy. The accident had scarred her face, and she was in a cast to heal her broken arm and shoulder. What was most appealing, however, even though she was emaciated, her eyes sunken, was the trace of innocence about her that amazingly belied that she'd spent a year on the streets. Unlike the other girls in the program, she wasn't hard.

* * *

Clive Brown was not really Jamaican. He'd grown up in a middle class neighborhood in Philadelphia and had become almost blood with Raoul Mais, the Jamaican boy who lived down the block. Together, he and Mais made their mark.

Clive considered himself different from most pimps, a fair and just man. He was secretly proud that he only had to kill one man to establish himself as someone who'd kill you if you got in his way or tried to take something from him. That one assassination had created a reputation that carried enough weight in the criminal underworld to keep his life moderately peaceful. He did not look for trouble; he liked and enjoyed serenity.

Prostitution, in his eyes, was a business. He was fair. He never broke in a girl himself, had personally no taste for prostitutes. Oh, sure, he allowed them to suck his cock, just to see how they worked when he inspected them initially. As they worked on him to get him up and to make him come, he delivered his "Be a good cocksucker" sermon: "You be a good cocksucker, and you will make a lot of money for your daddy. A good girl can suck five cocks an hour." Clive often spoke slowly, so that it would penetrate, and in a Jamaican accent, because that was part of his mystique.

And the less these girls knew, the better. They didn't have to know that where he lived had nothing to do with where he worked. He owned a house in Chestnut Hill, wore Armani suits, and drove a Beamer.

"'Cause most men won't be like me," he would tell them.

"Most men will come in five minutes. You gonna work on me twenty minutes. Now you belong to me; I own you, you understand? You will be treated well, but you will work. You do your job, you got nothin' to worry. You fuck up, you run away, I will kill you. You will now go to meet Mr. Mais."

And he did treat them well, provided they obeyed the rules, that is. Housing, food, clothing, drugs. Once he sold them, though, Clive took no responsibility for what happened to them. He had his niche, catering primarily to a lower middle class clientele, and he needed women who looked fairly good. Most importantly, they had to be young. Harder for an old broad to make money, and money was the name of the game.

Thirteen women were in his stable, and he rarely kept any one of them for more than five years. Usually, they were sold out of town, simply driven or flown to either New York or Chicago and given to some other purveyor of flesh for cash. Lately they were being sold locally, but for a time, they were working with an Asian firm that somehow got them out of the country. It never astonished Clive that once he sold these girls, they would really become lost. They could disappear without a trace and no one would go looking. Five years was all it took, from "lost and lonely" to completely lost. Clive knew intuitively, after five years most of the families had already given them up for gone. And no one ever came looking. Until Silky had done it, no one got away, because Mais always brought them back. Of course, no one had stepped in front of a bus before...

Clive pushed his swivel chair back and considered the issue. The girl had been put in a program in the neighborhood in which his people worked. That was a problem. Normally, if this happened—if she'd simply somehow left town—it would be easy; Mais would find them and bring them back. That was his forte. Mais was able to work the network as well as any, and as much as he disliked the idea, because the rehab program was becoming quite a force, the girl would have to be bought back and publicly taught a lesson. If he didn't, people might see, as a weakness, his failure to take back what was rightfully his, and that misinterpretation could lead to trouble. Would other girls follow her lead? Of course. But how many were likely to step in front of a bus? No, he had to get her back, bus or no bus. But how? That was the question.

* * *

In the small meetings where you were supposed to reflect on yourself and resolve your own problems, James always wondered what had gone wrong. In the beginning, he'd blamed it on the drug. How could he stand up against such a beast? They'd made it too powerful.

When it was his turn to talk, he always told them how his future had seemed so promising. He'd gotten a scholarship to college, and then it all went flooey. He could see clearly the first day he'd taken the hook, had allowed it to enter into his system. He was young, brave, under the false impression that he could not be hurt, that he wasn't vulnerable. He'd overestimated his own strength. That first day, it was as though an alien had immediately taken possession of his body and he was soon forced to feed the stranger. Since that day, nothing had been the same. "Kids take chances," he'd say. "I took chances. Who knew? Did I know? I don't know, maybe."

But he had known. He'd heard.

A year before he first smoked, he'd met a girl on a plane coming back from Florida. The University of Miami had invited him down to look at their program, and on the plane, the girl sitting next to him was wired, shaking, literally jumping in her seat. At first James thought she was just afraid of planes, but on the ride home, she'd told him about her real fear, her real flight: "My parents are bringing me home. I'm hooked, man. Hooked on a new drug. I can't escape. I'm trapped. There's never been anything like it before. It's a bitch. I'm fucked. It's called 'crack,' man, it's called 'crack.' You're not a NARC are you, man? Ha-ha. Good. You don't talk much. I can't stop. It's called 'crack.' My parents, they'll take care of me. It's beyond me, man."

So James confessed he'd known. He'd heard what it was and what it could do, but he didn't think it could do it to him. He'd always taken chances; that's what made him a great running back in high school. Even now, on the job with Segal, he took chances. At work, if he missed a step, he broke a leg; with crack, you lost your youth, your soul. Some could take it and simply escape. Two of his friends who took it with him that first time in college, as far as he knew, weren't hooked. What had happened to him?

As he looked around the room at the others who, like him, had also lost themselves, he wondered: What was the common ingredient in their bodies that made them susceptible to the beast? Soon, scientists would have the answer. Soon, they'd know how to cure it and make all of this aching desire go away.

People in the program immediately jumped on that kind of thinking. The false hope of every junkie, when he was really told that the only thing to make it go away was himself. It was his fight, and his fight alone. The program would give support, but the addict must want it. They were told to stop reflecting on what could have been; that was gone forever. Think only about staying clean and about the future. There still was a future. Huh. Apparently, everybody was a psychiatrist.

* * *

As they drove along from one job to another, Segal would verbalize his thoughts and feelings about the world. He listened to an all-talk radio program, and his own comments usually revolved around the topic of discussion for that day. James would listen and smile. Segal had a sense of humor that twisted things and made the serious problems discussed on air seem funny and ironic. For instance, he believed in a program he'd concocted called "The three C's": caning, castration, and cyanide. "If they graffiti," he said, "you cane them, just like they did to that kid in the Philippines. If they rape, you castrate them. If they murder, you zap them with cyanide. Get rid of the fuckers. Straighten this society out."

"What would you do with people on drugs?" James asked. "'Cause that's the thing that leads to the most crime."

"Were you a thief, James?"

James smiled, and Rocky took note. "Yes, I was," said James. "I stole, big time. From everybody. My parents, my wife—everybody."

Rocky shuddered. James now knew him, knew what he had, had been to his house. "James," he said, "if you ever start using again, you'd better let me know, 'cause if you steal from me, I'll kill you, I swear."

"Oh, don't worry. If I start using again, you'll know."

A long, uncomfortable silence followed.

"But right now, I'm in control," James said. "I don't feel the need."

"Good. Stay that way."

"I'll try. But what would you do with drug addicts?"

"Okay, here's what I'd do: I'd send them all to an island, totally out of their present environment, for two years. Make it totally free of drugs. They wouldn't have any access to the drugs."

"Yeah, sure."

"I'm serious."

"Who would make it that way?"

"The government."

"The government? Then the drugs would be there. There'd be drugs there. Just like in the prisons, they'd be there."

"Yeah, I guess you're right. But don't you see? That's the problem."

"Do you think everybody who does drugs should be on that island?"

"Yeah."

"All drugs?" James laughed out loud. "'Cause if that's the case, I guess you'd be sending yourself to the island." And Segal gave him a tight-lipped smile.

"Rocky," said James, "you don't think I don't smell the grass? Every time you smoke, even though you try to air out the car, I can still smell it."

"First of all, there's a big difference. And hey, I hope that doesn't bother you."

"No, that doesn't bother me," James said. "Look, you remember that time we were in that apartment up on Fitzwater Street, fixing that window? We had to remove that stuff on the sill—there was a small jar with water on it?"

"Vaguely. I know the apartment. Go ahead."

"Well, in that little glass vase was about fifty hits of crack. That guy was a dealer. If I was gonna steal, if I was gonna get back on, that would have been the time. That was the only time I was tempted on the job. I talked about it that night at meeting. It was a struggle to get back on track, but I did. I have to. I have to stay clean. I want it so bad."

* * *

Anna Marie Silkwood stood in the food line and slid her brown plastic tray along the counter rails, waiting for one of the cooks to put mashed potatoes, canned vegetarian baked beans, and a ladle of Chef Boyardee beef stew on a white china plate. James, who had, just hours before, become a Key, stood behind her.

"Hi," he said. He was feeling pretty good about himself. She turned her head slowly and looked up at him, blinked her eyes, then studied him. He was tall, sandy-haired, and smiling. For the first time in a very long time, she thought about how she looked. Having been run over by a bus just seven weeks prior had, in addition to giving her broken legs and two cracked ribs, left her face swollen and scarred. Her legs and ribs, the doctors said, were healing nicely; her face was taking longer. James didn't seem to mind, though.

"Do I know you?" she asked, thinking he might have been one of her many faceless customers. He just shook his head. "Then…"

"Just bein' friendly," he replied as the cook handed Anna Marie her dinner.

"Oh..." she said, turning away.

"Today I became a Key," he added as she walked away to sit at a table with four other women. The cook woke him out of his reverie by poking him in the arm with his filled plate.

Still smiling, he sat down with a bunch of guys from his house three tables down from where she'd sat. When her group had finished eating and they began to file out, she paused by his chair for not nearly a second and said, "Oh, by the way, congratulations." She didn't even look at him, but his eyes followed her as she left the mess hall.

Sparrow saw James watching her. "Hey, Key," he cautioned, "be careful. Don't fuck up now."

* * *

Raoul Mais leaned against a tree across the street from the Chew Street House and examined his nails, which he'd just had manicured. He blew on them and smiled. His father, who always had so much dirt under his nails they could grow things, would have been proud. "My boy," he would say, "puts polish on the tips of his fingers. He dress in fancy suits and drive a red Ferrari, but he no faggot. He shoot you if you look at him wrong."

Mais smiled to himself. The girl would be coming out soon; it was almost noon. Dirty Jerry, who'd been in the program and had actually stayed clean for two months, told him the schedule and where Silky would be. He checked his watch, and just as he did, the front door opened. Girls started to file out, one after the other, Silky was fifth in line. Her eyes darted around as she came down the steps to the sidewalk, and even though she tried not to show it, she saw him, and Mais knew it. He smiled at her, his upper lip curling to show his ultra-white teeth, and his eyes twinkled. *I got you,* they seemed to say. The girls marched across the street, passing close by him. He almost reached out to touch Silky, but Stacy Spears was behind her and intuitively stepped between them. He didn't say anything. Didn't have to. There was plenty of time.

In only five months, Stacy Spears had achieved a high status in the program—she'd become an important Key and the head of Chew House. Something had clicked for her, and she thrived. She loved being clean, feeling whole, and this hardened her will to fight the demon. She immediately knew who Mais was without knowing who he was and, following his eyes, she knew who he was after. She'd spent most of her life on the streets and she could both read the lines and between the lines with the best of them. This tree-leanin' sonofabitch was there for a reason: He wanted Silky. He had something on her, and damned if she was gonna let anything stupid happen on her watch.

* * *

Segal was pissed. Where the fuck was James? That son of a bitch had missed an entire week of work! He hadn't called, and he hadn't showed. The other guys who worked for Segal were basically worthless. They had no skills. James not only had strength, but he was also smart, teachable. You only had to show him things once. Segal had taught him how to plaster a wall, frame out a room, paint a perfect cut line, and James had easily taken to it. Segal had started to take him in, put his arm around him, invite him to dinner, introduce him to the wife and family.... But now, he was missing in action.

It was the last Friday in June. Days were longer; the heat, stronger. By noon, the crew—two schleps and a standby—were wilting from the intense heat. He considered calling it a day, but he was, thanks to James, way behind schedule. He tried not to think about it, because every time he did, he started to boil up. The rage within him was intense, and it was robbing him of his energy. His old lady, Missy, the love of his life, kept warning him about his high blood pressure.

"You're gonna blow a gasket, Rock. When are you gonna admit you're an old man and start taking it easy. Let it go."

Segal would look at her, smile, and blow out a puff of air.

"Yeah, you're right," he'd say.

Then she'd come to him, put her arms around him, and lay her head on his chest. "I don't want to lose you. We have enough money. You don't have to work the way you do. You don't need the aggravation."

Segal would smile and relax, but Missy knew—and he didn't have to say it—that it simply wasn't in his nature. If he didn't do what he was doing, what would he do? Sit at home and watch some stupid soap on TV? Not him. That wasn't who he was. It was, however, in his nature to blow a gasket every once in a while, and as long as Missy was there, he'd be all right.

But right then, Missy was at home, and he was with the three a-holes, not getting done what had to be done. Fucking James had fucked him, and Segal resented the dick up the ass. He yelled at one of the schleps, and decided right then and there to call it a day at five and to go find that sonofabitch. James owed him.

* * *

Many times, James, just like every druggie before him who faces a decision that will change his life and his future, will feel the urge to use. The tug of drugs is so strong in some people, it saps the life right out of them. James was one of those individuals. He'd failed so many times before, but now things seemed brighter than they had.

He'd been made a Key, plus he had a job he liked and a boss he admired and respected. He was trusted. He'd found that he could achieve a "high" on life. He had accepted things. He'd been clean for six months—longer than he could remember. He was, for all intents and purposes, happy. Segal, his boss, had decided to rent him an apartment in one of his buildings. Wasn't much of a pad—just a kitchen and a small bedroom—but the rent was cheap and, as Segal had put it, it was a start. So things were looking up.

Then, unfortunately, he got invited to a party, an outdoor barbecue, by a program graduate, Wes McConnell, and everything went blooey.

The party was in West Philadelphia, and McConnell was celebrating being clean for two years. There wasn't, of course, supposed to be any drugs there, yet they were there, in the hands of a beautiful young girl named Rochelle. She was long and slender, light skinned, chestnut hair. Her face was round and her teeth sparkling, and she had a body that filled out every part of her flowered dress. Nineteen-year-old Rochelle was McConnell's stepdaughter. When James had entered the party, it seemed Rochelle knew who she wanted to be with.

James couldn't help noticing Rochelle, especially when she immediately came up to him and gave him a beautiful red rose she'd just picked from her father's garden. She smiled up at James, and as she handed him the rose, she whispered, "This is the first flower I've ever given anyone."

"Thank you," he said, surprised. "But why me? I mean..."

"I like you. The way you look." She stared into his eyes.

He smiled and was about to reply, when another Key called him over to meet Rochelle's father. McConnell shook James's hand, then put his arm around his shoulder, leaned over, and whispered into James's ear, "I see you talkin' to my baby girl.... Don't!" then he turned away and went off to meet another guest. James was still holding the rose.

At that moment, James knew he should have left the gathering. He didn't know what was really going on, but he knew when McConnell had turned away, he should have left the party. Not long after that, when he was about to leave, Rochelle came up to him, tugged on his sleeve.

"You leavin'?" she said. "I got something for you." She leaned forward, accentuating her cleavage, and showed him a small package of crack cocaine in the palm of her hand. And that was all it took, almost as if the brown flat square package had arms that had reached out, grabbed onto him, and dragged him away. Six months of struggling to stay straight, thrown right out the window by the opening of her palm. Poof. Gone. People who don't use can never understand the tug, the urge. He didn't understand why she was doing it, but the reason didn't matter. The urge to take it, to devour it, was all that mattered.

He never did remember what happened next.

* * *

Segal drove his pickup into one of the parking slots of the Germantown building, where he'd allowed James to rent an apartment. The parking area was only a short walk from the front door of the ground floor unit; what was once a storage area for the larger units above, was now a small efficiency. Segal had cleaned it out, put in a small kitchen and a bath, pulled up the old floor, and reinstalled tongue and groove hardwood. The tenant before James was paying five hundred a month, but Segal had given it to James for considerably less. He figured he'd take a portion of it each week from James's paycheck. Rocky knocked at the door several times before he started pounding on it in frustration. Still no response. He went back to the truck and searched through a bag of keys for the set to that building. He knocked one more time before he let himself in.

The door opened to the small kitchen, where sat one chair and a small table. No dishes or anything else was in the cabinets, and the refrigerator was empty. Under the sink stood a wastepaper can filled with take-out food containers. The room was clean, though, and looked as if it'd been swept. Segal gnawed on his lower lip as he made his way down a narrow hall leading to the bedroom. He passed the bathroom, which was also empty. The shower had no curtain, but a mat lay on the floor.

He'd given James the keys to the flat two weeks before, but it looked as if James hadn't used the place. Segal walked into the bedroom, where a sleeping bag lay on the floor next to a single armless chair with work pants and a checkered shirt draped over the back. He stood there for a couple of minutes, contemplating. Then he let out a puff of exasperated breath.

This fucking business was killing him. Always one thing after another. He checked his watch. He could get a new lock for the front door at the hardware store nearby. Wouldn't take him long to change it out. That's what he'd do. If James came back and couldn't get in, he'd have to call.

Frustrated, Segal started to leave, but stopped in his tracks when he heard something. He wasn't sure, but it sounded like a whimpering coming from the closet. Segal knew the closet—small, and not very deep. Couldn't hold more than a couple of hangers. He swung open the door and … there was James! Hiding, sitting on the floor of the closet in his underwear, legs pulled up to his chest, hands clasping the back of his head.

Segal's lip curled. "What the bloody fuck?"

"I … I…"

"Get the fuck outta there, you simple shit!" Segal yelled, and he grabbed the druggie's arm, pulled until James came tumbling out. "Get the fuck up!"

When James got to his feet, Segal reached up—James was a head and a half taller than his boss—grabbed his shirt, and slapped him several times across the face. James took the punishment, arms at his sides. Then Segal punched him viciously in the kidneys, and James doubled over onto his knees. Segal grabbed him by his shirt collar and dragged him out of the bedroom, down the small hall, and through the kitchen to the front door. The old man was panting heavily now, trying to catch his breath. James had crawled out the door and collapsed outside on a patch of grass. Standing at the door gasping for air, the old man swallowed hard, then jumped onto the druggie's back. The impact sent James face-first into the dirt.

"I ain't through with you yet, bitch." He could barely get the words out. "You want to be a druggie…?"

But he never finished his sentence, because James, who was younger, stronger, and bigger, shook him off and was suddenly on top of his boss. The tables had turned. James had pinned the old man's arms and now stared down at him. Segal had no fight left. Next to the druggie was a rock the size of a baseball. James grabbed it and, holding it in his right hand, he raised it above Segal's head.

"I don't want to be a druggie!" James yelled. "I don't want to be a druggie!"

Still gasping for air, Segal stared up at him. "Then put that fuckin' thing down, and get the fuck off me."

And as if seeing the rock in his hand for the first time, James realized what he'd almost done. Tears filled his eyes, and as they ran down his face, he threw away the stone and rolled off of the old man.

Together, they lay in the grass and stared up at the sky.

* * *

Everyone who knew him, knew Rocky Segal was a stubborn son of a bitch. Usually if he said something or gave his word, he'd battle you to the ground to defend it. He had emphatically told James he'd fire him instantly if he did anything stupid. Well, James had done something "stupid," big time, and now, lying on the lawn, he was crying, sobbing—big time. When he was searching for James, he told himself that if he found him, he'd kill him, and he almost did.

"What the fuck were you doing in that fucking closet?" Segal said. "Were you hiding from me? You didn't think I'd find you?"

"I wasn't hiding from you. I was hiding from them," James said. "They're looking for me. They'll kill me."

"What the fuck are you talkin' about? Who's gonna kill you? Who's looking for you?"

So James told him about the party, about the girl, about the girl's father, about the dope.

"Do they know where you're livin'?" Segal asked. "Do they know about this building?"

"I don't know."

"All right, get any shit you got in there, and I'll take you back to the rehab joint."

"I can't go back there. They won't take me back. I tried. They threw me out."

"I'll go with you. We'll go together."

"I can't. They don't want me. They don't trust me anymore."

Segal stared at James and gritted his teeth. Others had quit him before, and he didn't care. But this kid was broken. If James was a horse, Segal would shoot the son of a bitch. "Okay," he said, "let me ask you a question, and don't, whatever you do, lie to me. After you left the girl, did you use again?"

James started shaking. "I wanted to," he said, "I want to, but … but I didn't. I swear to you, I didn't."

* * *

Two Keys stood guard outside the rehab center as Segal walked up the steps to the front door. One man, a burly fellow, stopped him before he reached the entrance, putting a flat palm on Segal's chest. Segal looked down at the hand in disdain, and then up at the man's face.

"What you want here?" the man said, removing his hand.

"To be treated civilly," Segal snapped.

"He all right," said the other man with a chuckle. "That's Mr. Segal. You ever unfortunate enough to work for him, he'll work your butt to the bone." Then to Segal he said, "What you doin' here, Rocky?"

"I need to see Sparrow. Need to talk to him."

"May I inquire as to what it's all about? That bird's a busy man, now that he's the new boss of the council."

"It's a private matter. Please just tell him I'm here."

The man asking the questions smiled. "I will, if you'd do me a favor." He waited for Segal to ask what that favor might be, but the rehabber remained mute. "I want to work for you again," the man said. "Can't you put me on the job?"

"If I recall, I fired you for sittin' around and whacking off too much. You lasted a week without doin' diddly, so you hid pretty good. I don't want to play hide and seek with you again."

The man laughed out loud, then turned to the man who'd put his hand on Segal's chest. "See? What I tell you?" He turned back to Segal. "Okay, Mr. Segal, come with me. You can wait in our visitin' room while I tell him you're here."

The room, just on the inside of the door, was sparse—two tables, one with a low-lit lamp, and two chairs. Segal took a seat and studied his cell phone. He had sixty-one text messages, and he started to go through them. Forty-eight of them were junk. He almost got through them all, when Sparrow came through the door.

"Mr. Segal, what can I do for you?"

Segal stood up and extended his hand. Sparrow took it. "Sit down with me, I need to talk to you."

"I'm pretty busy right now. I—"

"I heard about your new job. Congratulations. This won't take long."

Sparrow relaxed, took out a pack of cigarettes, and lit one up. He took a long drag and said, "I'm listenin'."

"Okay. I'm here about James," he said, searching Sparrow's eyes.

"The Greek?"

"Yeah."

Sparrow shook his head. "Yeah, that's a damned shame. He was doin' good, too."

"I want you to give him another chance."

Sparrow looked around for an ashtray, but there wasn't one. The ash fell to the floor. "What's that? Another chance?"

"That's right."

"No can do, my friend. This ain't kindergarten. You fuck up here, you out. A junkie has got to be in control. They say he got stoned at a party and gave some shit to a young girl. That is a big no-no!"

"That's not the way I heard it."

"How'd you hear it?"

"The young girl gave the shit to him."

Sparrow laughed. "You know you can't believe anything a junkie says."

"Look, James was straight when he went to that party. He went because he thought that that party would be the last place that he might find drugs and be enticed. The girl had the dope."

"But he took it."

"Yeah. Maybe. Maybe he did, maybe he didn't. I don't know, and neither does he. But, let's say he did. Okay, he made a mistake. He was doing good. You guys helped him. He fell down. Don't let him slide all the way."

Sparrow just shook his head. "I wish I could help you, but it's against the rules. He took again. He knows he can't come back."

"He has nowhere to go, nowhere to sleep."

"He can go to prison. There are doorways and park benches where he can rest his weary bones. That's where he belongs. We gave him a shot, and he threw it away."

Segal bit his lower lip and stared at Sparrow in contempt. "That's it, then. You're just gonna throw him away."

Sparrow was silent.

"Okay. I guess that's it. I tried." Segal slapped his legs and stood. "Oh yeah, by the way, I got four of your guys working for me this week. I'm gonna send them back to you. I'm sure you can find them work somewhere else."

A look of concern crossed the old bird's face. "Aren't they any good?" he said.

Segal snickered. "Truthfully," he said, "they stink. Just like all the other bums you've sent me over the years." He stressed the word *years*. "They work like druggies on relief. I'm tired of checking up on them. I'm goin' to tell them they can stick this place up your ass!" He turned and started for the door.

Sparrow stopped him. "Rocky, don't do this. These men need you."

"Fuck them and this place! After all these years, I ask you to do one lousy thing for me, and this is what I get? This is how I'm treated?"

"It's the rules."

"Fuck the rules. Yeah, the kid slipped, but he slipped because he was set up. Ask some people about that party. Do some investigation. Find out what happened. But take him back. Do the right thing!"

"Rocky, you know how much we need you, men like you—"

Segal held up his hand. "Then do me this favor. Let the kid come back in, give him another chance, and take care of him. Do it for me. Just this one time."

Sparrow let out a long sigh. "Okay. Okay. I'll figure it out. Tell him to come back."

"He's around the corner, in my car. Come with me and collect him. He won't come unless you're with him."

"Okay. What about those other guys?"

"You mean those guys working for me? Not to worry. They're doin' good, you know what I mean?"

* * *

Sparrow and James walked side by side toward the meeting house.

"Just act casual," Sparrow whispered as they reached the stairs.

Once inside the building, he walked James to the room where he and Segal had met just moments before. On the walk there, Sparrow had a soft face. Once inside the room, however, he turned hard.

"Listen, you son of a bitch, don't you fuck this up. You're lucky. You got a good man on your side. Now tell me what the fuck happened. And make sure it's the truth! I want to know everything. Who invited you to that fuckin' party?"

* * *

"I don't remember exactly who," said James. "Several people asked me if I was going. I remember the girl. She was Wes McConnell's daughter. I remember I decided to leave the party. It wasn't ... I don't know ... I guess I didn't feel right. I was, like, iced out. I was the only White-eye there, you know what I mean? Anyway, I started to leave—I was almost out the door—when the girl followed me out. I can't even remember her name, but she was McConnell's daughter. She showed me the package, took my hand, and started back to the apartment, and then … then … everything went black."

"Show me your arm."

James shrugged and bit his lower lip. "Yeah, the stab was there. I must have used, but I don't remember what happened. The next thing I knew, I woke up in a storefront maybe ten blocks away."

"It sounds like bullshit to me, but we'll see. I'd heard that Rocky had given you an apartment."

"He did, but I knew I couldn't stay there. When they put me out of the party, they threatened me, said they would kill me."

"I thought you said you didn't remember anything."

"Look, Sparrow, I'm telling you the truth. I don't know. Things keep coming back, keep fallin' away. I might have fallen over the edge. I don't know anymore."

* * *

When Segal found James hiding in the closet, he was infuriated. To see a grown man pulled up in that tiny space? It was ridiculous. The building was old. They were the original closets. They weren't deep. You couldn't even hang a suit, it was so narrow. But there was James, sitting on the floor, with his legs pulled up to his chest, sniveling. Sniveling!

Wow! Segal thought. *What that drug can do.* It was so powerful, it could turn a man—a real man—into a fucking baby. James, who could carry two bundles of tiles—a hundred pounds!—up to the third floor on a fifty-foot ladder, was hiding in a fucking closet.

Both he and James agreed that James couldn't stay in that apartment. It was behind the building, and it was dark back there. Made him too vulnerable. No. He had to go back to the center, had to stay in rehab. Nothing would happen if they just accepted him back in; no one would hurt him if he were inside that building.

As he drove home, Segal thought about the time he'd almost been pulled in. That was at least ten to twelve years ago. At times, once or twice, he'd experimented with cocaine, and he'd liked it.

After having done it, he wanted to do it again, but it was never available for him and he certainly wasn't going to chase it down.

Then one day, a friend of his came to him, said he needed a favor.

"I need you to take this package and hold it for me."

"What is it?" Segal had asked.

"It's a brick of cocaine," his friend told him.

And that's what it was ... a block the actual size of a paving brick.

So Segal took it and hid it in his attic. To get up there, you needed a ladder and you had to climb through a small door. Segal hid the stuff, went back through the small door, and climbed back down the ladder. But when he got to his living room, two floors below, he started thinking about that brick of cocaine....

He'd just take a little hit. His friend would never miss it.

So back up to the attic he went and scraped off a little of the brick.

Over the next seven days, he'd made twenty-two trips up to the attic, and during that time, he and his wife were so totally drugged out, they held each other one night and swore they'd never do it again. Because they knew if they kept scraping at that brick, they'd never be able to do without it, and there was too much at stake: their children, their lives.

The next morning, Segal called his friend and told him to come get what was left of his brick. They'd used a lot of the shit, and Segal had paid his friend. Turned out to be a lot of money, but Segal didn't care. He knew what the pull of it was. Luckily, he and his wife had each other to hold on to, to fight together against it. The thought of it, however, lingered for years.

* * *

The Alden Park Manor was built in the Jacobean Revival style back in 1926. The complex consisted of three towers that overlooked the Wissahickon Valley section of Fairmount Park. A magnificent structure filled with spacious, luxurious apartments meant for people of means. Clive Brown maintained an apartment there on the fifteenth floor of the tower closest to Wissahickon Avenue.

Raoul Mais walked into the Alden Park Manor wearing his green-and-gray checked sports jacket, a bright green ascot, brown slacks, and two-tone shoes. His boss, Clive Brown, didn't often ask him to come up for a visit, but the guard at the lobby desk recognized him immediately and watched him as he made his way to the elevators. Brown had a five-thousand-square-foot apartment on the fifteenth floor, and Mais was let into the apartment by Sherman Oaks, a former NBA basketball player. Oaks was a live-in personal bodyguard for Brown.

"He's on the terrace," Oaks said.

Mais nodded. He knew his way, and walked out to meet his boss.

Brown was reclining in a beach chair, drinking a martini. "Raoul Mais," he said. "You're on time. What you got to tell me?"

"Nothin' yet, boss."

"Nothin' yet. You crazy. What the hell goin' on?"

"Look, it would be much easier to just kill her."

"Kill her? Kill her? You crazy. I don't kill what I own. She still young. She still able to make money. And I don't kill what I own, you understand me?" Brown sat up in his chair. "I ask you to get her, and you still fartin' around. You must think I'm crazy."

"Look, I been hangin' around that fucking rehab for days. She ain't comin'. She pretends not to see me, and she's always with other women. There ain't nothin' I can do. I can't drag her into the car with all those other bitches around."

"Bullshit!"

"That's the truth. You worried about how it looks, her being on the street, about losin' face. Just let me shoot her fuckin' ass."

"No. I want to personally teach her a fuckin' lesson. You shoot her, I get no satisfaction and my other girls see me as weak. If she get away, others try it. And all de sudden, I'm dependin' on motherfuckers like Juice to find me workers. I want to fix her and put her back to work. I want the others to see her with de scars I put on her face and know what happens when you fuck with Clive Brown."

"Well, as soon as I get the chance to grab her, you'll get her back."

Brown looked closely at Mais, and his face scrunched up. "What, you goin' to some queer ball dressed like that? You turned faggot on me? No wonder you ain't grabbed her yet. Shit, people can see you a mile away."

Mais sneered. "I'm no poofter."

"Yeah? Well, you get that bitch, or I cut your balls off and make you one."

"There's a guy that I think is protecting her. I thought I got rid of him, but he's back."

"What fuckin' guy? The one you fixed at the McConnell's party?"

"Yeah, the big White guy."

Brown, who'd lit a cigarette moments before, smashed it into a glass-topped side table. "There's a bitch protectin' her, there's a White guy protectin' her, there's other druggies always around her. It's all bullshit! I want de cunt back here!"

Brown had finally lost his calm. He was yelling now, and Mais knew he had to do something.

* * *

The rules committee, in their weekly meeting, had decided that the ladies from Chew House could help the program if they'd would be responsible for cooking meals once a week, in order to give the cooking staff some time off. The ladies thought it was a good idea and that Thursdays would be the best day to fulfill that task. Their day would begin at six in the morning, and they'd work all day to prepare breakfast, lunch, and dinner.

At six that first morning, James was there to let them into the building. He'd been back only a couple of days, and when he saw Silky, his eyes lit up. She was beautiful. Their gazes met, and she smiled. He would have said something, but Segal had pulled up and waved to him. In an instant, Silky was gone.

Segal had agreed with Sparrow that for the next couple of weeks he'd pick up James, take him to work, then drive him home at night. The bird wanted to be sure James wasn't using again. James's Key status had been temporarily taken away until Sparrow could trust him.

James didn't see Silky again until Saturday lunch. He went over to her table and smiled at her. She looked up, and the corners of her mouth went up, too.

"Hello," she said. It was a soft hello.

"Hi."

"I haven't seen you in a while," she said matter-of-factly.

"Miss me?"

She thought about it. "In a way."

At that point, James couldn't think of anything to say. He just liked looking at her, and he stood there with a goofy smile on his face, trying to think of something interesting or smart to reply, but nothing came.

Just then, he was snapped out of his trance by Stacy Spears. "Hey," she said, "go find somewhere to sit. I don't want you talking to this young lady."

Startled, James stared at her, trying to determine if she was being serious. From the obvious stern look, however, she wasn't kidding.

"Why not?" he said.

Stacy crooked her finger, indicating he should come closer, and when he did, she whispered, "Because I heard you slipped, you know what I mean?" And then she moved in even closer and whispered directly into his ear, "Because you're a fuckin' junkie, a fuckin' bum, and can't be trusted. I don't want you to fuck up this girl. Don't pull her down." She backed away and, with the flat of her hand, brushed off his shirt as if dismissing him. "Now get lost."

All this time, Silky had been staring at the two of them. "Stacy," she said, "he was just saying hello."

Stacy had heard Silky, but never took her eyes off of James. "Do you understand?" she said again.

James let out a long sigh and, despite himself, smiled. "I understand."

* * *

The Chew Street house had a lot of physical problems. Built in 1760, the building had rotten eaves in which squirrels were nesting, and it felt like no one had been in the attic for over two hundred years. The girls who had rooms on the third floor heard the rodents scurrying around all night. It had a lot of small rooms, though, which made it perfect as a recovery home. It was safe—all of the windows had bars on the outside, and rule was all doors were locked coming and going.

Silky had a tiny, spartan room on the second floor—a single bed, a small writing table, a lamp, and a plastic folding chair. Management had spent very little money on furnishings. Most of the fixtures were purchases at Goodwill stores. Silky didn't mind. She didn't care. She knew it was temporary. Her thoughts were on her future. She was feeling good about herself, felt she'd turned a corner.

A soft knock came at her door and it opened slightly. Stacy saw Silky in bed. They looked at each other, and Stacy smiled.

"It's lights out," she said. "Get some sleep. We have a tough day scheduled for tomorrow."

She was about to shut the door, when Silky stopped her. "I have to ask you something."

"Sure."

"What was that all about today, with James? He wasn't doin' no harm."

Stacy let out a long sigh, then walked over to the plastic chair, opened it, sat down hard, and stared at Silky. "Girl, what's wrong with you? Are you looking for trouble?"

"No."

"Well, you better stop thinking about that boy. He ain't for you. He's a fuckin' junkie. He slipped and shouldn't even be here. He should be out on the street where he belongs." At this, Silky bit her lower lip as Stacy added, "You got to forget about him. Stayin' clean is about not slippin', bein' strong. If you two got together and he slips again, who you think would be slippin' alongside him? You! That's who!"

"But—"

"There ain't no 'buts.' It's tough enough to be strong for yourself, but" —she held up a finger— "it's so much tougher when the one you care about is suckin' you in."

"But—"

"You can't be with no junkie. You're gonna be fightin' this for the rest of your life. Get used to it, and understand men are all shits. Personally, I wouldn't give two shits for 'em. They don't give a damn about you. When you get whole, you got to look for someone who cares about you, who wants to protect you, who's willin' to die for you."

Silky stared at the Key. "I'm afraid," she said.

"What you afraid of? You'll find someone. A girl who looks like you won't have no trouble."

"No, it's not that. There's a guy who's hangin' around that—"

"I know the one you talkin' about. Don't you worry about him. I got me something that'll take good care of him. Now go to sleep. Wake up is at five."

* * *

Two years since Silky had left her home; almost two years since The Juice had put her on the street. Now, she wanted to go back home. But how? What would she do, what would she say? She tried calling home, but her mother had told her it was no longer her home. She'd made a mistake leaving, and now it was too late. She'd been raised in a lower middle class family. She'd gone to Catholic schools, and the nuns there had preached that suicide was no way to get into Heaven. But she didn't care. She just wanted to die. She wished the bus had killed her. Then, at least, it would be over.

If only she had enough money to escape, to get a job, to meet someone who really needed her, who really loved her. She knew things now that, when she was at home, she'd never imagined; things they couldn't show on TV, things you couldn't talk about with decent people. She'd seen men beat up, stabbed, shot, cut, clubbed; and women abused, used, and treated like shit. She had no money because, as hard as she worked, Clive Brown always said he was putting it away for her into some secret fund she knew she'd never get. The first time she'd asked about it, he laughed and said, in his Jamaican accent, "It be a retirement fund, for when you ready to call it a day." The next time she asked about it, he slapped her viciously across the face. "What, you crazy, girl? I told you, I takin' care of it for you. That's all you need to know." Then he curled his lip. "What, you thinkin' of doin', goin' someplace?" He started walking away. "You let me know when that be, so I can give you a goin' away present."

The last girl who tried to get away was quickly found and returned to Clive. She'd tried to leave with a man who'd said he loved her. She was severely beaten, and Clive had cut her cheek with his switchblade to teach her a lesson. No one ever ran away on Clive Brown.

After that, Silky (she hated the name "Silky," given to her because The Juice said her pubic hairs were so silky) on a daily basis she thought about dying. Degradation enhanced the depression. Fear was another growing cause. In her work, as hard as she tried to act tough, she was constantly worried some john would freak out. When she first started walking the streets, one sonofabitch went so nutso, she thought he was going to kill her. Now, she couldn't even remember what she'd done to set him off.

For a while, the hospital and rehab center had calmed her. Most of the time she felt safe, but ever since she'd seen Raoul Mais lurking around, she no longer felt strong and the anxiety had returned to make her captive. She knew who he was. She'd seen him huddled with Clive. Sometimes they would meet at a nearby coffee shop. Now, he watched her almost daily. She never looked at him directly, but always out of the corner of her eye, she would catch him smirking. He was so sure of himself, as if he expected her to break away from the line of other patients and go to him, like he was saying, "You gonna pay for every day you stay away. Who you think you hiding from?"

She had no friends, no one to protect her. Stacy had taken her under her wing, sure, and although she was well-meaning, Stacy was no match for Mais. Mais was a cold-blooded killer. Like a starving animal, he was lying in wait, biding his time, preparing to pounce.

God, how her life had turned! In the darkness of her room, thinking about her circumstances, she laughed out loud. Way back when she was fifteen (seemed like a long time ago!), a boy, Ronald "Ronny" Alberts, had asked her out. She was fifteen! Five years ago—three-fourths of her life! It had been her first date. He was going to take her to the movies, this tall, awkward, shy boy.

As she thought about it now, Ronny had an innocence about him that reminded her of ... of ... James. Maybe that's what had attracted her to James. For as much as James had been through, he still had that hurt look on his face that made her heart go out to him. She couldn't help it; she couldn't control her heart. Stacy, who was like a nurse, one who knew people, could see it. She saw the look in Silky's eyes and knew it was bad for the both of them.

* * *

In order to stay sober, Stacy Spears took her position at the Chew House very seriously. Before she'd become an addict, she'd been an RN at Temple Hospital. She'd voluntarily sought rehab because she loved what she did and was afraid she'd kill someone by being too high to react.

The women under her leadership were doing very well. More

than eighty-three percent of those who graduated under her governance were still drug free, and Stacy was proud of those numbers. But she was concerned about Silky. Stacy could read people; she knew Silky was suffering and worried, and both of those things had the ability to send an addict back to the streets.

And that's what Stacy had told the house managers at the weekly meeting, when the chair asked if anyone had any problems.

"Yes." Stacy raised her hand and stood. "I do. I got a girl at Chew House who has an asshole following her around."

"Does he got a name?" someone asked.

"One of my girls told me that they call him Mais. They say he works for the pimp, Clive Brown."

"You think there could be trouble?"

"Yeah, he's got her scared. I'm afraid he might grab her."

Sparrow asked the group if they had any ideas.

"I had me a problem like that at Ambler House," said one, "and we sent a couple of Keys to escort them back and forth."

"Did it work?"

"Hell yeah! We always sent two big Keys with them, and that sonofabitch disappeared right quick."

"Well, that's what we'll do," Sparrow said. "Is that okay with you, Stacy?"

"Yes, it is. That's what I was hoping for. I like it. Thank you."

* * *

What Stacy didn't like, however, was that Sparrow had chosen James as one of the escorts. He wouldn't of done that, had Stacy said something. But Stacy hadn't, and she'd silently cursed herself when she saw James was one of the Chew House escorts.

Sparrow, for his end, had chosen James to be an escort as a punishment. On the days the Chew House cooked, James had to be waiting at the residence at 5:30 a.m., but James didn't mind. He was an early riser anyway, and with nothing to do, he was always antsy waiting around for Segal to pick him up. Besides, he liked seeing

Silky. These days, she was especially beautiful in the morning. She'd gained back the weight the drug had robbed her of, and color had returned to her cheeks, replacing that sullen, drawn look. Her eyes no longer seemed dark and sunken. She and James always smiled at each other, but they never spoke. Stacy was always there to make sure of that.

One morning, as the group walked to the Bainbridge House, James saw Mais standing on the top step of a dilapidated brownstone recently converted into an apartment building. He wouldn't have thought much of it, had a familiar girl not emerged from the building, go up to Mais, and take his arm. It was Rochelle, Wes McConnell's daughter. James curled his lip, and so did Mais. Rochelle saw James, knew him instantly, and laughed as if it were some sort of joke.

Suddenly, James understood what had happened to him on the night of the party; understood why the girl had followed him, lured him into a bedroom. While he still couldn't remember what had happened next, he remembered seeing Mais in that fancy car, eyeing Silky.

He was about to say something to Stacy but saw she was already aware of Mais's presence. The look on her face was not one of joy; it was sinister. She turned toward Silky, but Silky hadn't seen him. Good. She turned toward James and tipped her chin toward the pimp. James nodded in understanding.

* * *

That afternoon, James, after arguing with himself whether he should or shouldn't, decided to ask Segal what he thought about what had happened that morning. He stopped what he was doing and told Segal he needed to talk to him.

Segal had been studying some floor plans, and so of course was irritated when James came to talk to him. "What are you, crazy? You stopped painting in the middle of rolling a wall to talk to me?"

James began to tell him, but Segal went on, pointing to the

unfinished wall. "Wallace, who ain't worth a shit, is finally cutting in correctly, and you just stopped. What the fuck! See me at the end of the day. Get back to that wall before the paint dries and we end up with a goddamned paint line that we can't correct!"

When James turned to finish the wall, Segal yelled, "Wallace only cut until you finished that wall."

When the wall was done and Wallace had gone out to catch a smoke, James went over to Segal and sat in a folding chair.

"All right, so tell me," said Segal.

"I'm scared," James said. "I found out..."

"Oy, yoh yoh! What now?"

"Okay, so you remember what I told you about this girl, Silky, being afraid..."

"And they put you on guard patrol, yeah, yeah."

"Well, today, while escorting her group to Bainbridge House, I saw the girl from Wes McConnell's party."

Segal suddenly became interested. "The one who gave you the shit?"

"Yeah. And she was with a guy named Mais. The guy's a drug dealer, and a known killer."

"Are you kiddin' me?"

"No. This is the guy who's after Silky."

Suddenly Segal was breathing heavily. He sat down and stared at James in disbelief. With James, it was one thing after another.

"I need a gun," said James. "This guy's gonna kill me. Do you have gun, Rocky, or know where I can get one?"

"Yeah, I got a gun. But you definitely ain't getting it. Why would he kill you, if he's after the girl?"

"Because I'm gonna protect that girl."

Segal shook his head. "I'm not gonna give you a gun. You must think I'm crazy. You shoot someone with my gun, where does that put me? Right in a fuckin' cell. No. No way."

"What am I gonna do? I gotta have something. Please!"

"Look, I won't give you a gun, but I will give you something. Wait here."

Segal immediately stood up and started walking to the door, and when he reached it, he yelled out, "Wallace, get the fuck back to work! Start cuttin' in." Then he went to his car, took out a policeman's billy club, and brought it back into the building. He handed it to James. "This is the best I can do," he said. "There's a loop here that fits on your belt. If the guy tries to grab the girl, hit him with this. It's the best I can do."

James stared at the club, then looked up at Segal. "You want to arm me with a club, when you know as well as I do that that sonofabitch is gonna be carrying a goddamn gun?"

"It's the best I can do. I don't want to see you spend the rest of your life behind bars."

"But Silky is in danger. This guy is gonna do something. I gotta help her."

Segal smiled. "You like this girl, don't you?"

"Yeah," said James. "I do."

* * *

The long white limo that Clive Brown used to convey him to New York cruised slowly down Wayne Avenue on the way to I-95. When he saw Mais strolling down the street as if he didn't have a care in the world, he told his driver to stop and pull over. Mais's casual attitude pissed off Brown, and he rolled down the window, crooked this index finger toward Mais.

Mais had seen the long car pull over, but didn't have to be told who was in the car and why it was stopping. Walking between two parked cars, Mais bit his lower lip and looked in the window, where he saw a pissed off Brown, and he was ready to take lashes. He'd been avoiding his boss, and Brown knew it.

"Where you been, motherfucker?" Brown said.

Mais swallowed hard. He wasn't afraid of very many men, but for some reason, Brown wasn't just any man. He was a stone-cold killer who didn't have to personally kill anyone anymore.

Mais let out a long sigh. "I just can't get to her."

"Bullshit."

"It's the damned truth. She's always surrounded by the other girls, and now they got two guys escorting her and the girls back and forth from Chew House to the main building. Plus now, they always got a guard. One asshole, the big guy, is even carrying a cop's club."

Brown didn't say anything, and the silence was deafening.

"I can't grab her," Mais said. "There ain't no way. You ain't getting her back alive, boss."

"Because they're always watching, is that right?"

Mais nodded.

"Because all eyes are on her?"

"That's right."

"Then what you do is create a diversion. You make them look at something else."

"How the fuck we gonna do that?"

Brown's eyes narrowed. "Get in here," he said, "and I'll tell you how the fuck we gonna do it."

When Mais had gotten in and heard the plan, he stared at Brown for a moment, and then started to smile. Of course. You create a diversion.

"I like it," Mais said, "but the only problem is, I can't actually be part of the grab. Too many people would recognize me."

"Yeah, you're right. But I need you to hold her. I'm going to be out of town for a few days. When this goes down, you got to be in your place."

"When's it goin' down?"

"Tomorrow."

* * *

Besides James, another guard escorted the group to the main facility for the dinner meal, a huge, imposing man whom everyone called Big George. Big George was delighted to be out on the street, and he smiled a toothless grin at one of the girls.

The women were straggling along down Green Street, single file, not really thinking about anything, when suddenly there was an accident. Right at the corner of Green and Haines, just as the women were about to cross, two cars had a head-on collision. One guy jumped out of his car and started banging on the hood of the other car. No one was hurt, obviously, but the racket that had ensued had stopped the girls' march to dinner.

James, like everyone else, momentarily stared at the crash, then tried to direct the girls around the logjam. When he turned, he saw Stacy running toward a man who'd grabbed Silky and was dragging her against her will into a car parked across the street. Stacy had a blackjack in her hand and was about to hit the man with it, when the man reached into his pocket, pulled out a gun, and shot her twice. The abductor threw Silky into the back of the car, where another man was waiting, then he then jumped into the front seat behind the wheel.

Before any shots were fired, James had seen the kidnapping and was already running toward the getaway car, billy club out, and before the driver could even put the car into gear, James had jumped over Stacy's prostrate body and had whacked the driver's side window, smashing it to smithereens. He was trying to open the door to drag the driver out, when the guy in the back seat pulled out a gun and shot James in the side. The shooter was about to get off another shot, when the driver finally floored it, and the car pulled away.

* * *

The bullet that hit James had had enough force to throw him back three feet, and he landed in the street, billy club still in hand. Big George picked him up and carried him to the sidewalk, then set him down next to Stacy.

"It's Mais," Stacy gasped. "It's Mais. He got her. That sonofabitch got her."

The pain was intense as they waited for the ambulance, and

when it came, they took both James and Stacy to Temple Hospital. Stacy was rushed immediately to the ICU. James was able to walk to a room, where a doctor bandaged him up. He'd been lucky. The bullet had passed right through him without hitting any vital organs.

* * *

Mais heard the banging on the garage door that led to the interior of his house. He'd left the garage door open, and they'd driven right in. The man in the back seat had used a chloroform cloth over Silky's nose after they'd taken her, and he was now carrying her over his shoulder. Mais knew the man was one of Brown's collectors, a big thug they called Crunch, with a pockmarked face and a mean expression. He carried Silky up the stairs, into Mais' living room, and threw her on the sofa. She was still under and looked dead.

"Is she all right?"

"She'll be fine in about fifteen minutes."

"How'd it go?"

"We had a couple of problems. You wanted her, you got her."

"I don't fucking want her. She belongs to Clive."

"Clive said to bring her here. She's yours until he says different. He's out of town until Saturday night."

"What kind of problems?"

"Look, I told Buzz to stick around because we have to get rid of the car. His face took some glass. Some asshole with a police nightstick busted the front window. We'll drop it off a couple of blocks from here—"

"What problems?"

"Don't worry about it; ain't no big thing. I gotta get going. Once we drop the car—"

"What fucking problems!?" Mais yelled. "Tell me, tell me now!"

"I had to shoot a few fucks. But everyone got away clean, not to worry."

Mais started stomping around. "Fucking bullshit! Fucking bullshit! Should have just killed the fucking bitch!" His anger kept him moving in a circle, cursing.

Crunch watched him for a couple more seconds, then snapped, "We gotta get going! This car is the only thing that can tie us to it."

"Yeah," Mais said. "You're right. Get rid of it. Wipe it down and then lie low till dis blows over."

"Brown will be in touch with you."

"I'll walk you down to the garage and shut the door after you leave." He glanced over to Silky, who was still prostrate on the sofa.

Crunch looked at her, too. "She's a beautiful piece of ass, but she ain't worth this kinda trouble."

"Yeah," Mais said, "tell that to Clive."

* * *

Long after Crunch had left, Mais was still pacing. He was worried, and that didn't happen very often. Mais didn't mind killing people—he'd put a lot of them down—he just didn't do it out in the open, in fuckin' broad daylight.

That stupid shit, Crunch. The motherfucker had shot two fuckin' people, and the girl they'd kidnapped was still out cold on his sofa! What a stupid fuckin' way to go down. He had a cell number for Brown, but there was no answer.

The girl started to stir. Mais curled his upper lip as she opened her eyes and slowly started to focus on where she was … then she jumped up with a start. She saw Mais, and everything that had taken place earlier came flooding back to her. She began to sob. She saw the crash, the big man who grabbed her and had pulled her away; she saw Stacy run at the guy, saw the guy shoot her. Stacy had gone down, and then she saw James smash the car window … then it all went black.

Now, she was staring at Mais, and she knew wherever she was, it wasn't where she wanted to be.

"What the fuck you crying for, bitch? You know this is where you belong. Brown, he gonna come and get you. He gonna make you feel good."

"Oh, dear God," moaned Silky, and her face fell into her palms. With tears running down her cheeks, she looked up at Mais and pleaded, "Let me go, please. I don't want to do it no more. I don't want that shit no more. Please."

"Girl, I don't want to hear that shit. You belong to Brown. He owns you. You know history? You know back in the day, White people owned Black people? Well, now it's the other way around. Brown, he owns you. He paid for you, so he owns you. Now shut the fuck up. If you say another fuckin' word or do anything stupid, I'll kill you, you understand? I should have killed you before. It would have saved me all this fuckin' trouble."

"Why did you kidnap me?"

"For him, for Brown. And remember this: I didn't kidnap you; I found you drugged at my front door, bitch."

"Then you can—"

The glare in Mais's eyes told Silky she'd made a mistake. He immediately went over and smacked her hard across the face. "What I say to you? Didn't I say to you 'shut the fuck up'? You stupid or somethin'?"

* * *

That morning, Segal pulled up in front of the center. He had a job downtown and needed to get James there. It would have been too hard for the kid to get there on public transportation. The Key at the door spotted him, and he walked down steps, tapped on the car window. Segal rolled it down.

"You looking for the boy?" the Key asked.

"Yeah," Segal said.

"He won't be comin'."

"Why the hell not?"

"He's in the hospital."

"What? What happened?"

"He got shot, is what."

"What the f— How? When?"

"I don't know. Nobody tells me nuttin'."

"Do you know what hospital he's in?"

"Yeah, Temple."

Temple Hospital, part of Temple University, was on Broad Street, only fifteen minutes away. Segal found James's room and pulled up a chair by his bed. James was sitting up.

"What the fuck happened?" Segal asked.

"I told you I needed a gun. They got Silky. I got lucky, though. There's another girl who got shot. I don't know what happened to her."

"Jesus Christ! I'm sorry, kid. I just didn't want you to get into trouble. I … I don't know. Was it the guy you told me about? Did he do it?"

"Nah, he wasn't there. These—I don't know who they were, but Stacy said it was him, Mais, that was behind it."

"Do the cops know about it?"

"Well, they came to the scene and got me here, but nobody even asked me what happened, almost like they weren't interested. Can you believe it? Anyway, there was a doctor in here a little while ago who said they were going to discharge me soon. Can you hang around and give me a ride to the center?"

Just then, Sparrow walked into the room with Woodrow Hall, who was the executive director of the entire program. He saw Segal and whispered to Hall.

"Mr. Segal," Hall said, "could you please give us a minute? We'd like to talk to James."

"What could you possibly say to him that's so privileged I can't be present?"

"I want Rocky here," James said, emphatic. "What is it that he can't hear?"

"I'm concerned about the integrity of the program. You seem

to bring nothing but trouble. Mr. Byrd here tells me that you broke the clinic's rules when you recently got stoned."

"What the fuck? This kid got shot trying to protect your people. He's one of you, and you come in here with this bullshit?"

"We've got a young Black girl, a Key, in intensive care, fighting for her life, so don't tell me about bullshit."

"Do you have any idea what's going on here? You've got to do something."

"We are aware of what's going on here. The police have been notified, and they will handle it. There's nothing we can do."

"The police! Give me a break. By the time the police get involved, that girl will be shot up again and back out on the street. You know who's involved. You can find out where he holes up, and you can get that girl before it's too late."

"Would you feel as strongly if it were a Black girl who was taken?"

"Silky is Black!" James shouted.

"She ain't that Black."

"Damn it! This isn't about Black and White. Don't make this about race. By thinking that way, you're losing your community."

"Community? What do you know about our *community?*"

Segal looked at Hall, and he couldn't keep from curling his lip. Hall was a meticulous man: his nails were polished, his hair neatly trimmed, his Armani suit scrupulously tailored.

"You mean the ghetto?" Segal sneered. "I probably know more about the ghetto than you do. You think that Blacks are the only ones who come from the ghetto? I grew up in the ghetto, I work in the ghetto, I hire your fucking druggies to give them a chance. I'm not helping this asshole here because he's White. I'm helping him because I think he has a chance to break away, be clean. Now there's a girl that's been taken. Doesn't matter if she's Black or White. By the time the cops get around to checking this out, she'll be gone. She'll be back on drugs, lost."

Hall turned to leave, but Segal grabbed his arm. "It's up to you to get that girl back. She's one of your patients, for Christ sake!"

"The police will handle it."

"Good fucking luck. All you care about is making money, asshole."

Unable to hide his contempt, Hall turned and walked away without looking back.

But Sparrow didn't. "Look," he said to Segal, "do me a favor and take James to Bainbridge house. Wait for me there. I want to talk to you. To the both of you."

* * *

By the time James had received his discharge from the hospital, Sparrow had already arrived at Bainbridge House. James and Segal got there a few minutes afterward. Sparrow told an assistant to tell all of the Keys to meet ASAP in the gathering room, and it took less than ten minutes for everyone to gather.

Once they were all seated, Sparrow began. "You all heard about what happened. One of our dear lady Keys, Stacy, got hurt, bad. She took two bullets in the gut and is now in critical condition at Temple Hospital. You know James here, he also got shot. But he got lucky. Some of you might know Rocky. He's James's boss, and others of you might have worked for him.

"The reason two of our people got shot is because they were trying to protect one of our own. Some of you might know her: a White-ish girl named Silky. Silky was a junkie, just like all of us, and just like all of us, she was tryin' to get and stay clean.

"Now, before she came to us, she was a whore, a girl of the streets. You know how —we all here know how— crack can do you. It makes you fall down hard. Well, she fell—hard. She fell so hard, she threw herself in front of a bus. But she must have been a good worker, because now, her pimp wants her back, so he sent some of his thugs, who grabbed her and shot up some of our own."

The room exploded as everyone started talking at once. Sparrow held up his hands. "Now, I'm asking you: What do you think we should do?"

Once again everyone started talking, and once again Sparrow had to calm them down. "Raise your hand and I'll call on you."

Every hand shot up. Sparrow decided to start with the first person on his right. "Isn't it a rule that if one of us breaks a rule, we just let that person go fuck hisself?"

"This girl didn't break a rule; she was forcibly taken. Kidnapped."

Sparrow started to go around the room.

"What do you expect us to do?" the next person grunted. "Call the police?"

Segal spoke up. "By the time the police get around to it, it'll be too late."

"Then fuck her. She got to be responsible. She a fuckin' whore."

"She's one of us! We got to do somethin'."

"Bullshit."

"Listen, we can't let this fuckin' pimp dictate to us."

"Who the fuck is this pimp, anyways?"

James gritted his teeth. "They call him Mais."

"Sheet, he a bad fuck. They say he killed a whole bunch of fuckers."

Sparrow put both hands down on the table. "Does anybody know where this pimp might hole up?"

"I know where his place be. About ten blocks from here."

Segal exploded. "Then we should go see this Mais, en masse. If we all go together, then maybe he'll listen and let her go."

"You fuckin' crazy. That bitch a stone-cold killer."

"Listen, if we all go together, all of us, and stand outside his window, I think he'll listen."

"He ain't gonna listen!"

"He can't kill us all. I'll go talk to him, if you guys go with me. I'm livin' on borrowed time right now anyway."

"What you gonna say to him?"

"I don't have the slightest idea."

Sparrow stared at Segal. "You don't have to do this, but I think you're right. I think he may cave if we go as a force. I'll go with you.

Anybody else?"

To Sparrow's absolute surprise, everyone in the room raised their hands.

In approximately twenty minutes from the time the committee had agreed that everyone meet to visit Raoul Mais, the size of the group had grown to forty-two people.

They marched two abreast to Mais's residence. Halfway there, they were met by almost all of the women from the Chew House, and before they reached Mais's street, they were instructed not to talk. Silence was more ominous than noise and yelling.

When they arrived, they lined the opposite side of the street and stared at the large factory's second-story windows. Sparrow started to walk to the one door of the building, but Segal stopped him.

"Listen, Byrd," he said, holding him by the arm, "I think only one of us should go to the door to talk to him."

Sparrow scoffed. "You ain't even one of us. What the hell, man?"

"Byrd, I have nothing to lose. You do. Two of us, we look like cops. Let me do it. I think I can get to him. I'm a great bullshitter."

"You could get your ass shot."

"Hey, I'm White. Black people don't kill White people."

"Well, we may have to change all that, motherfuck."

"I'm goin' over and ringing the bell."

"Be careful."

* * *

Mais lived on a dead-end street, in a building he owned that once manufactured cheap sofas and reclining chairs. Next to the garage was a door that led to the second floor, which was huge, and except for the bath and bedroom, everything was pure open space.

When Mais heard the doorbell ringing insistently, he at first tried to ignore it. But the ringing was persistent, so he walked over to the intercom, and before clicking it on, he cautioned Silky not to say a word.

"Yeah?" he said.

"Mr. Mais," replied a voice, "I need to speak to you."

"Who the fuck is this?"

"My name is Robert Segal. People call me, Rocky."

"What the fuck do you want?"

"I'm trying to help you. But before we talk, and before you get all excited, I just think you ought to look out your window and see what's happening in front of your house. I'll be here when you hurry back to talk."

The bank of windows looking out over the street was just a few feet away. The amount of men congregated across from the building, looking up at him, startled him. They all stood there in absolute silence.

He went back to the intercom. "What the fuck?" he yelled into the box.

"Yes, I'm still here," said Segal. "Okay, you see what's happening. What we'd like you to do ... for the good and for the welfare of all concerned ... is release the girl we think you are holding."

"Get the fuck away from my property—"

"If you release her, we will. We will leave, peacefully."

"I don't have no girl. What girl?"

"Look, let's not bullshit each other. We believe you have the girl. You ever hear of a guy named Drizzle? He was the guy drivin' that car. Somebody recognized him, and some folks paid him a visit, and he said she was dropped off here. People know what's goin' on. Just release her, and we'll walk away."

"Listen, you motherfucker, I'll blow your fucking brains out."

"Now, that would bring the police. And you can't kill us all. You let the girl go, and we'll just walk away. We won't call the police. That'll give you time."

"Time? Listen, motherfucker, I didn't have anything to do with what happened. Somebody just dropped her at my door, you know what I mean?"

"I believe you. That's why I'm offering you this way out of a lot of trouble."

"How do I fucking know I can trust you?"

"I'm giving you my word. I'm not a cop. Releasing the girl would be your best move."

"Nah, I'm not doing it. Go fuck yourself."

"Okay, so what we'll do is call the cops, and they'll come and knock your fuckin' door down. Maybe you'll get off a couple of shots, but in the end, they'll kill you. Letting the girl go is your best bet. No one is going to say anything. Trust me, it's the smart thing to do."

Mais spun around to stare at the girl sitting on the sofa. She'd heard the whole conversation. She didn't verbalize anything, but her lips said, "Please."

Mais made a quick decision, and he spoke into the intercom. "Hey, you still there?"

* * *

Two months later, James, using Segal's pickup, drove Silky to the Greyhound bus station. He parked the car, removed her small suitcase from the back, and carried it into the complex. When Mais had set her free, James was the first one to greet her, and as much as his wound hurt him, when she'd almost collapsed, he'd caught her and carried her to the Chew House. From the way she lay in his arms, everyone saw a potential growing love that couldn't be denied. And they were right. A bright light glowed whenever they were in each other's company.

He was right behind her when she got her ticket, and she held his free hand as they walked to the bus. They stopped before she boarded.

"I'm gonna miss you," he said. "Enjoy being home. I'm so glad your parents want you to go home. Don't let anything bring you down. Stay clean. That's what I'm gonna do. Think about what we could have together if we both stay clean."

"I will. I'm gonna give it everything I got. Don't be too long in coming. I ... I ... love you." First time she'd ever said it, and a tear rolled down her cheek.

"It'll take a couple of months," he told her. "I'm gonna save my money, and then I'll be coming for you. Don't worry about me. I'll be true. I never felt about anyone, the way I feel about you, Anna. You will always be my one true love."

* * *

Mais disappeared. After he'd released Silky, he hurriedly packed some clothes, his considerable stash of money, and drove away. He was not heard from again. The police are currently looking for him. He left behind Rochelle, Wes McConnell's daughter who, ironically, ended up at the Chew House as a patient.

Stacy never quite recovered. She'd suffered a spinal injury from one of the shots. The prognosis of her ever walking again was not positive.

Sparrow stayed sober and became the director of the program.

Brown was indicted, but the case never went to trial.

Segal sold his business and retired with his wife in Florida. James, when he was emotionally strong enough, sought out Silky, and he married her in a City Hall ceremony. Together, as husband and wife, they traveled to California and opened up a small restaurant. They now have two children and seem quite happy.

Out to See/Sea

After twelve years, I was back in New York. This time, though, I was sure it would be different. This time, I was dressed in a suit and carrying a briefcase on the street of musical dreams, headed for one of the biggest record companies in the business, to see their biggest producer: Gregory Vance of EMI.

In front of the main entrance at 444 Fifth Avenue stood a guy with a tambourine on his foot and two cymbals around his knees, playing the hell out of a banjo. Talk about a one-man band! In the lobby, a trio was playing furiously, hoping an exec from one of the several companies who had offices in the building might hear something that would turn them on.

But the lobby was as far as they got. Nobody who even smelled like a loser was getting by the guard at the elevator. The big guy in blue nodded to me and pointed to the open car.

I smiled. "Does he play here all day?"

"Nah, he gets one hour, once a month."

"You're a good man."

"Hey, ya never know, you know what I mean?"

I knew exactly what he meant. A dozen years before, I had taken my licks. But now, I wasn't toting a guitar and playing for nickels and dimes. Now, I was carrying a briefcase with something in it I considered dynamite.

For me, it had been a crazy time. The music world had gone from Folk to Rock, and I had changed as well—from a hippie playing Irish sea shanties, to a businessman running a one-hundred-fifty-seat restaurant. Everyone had to make a living, and I was no exception. I remembered going to Gerde's Folk City in the village and hearing Dylan.

"How the hell did this guy get this gig?" I'd said to Andy Babbish, my apartment mate. And Babbish just raised his eyebrows and shook his head.

"Andy," I'd said, "I hate to tell you this, but I'm leavin'. This town is killing me. I'm not having fun. Working all day waiting on tables just to pay my rent is not what I want to do."

Babbish nodded. "Don't worry," he'd replied. "I'll get someone to pay your share of the rent. Where are you going?"

And I told him. Europe. I'd been there for six months, street singing, and having a ball. When I had gotten back, Dylan was a star. What the hell did I know?

Disillusioned, I'd stopped playing guitar, stopped listening to any kind of music that had an acoustic guitar, and had gotten down to making a living. It killed me inside, because music is what had previously kept me going.

In the years that followed, I'd drifted from teaching elementary school to running restaurants—turning around places that had, for one reason or another, not made it, and that's what brought me to La Terrasse.

This beautiful restaurant on Penn's campus was dying, and the owner had no idea how to save it, so he gave me twenty-five percent of the business. Of course, at that time, the place was losing six-thousand dollars a week, but I saw what it could be.

I fired the chef, a Frenchmen, who came out of the kitchen to greet the patrons in the same dirty apron he'd been wearing for weeks. The soiled bid, no longer white, was so disgusting, it was surprising more people didn't puke than the ones who'd finally precipitated the Frog's dismissal. When the five people who were at the table refused to pay, I pointed to the kitchen and yelled at the chef, who shrugged, not understanding. "Get the fuck out of here!" I shouted. The Frog cried in his dirty apron all the way back to France.

I changed the systems, the menu, the pricing, and I stopped the thievery—the help, mostly Penn students, felt the restaurant's dishes, silverware, glasses, tablecloths, bottles of wine, were like a stash from mom's cupboard. The demi-chefs who went to the market each morning to buy the day's meats and vegetables had special deals with the suppliers. Everybody was making money ... except for the owners.

I changed all of that; still, I couldn't stop the bleeding. La Terrasse needed something more. It had no ambiance; it had no vitality, no vibrancy; it lacked that intangible quality all great places have. I had to somehow let people know that the place had changed, that it was now markedly different from the place that had been staggering and ready to fall.

So I started a poster campaign.

A conductor in a chef hat: *Every meal a production!*

Nothing.

A crazy guy dressed up like Napoleon: *Is this any way to run a restaurant?*

Nothing.

I was ready to call it a lost cause, when one Saturday night, in walked three guys looking like they'd just come out of the mountains, trapping beaver. I thought of the old joke *"I shot him 'cause I caught him fucking my board,"* and smiled. I would try to get rid of them as quickly as I could.

They were longhaired, scraggly bearded, and looking for the manager, so Jesse the bartender pointed them down the bar to where I was. Jesse shrugged and shook his head when he saw the look on my face. They wanted to know if I wanted to book them. Book them? They were a band. The instrumentation? Two guitars and a fiddle.

"What," I said, "hillbilly shit? This is a French restaurant."

They looked at each other, wondering what to say.

I sized them up. "Can you play?"

They just smiled. That said a lot. What did I have to lose? The place needed something, and besides, they were Penn students. And while I knew most places that turned to music were desperate, I had a feeling about these guys, and well ... I was desperate.

Still...

"Look, tell you what I'll do. Come in next Friday night. You start at eight-thirty. If you can play and it sounds good, and you can do four forty-five minute sets, I'll pay you a hundred bucks. Tell your friends. Put some people in the place. I'll put you in that corner of the bar. If you stink, I'll pull the plug immediately and not pay you a dime."

They left, shaking my hand profusely.

The following week, I had almost forgotten about them, until Jesse left his bar duties to tell me those three hillbillies were setting up. Disjointedly, I stammered, remembering, "Oh, yeah, yeah. Let them set up near the back of the bar, right before you enter the dining room. Let's hear what they sound like. If they can't play, we'll pull the plug."

Jesse nodded. "Gotcha, boss."

I hadn't even had time to see if they'd set up where I wanted them, when I heard the fiddle ... which was more violin than fiddle, really. At that moment, I was in the main dining room, schmoozing some guests, when the sound had drifted through the restaurant. Definitely not what I'd expected.

Then, moments later, I heard the rhythm guitar, which came in behind the violin, and it all pulled together when the lead guitar entered the mix.

And then came the voices—the blended harmonies. Different, brooding, magical. I'd never heard anything like it.

I stopped talking. So did the rest of the customers. Neither I nor the thirty-five diners in the one-hundred-fifty seat restaurant could see them, but they could hear them, and when the trio stopped playing, even though the audience had no idea who was creating the sound, the whole room broke into applause.

"Holy shit," I muttered, a huge smile on my face. Before I could excuse myself from the people I'd been talking to, one guy at the table asked, "What are they called?" and I laughed, replying, "Now that's a good question."

"Hey," he said, "I like that name."

I nodded, then left to find out what they were indeed called.

By the time I'd worked my way into the bar, the trio was already into their second song and the dozen or so drinkers were already into them. It wasn't just the sound, which was different from anything I'd ever heard before, they also had a look.

The fiddler/violinist was clean-shaven, wearing a long, tan doeskin coat tasseled at the sleeves and a big leather, brimmed hat. He had huge eyes that glared out at the audience and seemed magnified behind horn-rimmed glasses. He stood to the left, his right leg bent at the knee. Leaning forward, he bowed violently at times, softly at others, and when he wasn't moving his bow arm up and down, finessing the strings, he was picking.

The guy on the far right had a Cat Stevens look. Like Stevens, he sported long, black hair down to his shoulders, and a silky goatee. His voice was high, sharp, piercing and, at times, brilliant. He was the rhythm guitarist. But he was far from a mere up-and-down player; he did things rhythmically that few others could do. He was the bedrock, and he was precise, played it right every time.

The guy in the middle was the tallest, with long, black hair that ran past his shoulders, and a thick woolly beard. He had more than a decent voice, but he could play lead guitar like I'd never seen before; his fingers literally flew up and down the neck of the guitar.

I was stunned by the quality of what they were putting down. They were great. I looked around the bar and I knew I wasn't alone in my assessment.

Another round of applause followed the close of the second song, and it went on like that all night. The big guy in the middle looked at me and smiled, and I gave him a thumbs-up and smiled back at him.

Two weeks later, you could not get into the place.

The group was called Tyger—with a Y. The big guy in the middle was Bill Carpenter, and his brother Dick was the violinist. Steve Hastie was the rhythm. The three of them had never played together in public before, which amazed me even more.

"You know why we spell it that way?" the fiddler asked, sticking his face into mine.

I smiled at him. "Because Blake thought it'd be a good idea?"

The big guy, the fiddler's brother, laughed out loud goofily, almost a guffaw, and slapped me proudly on the back. "That's right," he said. "Hey," he shouted to the bar, "I like this guy."

The fiddler didn't remove his face from mine. "And we're burning bright!"

"Well, I want you to burn bright for the next two weeks when you're playing here," I said. "And you know why? So you can buy some mouthwash."

This time, Steve Hastie laughed.

They would play every Saturday night for the next two years.

That night, and for the next couple of days, I changed my usual radio station featuring the likes of Frank Sinatra and Mel Torme, to one playing the latest hits as I tried to find a sound similar to Tyger's. Nothing I heard even came close.

I'd rolled the dice with this trio and it seemed I'd thrown a seven. Everything started to click; I was on a roll. The place was continually packed. Within a month, we were turning a profit, although I knew it wasn't just Tyger. Later, though, I'd tell people it was.

Everything was simply coming together; everything—just like the band—was singing in perfect harmony. The new employees, the new menu, the new systems—everything played a part. The staff, because of the crowds, started to make serious money and started to take pride in the place.

Success is contagious. People loved La Terrasse, and I felt I could do no wrong. I put a classical string quartet in for Sunday morning brunches, and within weeks we were doing four hundred fifty brunches; the waiting line for a table went out the door and down the block! Suddenly, there was a vibe, and five months later, the restaurant was making serious money. I loved making money.

But as much as I loved the money and the place itself, I loved the band more. For I loved music. My best days? When I woke up with a tune whirling in my head, and lately, it had been Tyger songs. These were the kind of guys I wished I'd known growing up. My boyhood buds were fighters, not singers. Oh, they'd hang out on the corner, night after night, and harmonize ... but not one of my old friends had ever played an instrument. Hell, I didn't pick up a guitar until I was seventeen.

These guys, though ... these guys were different. They'd started playing when they were eleven and twelve, and they were real musicians. I envied their musical talents. And the songs were so incredible; ninety percent of the tunes they played were their own—beautiful, haunting melodies with deep, brooding lyrics. I would go in on weekends and sit at the bar just to listen. I loved the stuff.

La Terrasse's offices were above the restaurant, but I was hardly there once the place had opened for business. I maintained a table in the far corner where I could see the entire dining room, and rarely did I relinquish it, no matter how busy the place was.

Sometimes, before they started playing, Bill Carpenter would come over and say, "Hi, boss!" always with a big, friendly, goofy smile. "How's it going?"

I'd invite him to sit down, and we'd talk. I'd always ask probing questions, mostly about the band. I learned that Carpenter and Hastie had gone to the same high school, and while they both had been playing for several years, they didn't start playing together until they'd met at Penn. They lived in the same dorm. Dick, Bill's older brother, rounded out the sound.

"Listen," Carpenter said this time around, "would you mind if we did the first set strolling through the terrace?"

"If you keep it soft," I replied after some consideration, "I think it might be fun. If it works, we'll do it that way every Saturday night."

The patrons' response to this was very strong. Three months later, Carpenter had another request. He stood by the table and shifted his weight from foot to foot. I motioned for him to sit down. He hesitated.

"Got a problem?" I asked.

"Well, yeah."

"What?"

"How about a raise? I mean, it's been four months, we do four sets…"

I raised my hand. "Sounds good. I'll give you an extra hundred a night. That's two hundred a night. The best I can do. Well?"

Carpenter's response was another big goofy smile.

Two months later, he was shifting at the table again, and this time, Hastie and his brother were with him. I invited them to pull up chairs and sit down. Hastie did the talking.

"Listen, Ted, we know you like the music."

"I love the music."

"Well, we need a manager. We need someone to get us gigs. We need someone who can get us to the big boys. Would you be interested?"

"How much can you pay?"

"Pay?"

I laughed. "Okay. Just kidding. What are you willing to give up?"

"Five percent."

I laughed again. Thirteen years earlier, in New York, I knew guys who were willing to give up anything to have someone get them out. I knew a good agent could get a minimum of twenty-five percent, and I was about to tell them that, when a waitress came to me with a problem that needed my immediate attention.

"Listen, guys, I'll think about it," I said. "Give me till next week."

And think about it I did. I knew that one gig, though a success, didn't make a career. Tyger had obviously tried to get other jobs and saw it wasn't as easy as it had been at La Terrasse. Few other places in Philadelphia were willing to give them a shot, and a lot of other bands were competing for those places. Once people had learned that La Terrasse had music, I was besieged by one or two bands a week—most willing to play for free. I'd found another group, Thomasson and Tinkleman, that played every third weekend, but no band had a sound like Tyger's.

One week later, I came up with a proposal, which I'd spent considerable time thinking about. I considered myself a patron of the arts. Actually, I considered myself an artist. Even though I'd gone to New York and had hacked around Europe, street singing, making enough to live abroad for six months, I knew I was not a musician. Not like the Carpenters and Hastie, at any rate. But I'd majored in creative writing in college and lusted to write. I considered myself a storyteller, a writer—I saw a story in everything, and I'd spent my late nights writing. After Europe, I taught for ten years and wrote a book about teaching in the Philadelphia Public Schools. It had taken me four years, and though I'd sold several of the stories to the *Philadelphia Inquirer,* my total compensation was three hundred dollars—about seventy-five bucks a year—which is why I took the job at La Terrasse.

The following Friday night, the four of us sat down together, this time in the office.

"Okay," I said, "I thought about it. I don't want to take advantage of you, but I can't do it for five percent. It's too much work, and to be honest, I'm not sure I can help you. But if I do take you on, I want ten percent, which is a lot less than most real agents get. And we've got to trust each other, we've got to protect each other, we've got to be a team. Of course, this place won't count. And there won't be a contract; your word will be our bond."

They looked at each other.

"Hey," I added, "why don't you go think about it and let me know?"

They thought about it for all of fifteen seconds. What did they have to lose?

Initially, I got them some jobs at a few New Jersey community colleges and had actually driven them to the gigs, but I never took any cut of the two or three hundred they made. Thirty bucks wasn't what I was looking for. The guys seemed happy, the road was fun, and the bucks weren't bad.

Then, a gig came that was an absolute disaster.

Actually, it was a riot.

Because of who I was and what I'd created at La Terrasse, people in Philadelphia answered my calls, especially other restaurant owners. I talked to one guy who had a Bistro in South Philly; I told him about Tyger and asked if he wanted to hire them. This guy, an actual Frenchman named Claude, told me that while his place was too small to host them, he was on the entertainment committee for an upcoming annual street event and it could be great exposure for Tyger. He'd already booked two bands and needed a third to fill out the card. Tyger could go on and do twenty minutes between the two other groups. I jumped at the opportunity. I'd heard of the event and knew it attracted thousands of people.

Initially, both the band and I were excited. It was a beautiful spring night, and the crowd was huge. What I didn't know, however, was that the two other bands were electric, putting Tyger at a distinct disadvantage. Being acoustic, Tyger should have gone on first, but the organizers had insisted that the format was set and the trio would go on after Madd Junkyard Dogs, an eight-piece heavy metal biker band.

The Madd Junkyard Dogs got the crowd crazy. The lead singer, a Mick Jagger wannabe and his bad band knockoff, finally quit the stage, screaming obscenities and cursing at people in the crowd. When Tyger took the stage, there was a sense that something was going to explode—there was a vocal rumbling, an undercurrent of anger. Tyger began to play, while the people directly in front of them were screaming at the people behind them. Even with a sophisticated sound system and the mics boosted up to their limit, there was so much crowd noise, no one beyond the first few rows could hear the acoustic trio.

Then somebody from the Madd Junkyard Dog's crew threw a punch ... and there was chaos. Everyone was fighting. Some jerks had begun throwing bottles; the pavilion began to shake. I saw Hastie's eyes go wide. Bill Carpenter's were shut, oblivious, as if still trying to concentrate on the music. I ran up on stage to pull them off. At first, they were reluctant to leave, but I finally got them to listen. They ran off stage and had almost made it to the safety of a nearby store, when a thrown bottle hit Mary, Dick's wife of six months, in the mouth, breaking her jaw and knocking out two teeth. Everyone watched, dumbstruck, as thousands of people brawled in the streets.

Now, because of the incident and because of what happened to Mary, I thought I really owed the trio something. The riot hadn't been my fault, but I felt I should have known better. The small gig stuff wasn't working. I needed a plan.

About eight years before, during my teaching years, I'd met John Mobley, an African American man, who was a line chef in a place I often frequented for lunch. I loved to talk to people, and so did Mobley. Somehow, we'd started talking to each other.

Mobley had a dream: to open a restaurant of his own in a predominately Black North Philly community. No one made ribs like him, and I, having tasted Mobley's delicious ribs, agreed, and if the other food he made was anything like the ribs, people would come from all over. He just needed someone to pull it all together.

I put up a grand, put the deal together, and built my new partner a barbecue joint with a western motif: the Rib Ranch. Eight years later, I still owned half the place, and still hadn't made a dime. But it really didn't matter. I liked Mobley, and the ribs were fantastic. Mobley however, had been an R&B front man in his youth and a singer of crazy comical songs, and he was still friendly with a really important producer named Bobby Martin.

Mobley set up a gig and invited Martin. The group would play at two o'clock in the morning, just after the Rib Ranch had closed for the night. Mobley invited about twenty people; everyone, except for the band and me, was Black.

The smell of barbecue sauce was thick in the air as Tyger tuned up. They'd just finished four sets at La Terrasse. I was standing in the back, while the audience sat on backless wooden benches. Martin, who was tall, immaculate, and smartly dressed, shook hands with me, then immediately excused himself to make an important phone call at a pay phone on the wall across the room. He was still on the phone when the band began to play. Just minutes after they'd started, he swiveled his head to stare at them and, without taking his eyes off of them, he hung up the receiver. The place loved Tyger, and so did Martin. I was watching him closely and noticed with delight that his mouth had dropped open.

Martin was excited. He loved the band and wanted to record their stuff. He said he wanted to take them into Sigma Sound, a famous recording studio, and lay down their tracks. We—Mobley, Martin, and I—would each put up fifteen hundred dollars.

Two weeks later the band came, ready to play twelve songs.

Martin laughed. "Do you read?" he said. "Do you have charts?"

No, they didn't read, and no, they didn't have charts.

Martin came into the sound booth where I was sitting, scratching his head. "They can't do twelve songs," he told me. "They'd be lucky to get three down tonight. Do you have any idea how long it can take to do one song?"

Martin reassessed his prediction, however, when they laid down their first track in fifteen minutes. Then Tyger really got going—they did twelve songs in two nights and put together what I called The White Album because there was no picture and the 78 was in a plain white sleeve.

After listening to the tracks, Martin wanted me and the boys to meet a producer he worked with in New York, Joel Claymond, who, Martin confessed, worked with bands like Tyger. Martin, after all, was an R&B guy, and Claymond was the type of guy who could take them to where they needed to go.

I considered the logistics and told Martin I'd get back to him. I didn't want to take them to New York just to meet this one guy, so I got them twenty minutes at the Bitter End, a famous spot in Greenwich Village, and then they could go meet Claymond. The whole group, plus my wife, Ruth, drove to the Big Apple in a friend's huge Cadillac.

The ride up the NJ turnpike was fun, the gig at the Bitter End was exciting, and the meeting afterward was interesting, to say the least. Claymond lived on the West Side in a one-bedroom on the eighth floor of a well-maintained high rise. The lobby was in good taste, the foyers were well kept, but Claymond's apartment itself was totally gauche. Claymond was trying too hard to look well-to-do, and the attempt at being hip failed miserably, the epitome being a fake waterfall that dominated one corner of the foyer. It looked as if it had been made from a kid's train tunnel kit. Still, the apartment was in Manhattan, and any apartment in Manhattan was expensive.

Claymond was young, maybe thirty-five, and like the décor, he was trying too hard to look like a New York guy. He was just under six feet tall and slim, and though he tried to be friendly, he wore a smug look of condescension. He seemed to dislike the group as soon as they'd walked in, and it had only gotten worse when Ruth, my wife, had asked if he was the same Joel Claymond who once took out one of her girlfriends from Paterson. At that point, he went mute and stopped listening.

Then, David Clayton Thomas from Earth, Wind & Fire walked in. Thomas sat down on the sofa for about ten minutes and couldn't take his eyes off of Bill's flying fingers. Bill laughed and said, "Damn you look so familiar." Claymond told Thomas he needed to talk to him privately, and as he pulled him away, I asked if I could talk to him for just a few minutes. Claymond dismissed me, saying I should talk to Bobby Martin, and Martin said, as the guys packed up their instruments, that he'd call.

I never heard from him again.

I knew we'd missed a chance. Maybe if Ruth hadn't said something about being from Paterson to a guy trying so hard to disassociate himself from it, or if David Clayton Thomas hadn't walked in to pull him away from what Tyger was putting down, things might have been different. But that's the way it was. Still, there were other people, and I would keep trying.

The ride back to Philly was a sleepy one.

Now, I was once again in New York. It had taken me weeks to set up this appointment with Gregory Vance.

The secretary smiled and buzzed her boss, who told her to send me in. The office was beautiful, and Vance was cordial. His suit jacket hung over the swivel chair behind his desk, but he still wore his tie, knotted at the neck, and his shirt cuffs were down. Yes, he'd heard of Bobby Martin, and considering the instrumentation, he couldn't wait to hear it.

Swiveling round in his chair, he put the album on the recorder behind him. He listened briefly to the first cut, then moved it to the second, which he considered for two minutes. I said that I personally loved a tune called "Sunday In The Country," and Vance listened to the whole cut. When it ended, he smiled.

"I like these guys," he said. "I like the sound. How old are they?"

I smiled. My heart was pumping fast. "Twenty-one," I told him. "They're graduating from college."

"Ah, that's a shame. I really like them."

My smile fled from my face. "A shame? These guys are ready to go."

"They're too old."

"Too old?"

"Yeah. I was hoping they were sixteen, seventeen."

I was stunned. My mouth dropped open. "Why?"

"Why? Because the only people buying records today are girls who are thirteen and fourteen." He shrugged apologetically. "Sorry, but I can't use them. Wish I could. I'll tell you what," he said, "leave your album on the table over there, and maybe, if I hear of something... Here. Here's a magic marker."

I turned and looked at the table that, in my excitement, I failed to notice coming in.

Five hundred albums must have been piled there.

* * *

The pile of rejected albums had told me all I needed to know: Getting Tyger out would take everything, and probably more than I had. They needed a guy who was really in the business—in the business, full time. With the gobs of time I was putting in, just thinking about them was more than I had to spare.

Still, I persisted. I got them a gig here and there, and they were still playing at La Terrasse three weekends a month. I didn't really know where to go, though, or who to talk to, until I got a call from a friend who had a boutique-advertising agency. His small firm was pitching a company who planned to open an elaborate bistro called Speakeasy and they needed a promo song and a band. The agency owner had heard Tyger and thought they'd be perfect.

I told the band, and two days later, we all went to the agency's offices and did a couple of songs including "Sunday In The Country" and ended with a song they'd written especially for the occasion called "Speakeasy." The song was fantastic. The agency loved it, but ... they didn't get the account. The client had decided against opening the place.

Three weeks later, the owner, my friend, had called me in and told me the bad news. It had nothing to do with the song—the song was great—and he loved the group. Then he told me he wanted me to hear something.

The next day, I went back to the agency and sat down in my friend's office. My *buddy* had just written a new song with a guy who was taking it to Nashville. He put on his demo and, what do you know, it had the same exact opening as Sunday In The Country. I went to ice.

"You can't use that," I said. "It's Sunday In The fucking Country!" At that moment, I realized my friend had called me in to see if I would recognize it and if I would say something. Say something!

Shit, I had plenty to say.

The guy hemmed and hawed.

"Just rewrite it," I told him.

"I can't. It's on its way to Nashville."

"Nashville! Call it back."

"I can't."

I stormed out of the office.

To try to soften and placate me, my *friend* had the guy from Nashville call me. "What are you so upset about?" the guy from Nashville said. "We steal shit like that all the time."

I never spoke to my *friend* again.

Shortly after agreeing to take the group on, Bill's mother and father came into the restaurant for dinner, and I sat down with them for a few minutes.

Mrs. Carpenter took my hand and looked me directly in the eyes. "You're not going to take advantage of my son, are you?"

Thinking back, I raised my eyebrows and shook my head. "Take advantage of *them!*" So far I'd invested several hundred hours, many hundreds of dollars, and hadn't received a single dime. And they hadn't listened to anything I'd said. Yes, they'd cut their hair and had changed their look, but not because I'd suggested it. At that time, grizzly and scruffy were out. Spruced up, they actually looked a lot better. And of course, I couldn't tell them anything musically; they knew everything there was to know.

Inwardly, I smiled. In my mind, they were still geniuses, but it was taking too much out of me. I was missing things at La Terrasse, and I was starting to get tired. I'd thought seriously about letting them go.

It was a decision I didn't have to wait too long to make. A month later something occurred that told me it was time.

The group had written four new songs and wanted to record them. I told them I really couldn't afford to take them to Sigma Sound again. They said they had a friend who would record them free, but they needed a space. Could they use my living room? Ruth and I had just bought an old historic, four-unit fixer-upper in the city's Germantown section. We occupied the whole first floor and rented out the second and third floors. Tyger wanted to know if they could use the huge living room. It would take a whole weekend. I thought about it. Sure, it would take some doing and I would have to clear it with Ruth and inform the tenants, but it was doable. Yes, definitely doable.

The boys set up on a Friday night. They moved the furniture around to accommodate the speakers, the microphones, and the soundboard. When I returned from La Terrasse that night at eleven, they had already gone home.

I told Ruth to invite some people the next day to sit in as an audience.

"Well," she said, "Holly Maddox and Ira Einhorn are coming over for a late dinner, and I think the band is bringing some of their friends."

The session was supposed to start around nine, but it was running late because the soundman was having some trouble. I went over to him to tell him not to worry, to take his time, but the guy saw me coming, and before I could say a word, he was yelling in my face.

"What the fuck do you want? I heard about you and all your bullshit."

This guy was actually yelling at me!

I stared back in rage, but did nothing. Had it been any other place or time, I would have punched out the sonofabitch. I expected Bill or Steve to tell him to go fuck himself. But Bill turned away, and Steve pretended not to hear it. Dick was looking over his glasses, tuning up. They'd all heard it and had said nothing.

Suddenly I realized these guys were not my friends. I'd grown up in a neighborhood where friends always had your back. If someone said or did something to one of your friends, or did something to one of your friend's friends, he was immediately straightened out. Somebody from the trio called Tyger should have told this guy to shut the fuck up.

I turned abruptly and walked out through the dining room and into the kitchen, out the back door and into the yard.

Sitting in the middle of the yard was a low-slung Mimosa tree. I leaned into the crook of its big, poppa limb and seethed. How dare that motherfucker yell at me, embarrass me … in my own fucking house, no less! Who did that sonofabitch think he was! I should have thrown him and them right the fuck out.

I fought to control myself, though, to resist the urge. I bit my lip, seeking control. It hurt like hell. I had to let this go. Maybe it was the booze, or the smoke, but I began to feel sorry for myself. I let out a big sigh, though it might have come out as a sob, and a tear rolled down my cheek from the anger. I wiped it away.

At that moment, I felt a hand on my shoulder. It was Holly Maddox. "Are you gay?" she asked probingly, looking at me with those big, beautiful eyes.

Her voice abruptly woke me out of my reverie. I turned to her, "Where the hell did that come from?"

"It's an observation. Ira said you've changed. That there was a time when you would have punched that guy right out."

"Yeah, Ira and I fought back to back a couple of times when we were kids, but we're supposedly grown up, now."

"It's okay if you are gay. Sometimes it feels good to let it go."

"There's nothing to let go. I'm as straight as a gate. I love women, but I also love the music, and I don't like being taken advantage of."

She reached up and touched my cheek. "You've got a tear running down your cheek."

"Yeah, it's a tear of loss."

"What did you lose?"

"A couple of friends."

Right then and there I knew how a soldier on the battlefield feels when the man along side him takes one.

For the next few minutes, I tried to explain about the music and how important I thought it was, and even though she nodded, I felt that she really didn't get it. Ira must have said something stupid.

What? Men can't feel- men can't be sensitive- men can't shed a tear? Sure, the old Ted Ira knew would have been all over that asshole, thrown them all the fuck out. Sure, Ira and I had grown up together, fought pitched battles as allies, so in his eyes I'd changed.

Holly just smiled. (Four years later she would go missing and eventually be found dead. Stuffed in a trunk that was stashed in a closet on Ira's back porch. I shed a couple of tears then, too.)

But, after she went back to the house, I thought about what she'd asked, and recalled a conversation I had about six months earlier with Tom Charters the bartender at La Terrasse. That was back when the band still had the shaggy, long-haired look. I'd been at the bar, listening to what had become my all-time favorite Tyger song: "June Brown Wheat." The song starts out soft—Steve singing the first two verses high—but then the pace shifts to a driving bridge filled with harmonies, until it finally collapses once more into Steve's solo voice.

Directly behind me were two guys with loud voices and too much booze. "Do you believe these fucking long-haired faggots?" one said. "*Sucking the microphone.* They should be sucking my dick." And the guy on the other side of him laughed. He'd said it way too loud.

I swiveled around to him. "What did you say, motherfuck?"

As I said it, he slipped off of his stool. His friend looked at him, and he too got off of his own stool. He had a good head on me, and he curled his lip to show his displeasure with the barkeep. But before he could say anything, I raised my hand above my head and snapped my fingers.

Suddenly, two guys, who you might say were the bosses' assistants, were at my side, and the guy with the big mouth was kind of quickly quiet. Earlier that day, I'd hired these special assistants because there'd been a rumor that some sort of disruption might occur. I was taking no chances. The two assistants at my side were there to maintain order.

They didn't say a word, but I did. Never taking my eyes off of the asshole with the big mouth, I hissed under my breath, "Take this sonofabitch and throw him in the street. And if he says one word, take him out back and beat the shit out of him."

My two assistants smiled at the delightful thought.

Then, snarling, I vacated my stool to check out the dining room. But before I could get there, Jesse pulled me aside and asked me what happened.

"Were they the guys?" he asked.

"I don't think so," I said, gritting my teeth.

"Then what happened?"

I liked Tom Charters and considered him an important piece of the enterprise. I'd made him head bartender and liked the way he took charge; he was honest, and his accounts were always on the money. I trusted his opinion.

"I didn't like what he was trying to say," I told him. "He was trying to accuse those guys in the band of being faggots, and I didn't like it."

Tom raised his eyebrow sarcastically. "Why would he think that? Because they have long hair?"

I stared hard at Tom. "Do you think they're gay?"

"I don't know. Are you gay?"

I was astonished. "Me?" I said, checking myself out. I laughed. This was actually funny. I'd spent my whole younger life chasing girls and loving every minute of it. Nothing more delectable than a beautiful woman. Never for one minute had I ever doubted my masculinity.

I held my arms out wide. "Do you think I'm gay?"

Tom hesitated.

"Go ahead," I insisted. "Say what you think."

"Well, you do fit the mold."

"The mold?"

"Yeah. You're older, and older guys like younger guys."

I'd never even thought about it. I gestured that Tom should go on. "And," he said, "you have to admit, you do have a softness for those guys. You storm around here yelling at people and cursing, but not at those guys. No one is allowed to sit at your special table, but those guys do. Instead of doing your work, you take the time to talk to them. You don't think people notice?"

I folded my arms across my chest and studied my head barkeep. He was big, clean-shaven, with a head full of curly black hair. When he wasn't behind the bar, he mostly wore wife-beater T-shirts over his excessively hairy body.

"Those guys are different. They're artists. Geniuses."

Tom nodded. "Yeah, so's my Uncle Louie. And the music, the lyrics..."

"The music! The lyrics?" I said totally confused. "What are you talking about?"

"Listen, I'm doing a PhD in song lyrics", Tom continued. I could never decide if Tom was the best bullshitter I'd ever met, or whether he knew what he was talking about. "Interpreting the psychology behind lyrics, trying to find out what the artist is really saying. That big guy ... he has doubts about who he is."

"Tom, I think you're crazy."

"Well, phrases like, '...the other side of me,' and ... what was it ... oh, yeah ... 'looking at the other side.' What do you think he means by that? Subconsciously, I mean?"

"I don't know. Until now, I never thought about it. It's ... it's head music."

Tom smiled. "Which one?"

I was about to reply, when a waitress came up to me with a question. She should have already known the answer, and I was about to snap at her, but didn't. Instead, I overly smiled and answered her in a gentlemanly manner. Tom was about to leave, but I stopped him.

"Hey," I said, "let me ask you a question." Tom poured a scotch and a white wine, but concentrated mostly on what he was about to be asked. "Are *you* gay?"

Tom grinned. "Yes, I am. When I go out on a date, I usually dress up like a drag queen." I held up a finger and was about to say something, but didn't. Tom turned with the drinks and headed back down the bar, yelling over his shoulder, "Just kidding!"

After Holly had left, I leaned on the tree in my yard and smiled, remembering. The sky was as clear as a brand new bell, and so were my thoughts. No, I was not gay, but I felt as if I'd just been fucked. I'd spent a lot of hours working for Tyger, putting out a lot of energy. Now, I felt used, taken advantage of, not appreciated. These guys were not my friends. I'd been stabbed in the back. I gritted my teeth and made a promise to myself: I'd let my anger pass and not ruin the night, but I would never again do anything for the group called Tyger. It was over.

I'd always been an impulsive guy, running headlong into things or away from things, then later regretting my actions. With Tyger, I'd waited a month to mull over my decision, and when I told them, it seemed they were relieved. They merely shrugged and went on their way. I wasn't at all surprised.

Two months later, I left La Terrasse. I was exhausted. The only thing harder than trying to sell a musical group, I admitted to myself, was running a restaurant. It was constant, never ending. You were only as good as your last dish, and trying to maintain a continually high quality of food was incredibly difficult. My one major fault? I didn't really trust anyone but myself, and I refused to teach people how to do my job. In the end, it just wore me thin.

I did, however, leave with enough money to launch a new business, and those funds provided me with enough to survive while I tried to launch that start-up.

* * *

This new enterprise was called Bicentennial Host Houses ... but I'd been stupid, blind.

Like so many others, I'd been taken in by a bogus survey that predicted that, in the summer of 1976, forty-five million people would be coming to Philadelphia. If that happened, one hundred seventy-five thousand people would be sleeping in the streets every night during the one hundred days of summer.

Believing that statistic, I put together a company that had two thousand rooms ranging from college dormitories to Chestnut Hill mansions. This was twenty years before Airbnb. Anyone who knew anything touted my company, to make millions, and during those years, I saw very little of Tyger. I missed those guys. But more than that, I missed the music.

And Tyger missed me. They immediately got other managers, but those new guys couldn't get them anywhere. They basically had no contacts, and unlike me, they suggested changes that made Tyger lose their original sound. They added pieces—drums, bass.... Eventually, they went electric.

Dick, the fiddler, who'd never been a people person, became disgruntled and left the band. Bill got married. The band refused to go on the road, to take the beatings that most bands have to go through; they still firmly believed that one night, someone important would hear them and they'd be discovered. The stuff from which movies are made.

All of this was happening, while I was slowly going down the tubes. The bicentennial was a bust, and so were my Host Houses. I needed seven million to come, but the survey the city had hyped had been so bogus, it was off by a factor of twenty. Fewer than three million people came to Philadelphia during the summer of seventy-six. Ninety percent of the bookings had vanished two weeks before July 4th because Frank Rizzo, idiot mayor that he was, announced he would call out the National Guard because he feared rioting in the streets. And then there was Legionnaires' disease, a totally new and unheard of affliction. People started dying, and even more people started canceling. Even the Pope, scheduled to come in August, had said "no way."

It was a total disaster.

I found myself totally broke and, to make matters worse, Ruth was pregnant. The baby was due in October. So, angry and depressed, I started looking for a job. Three months later, I found myself on an eel truck headed down the highway to North Carolina.

Once again, a company called Superior Fish, who specialized in buying and exporting the American eel, offered me a piece of the business to become their buyer. They needed someone who was tough, fearless, and (as I put it) dumb and desperate enough to deal with fishermen and trappers in the backwoods. It was a cash business, a dangerous business, but I had no alternative. I needed to survive. I'd be away for days, weeks at a time, riding shotgun on a foul-smelling truck, dealing with guys who could barely spell their names but who made tons of money.

I bought millions of pounds of eels. Some days, I'd leave the plant with a hundred thousand dollars in cash, paying eel fishermen in Virginia, South Carolina, New Jersey, and New York ten to twenty thousand a week. I found myself in dingy motel rooms, grimy gasoline stations, shabby restaurants, waiting for the next driver to bring down more money and another empty truck. I berated myself for wasting my time, energy, and the money I'd made at La Terrasse on the Bicentennial Host Houses. How could I have been such an asshole, such a complete idiot to gamble it all on such a fiasco? I should have known America wouldn't come to the party.

I fell into a depression that lasted a long time. The only thing that kept me going was my wife, who was strong at my side; my baby girl, who was as sweet a kid as any who'd ever held a pacifier in its mouth; and pieces of Tyger music that kept whirling around in my head as my eel truck bounced down the road.

At first, I kept thinking about the "if onlys." If only Bobby Martin and Joel Claymond had listened; if only this, if only that... Then I stopped with the "if onlys" and just thought about the music.

One night, while walking down a lonely road in New Bern, North Carolina, I passed a pawnshop, and because there was absolutely nothing else to do in the town, I found myself staring in the window, shaking my head at the utter crap on display: trays of dime store rings, old pop-up toasters, Big Ben alarm clocks, pistols, rifles.... Everything seemed to reinforce where I was and, now, what I was.

I started to walk away, but stopped and turned back. Something had caught my eye. To the right of the display, almost hidden by a rack of old lady clothes, was a beat-up guitar that looked like the one I'd had in Europe.

Suddenly, my mind was flooded with thoughts of Paris; Anita Longstrom; street singing; the songs I use to sing; and happier, youthful days. I walked into the store and paid twenty-five dollars for the old piece of junk. It was badly worn, the sound box had a crack, and it could never hold a tune for any length of time, but that didn't matter. And it didn't matter that it didn't have a case; I'd stash it behind the seat in the cab of the truck when I was driving, and sometimes it would bounce around, making music all by itself. At night, in those seedy motel rooms, I'd sing and play that beat-up guitar until people in adjoining rooms had pounded on the walls, yelling for quiet.

From January to the middle of March, I led a normal life. Eels are tough to catch in frigid waters—they go into an almost hibernated existence—so during those months, I was rarely on the road.

One night, in 1978, during that quiet stretch, Bill Carpenter had shown up on my doorstep, wearing a big, bearish smile and carrying his guitar. I was genuinely glad to see him.

"Hey, m'main man, how goes it? Come on in."

Carpenter said he was in the neighborhood so he thought he'd stop in. I couldn't have been happier. Ruth made us some coffee, and we moved out into the living room, where Carpenter began to play. He saw I had my old Martin out and asked if I'd been playing, and when I told him I'd been hacking away while on the road, he said he wanted to hear what I was putting down. So, I started playing rhythm, and soon, Carpenter was putting lead behind it.

I was ecstatic. I knew I could never play like Hastie. He, like Carpenter, was a virtuoso. But I didn't care, and Carpenter wasn't complaining. I'd never played ensemble with anyone before and it was exciting. Carpenter smiled at his old manager's mistakes but said nothing; he could anticipate the parts where I had trouble or broke down and compensated for them.

Carpenter just loved to play, and in truth, it didn't sound half bad. That night, we played for about two and a half hours.

The following week, Carpenter was back, guitar in hand. Once again, we talked over coffee and then played, and for several months, the once-a-week sessions became a ritual and only ended when the eels started running and I'd returned to the road.

It was on the road, as I bounced around from rural community to rural community, that I started writing; not just music, but prose. I figured there were two ways I could go: I could either hate what I was doing, and despise myself for doing it; or, I could discover and appreciate the uniqueness of what I was doing and be a part of the adventure.

And it was an adventure. I'd never met people like these before—country folk who worked the wilderness and knew its waters—nor had I ever been in the backcountry. There were stories there to write, to tell, and to even sing songs about. And that's what I started doing. As pissed off as I was that I'd fallen so considerably, I recognized that grueling time as an opportunity to describe what few city folk couldn't possibly imagine.

The next time I saw Carpenter, I told the big guitarist I'd written three songs while I was on the road, and Carpenter loved putting lead guitar behind them.

And we talked. We discussed books and music, and the business of music. Carpenter talked about the band, how it was changing, how his music was evolving, about the dynamics of the pieces. He wondered why I hadn't come out to see them.

"Listen," he said, "we're playing at a place close by next week. Actually, it's only two blocks away from here. I want you to come hear us. Okay? Okay! It's called Takers Place. Next week."

So, the following week, Ruth and I went to see the new band called Flambeau. Dick Carpenter was not a part of the group, and I felt the new group missed him. Even though they played Tyger tunes, something was lacking, and I felt as if this new band was just some cover band playing Tyger classics.

The drummer—just a young kid of maybe eighteen—didn't seem to know how to play in an ensemble, and he was playing way too loud. The bass player was playing his bass like it was a guitar, and while he was exceptional mechanically, he was all over the place, clouding the other leads.

But sadly, what Carpenter wore bothered me the most. He had on a washed out, stained white jumpsuit, which looked like he'd chased some meatpacking employee a couple of blocks to get it. It was dirty, and wrinkled, and about three inches too short.

Ruth leaned over and whispered into my ear, "What the hell's he wearing?" I just shook my head as she added, "He looks terrible."

"They never really cared about how they looked," I said. "In their minds, only the music is important. But you're right. This doesn't work."

When the band took a break, Hastie and Carpenter came over to say hello. The bass player, a young African American kid, came up behind them. "Hi," he said. "I'm Bog. So you want to be our manager, huh?"

I laughed. "No. I don't think so."

Carpenter's face dropped.

"I mean," Bog went on, "you want to manage the band."

"No," I insisted. "I'm just here to listen. I'm no longer in the management business."

Carpenter laughed it off as if he'd been caught with his hand in the cookie jar, then said he had to take care of changing a string. Hastie followed him, and Bog was left standing there with nothing to say.

Ruth and I left halfway through the second set. It was disappointing, to say the least. The remnants of Tyger were there, but for me, it just wasn't the same.

* * *

Twenty-five years later, I found myself on a plane headed to Seattle.

In that span of years, my fortunes had changed drastically. I left the eel business in 1981 and had etched out a fairly comfortable life for myself. I took a summer off in 1983 and built myself a house in Chestnut Hill, bordering on Fairmount Park and overlooking Valley Greene. I was extremely proud of the place and delighted in telling people that, in fact, I'd hammered in every nail. This house was the kind that, when people dropped in, their jaws often dropped down. It was gorgeous. The back wall was practically all glass and looked out onto the woods of Fairmount Park. I'd never worked for a carpenter, nor read a carpentry book, nor took a commercial course on the subject, but I'd built myself quite a house. I instinctively knew how it had to be constructed. I had a lot of my father in me. He'd taught me how to see it.

From that experience, I'd developed a small real estate business that specialized in restoring historic buildings. This business allowed me the time to do the things I loved the most: I wrote every morning and played guitar every night; I had two children who were doing well, and a wife I still loved with all my heart...

But now, as the plane cut through the clouds, my heart was heavy. Steve Hastie sat next to me, but conversation was sparse, each of us caught up in our own thoughts.

"The hardest thing an agent can do," a friend had told me a long time ago, "is to keep a band together. Egos finally get the best of them all, and it makes no difference who's writing what, or who's playing what, or how good they sound together."

The years had flown by and the band hadn't played together in twenty-two years.

Bill had met a doctor named Debbie and instantly fell in love. He was smitten, and so was she. Not only was she a beautiful woman, but she was also a psychiatrist. They immediately had a kid—a boy, the first of three. Debbie loved their music, but felt it was too much of a struggle and, in essence, both Bill and the band would never make it. She was a realist, and she knew, in a matter of months, what it took me years to admit. Plus, she was practical. Yes, Bill was a brilliant musician, but he was also a brilliant scholar, and she felt he was wasting himself.

She also saw the band was having emotional trouble, and once again she was right.

Steve, as it turned out, was frustrated with the way things were going, musically. He was tired of exclusively playing rhythm. He wanted to play lead, and this left Bill with a conundrum. Next to Debbie and his newborn son, Steve was the person Bill loved most in the world. It was a music thing—they were perfect together, but Bill was a lead guitarist.

So the two guitarists began to battle, until, out of the clear blue sky, Bill dropped a bombshell: He told Steve he'd decided to move to Seattle.

Steve was dumbfounded. "Seattle?" he said.

"Yeah. I got to go." Debbie had landed a job there, and that left him with no alternative. He'd been paying the bills as a floor sander/refinisher; something he could do without thinking, something he didn't have to take home with him, something that had allowed him to devote himself to the music.

"Seattle!" said Steve. "I guess practicing twice a week is out." After this, Steve never said another word, but Bill knew his silence was saying, "What about the band, you motherfucker! I put ten years into this thing!"

I only saw Bill once before he, his wife, and his kid all pulled up stakes and drove out west.

"He has every right to be pissed," Bill confessed over a goodbye beer, "but what could I do?" He gritted his teeth. "The only thing I'll really miss is Steve and the music."

"Look," I told him, "you've made the decision, so make the most of it. Do what you have to do, but don't let the music you guys made together slip away."

"Yeah, I'm gonna write a lot of music. I can feel it. And I'm gonna write a novel," he said, eyes glazed. "That's what I really want to do."

"I'll be looking forward to reading it."

"Hey, man, you're a writer. I'll want you to read it. I'll send you some chapters."

"Cool."

"Hey, man," he said, with a lilt of enthusiasm in his voice, "I just finished the *Dubliners*—for the fourth time." He laughed at how absurd that sounded. "I tell you that Joyce could write. He turns me on. He makes me want to write."

"Go for it," I told him, thinking a guy who writes lyrics like the ones he's written might actually write a fantastic novel.

* * *

The years passed steadily, and I occasionally heard from Carpenter. His family had grown; Debbie, while maintaining a lucrative psychiatric practice, had given birth to two more boys. The big guitarist, however, wasn't faring quite as well. He was still just sanding floors. His writing music, for all intents and purposes, had stopped. The same could be said for Hastie, whose writing had fallen off to less than a handful of songs.

By losing each other, it seemed they'd lost their creative muses, as well. Yes, they'd appreciated the public's applause, but an audience's opinions weren't really what mattered. In essence, Carpenter had written for Hastie, and Hastie had written for Carpenter—for only the one could really judge and understand the other. And to make matters worse, after close to twelve years in Seattle, Carpenter hadn't gotten past the second chapter of his book. I had to confess, after reading those initial pages, I had been wrong in my original thinking; the stuff Carpenter had sent me was not very good.

I'd come to understand that novel writing and song writing were two distinctly different things. The poetic beauty of language that dominated Carpenter's music was nowhere to be found in his prose, and worse, he could not tell a story; nothing in the first fifty pages made a person want to read further, and upon wading through the first two chapters, I was left feeling empty. I didn't know how to respond. So, I avoided calling Carpenter, and when I did finally talk to him, I said, "Listen, you haven't found your own voice. I know you love James Joyce, but you're not him. People are going to have a tough time reading this."

Carpenter was disappointed in what he'd surmised without

my actually verbalizing it. A couple of grunts had said it all. We didn't talk again for over a year.

In 1983, when my daughter was seven, Ruth gave birth to a boy, Matthew. Six years later, our entire family flew out to Seattle and stayed for about a week with the Carpenters. Dick and Mary had moved out there several years before, and it was a nice reunion. The only piece missing was Hastie and his wife, Julie.

As things turned out, in Carpenter's absence, I'd become closer with Hastie.

After leaving the eel business, I felt my writing had started to blossom; my stories had more substance and body, and my characters had started to live. What I discovered, though, was as difficult as it was to publish a novel; it was almost impossible to publish a short story. So I decided to tell my stories at cafes and clubs. I considered myself a storytelling performance artist. I told original adult adventurous tales, and people liked them. Between each story, I played a song or two, and on many occasions, Hastie backed me up, playing lead guitar and singing harmonies. A lot of people liked the way we sounded. But I knew Hastie never considered our working together as a viable, permanent reality. Yes, Hastie liked some of the songs I wrote, but my lack of musicianship left him unable to play the complicated stuff he'd written, and Hastie wanted to play his own music. Consequently, he never told anyone he was appearing with me, almost as if he were ashamed of playing with me and was doing it on the sly.

Then, in the nineties, Carpenter started having marital troubles. Debbie was unhappy and disappointed. Bill was still hacking around sanding floors, and there was no future in refinishing hardwoods. Sure, he was bringing in some money, but she still felt he was wasting himself. He wasn't writing, he wasn't playing, so what was he doing? Where was he going? What would it lead to? This was not what she'd opted in for. She wanted to be intellectually stimulated, and after ten years, what was there left to say about pine and oak flooring? Debbie wanted a divorce.

Around that time, Carpenter had begun to call, sometimes once or twice a week, and the conversations would go on for hours. What was he going to do? What could be done? She'd asked him to move out. He was still in love with her, of course, but he couldn't talk to her anymore and she wouldn't listen anyway. He was miserable.

It went on like that for months, until he'd finally found a small apartment and moved out. Now, he told me, he was alone and depressed. His moving out had made it so much easier for her to get a divorce. He missed the kids; he missed Debbie. What could he do? What could he do…?

I felt like Theo, Van Gogh's older brother. I still considered Carpenter a fantastic artist, and Ruth and I still listened to Tyger music. No lead guitarist played like Bill. Carpenter had no one else to talk to, and he needed an ear, needed to vent. How could Debbie do this to him? What did she expect of him? What could he do if he didn't sand floors? Did she really expect him to go back to school? That would take years!

These late-night conversations lasted until I ended them, pleading exhaustion and needing to get to sleep so I could work the next day. I'd stagger down to the bedroom to find Ruth waiting for me.

"Same thing?" she would ask.

"Same thing," I would tell her.

Then Bill and Debbie got a divorce.

Carpenter's phone calls continued for a couple of years, and his emotions had come out in one of the few songs he'd written while in Seattle called "Ain't Got Nothin'," a blues tune with a first line that said it all: "I ain't got nothin' and nothin' got me."

During this time, Debbie started seeing other men, and Bill tried to see other women but he couldn't find one who understood what he was all about. And, of course, I kept getting lengthy phone calls, running up enormous bills to prove it. The conversations rarely varied. Even though they'd been living apart for more than two years, Carpenter's thoughts were still wrapped around Debbie. He still missed her, still loved her, and still hated her. What could he do? What could he do...?

Then, out of the clear blue sky, the calls abruptly stopped. A couple of weeks went by before I realized I hadn't heard from Bill. At first I was relieved, but as time rushed by, I became concerned. I called him several times and left messages, but never got a return call.

One Saturday, Hastie called and asked if Ruth and I wanted to come over for dinner. When we arrived at Hastie's house, we were totally surprised to find Bill there, and even more astonished to find Debbie was there with him, and we were totally blown away by the fact they'd gotten married—again! When? Oh, about seven months ago.

I laughed out loud. That son of a bitch! He'd spent hours on the phone, running up bills with nothing but bad news and bad vibes, but when something good, something incredible happened, he didn't call. And now he stood in front of me and shook my hand like we hadn't heard from each other since the La Terrasse days.

I looked into his eyes as we shook hands, pulled him to me, and gave him a hug. Carpenter gave me that big, goofy laugh, and the six of us sat around the dinner table, laughing, joking, and telling stories as if nothing had happened.

On the way home that night, Ruth said, "That was the strangest thing I ever saw. He pretended like he never talked to you."

"Yeah, I was kinda dumbfounded. And not to tell me they got remarried?" I shook my head and laughed. "I guess he was ashamed, or felt stupid, after bad-mouthing her for so long."

"Well, I'm happy for them."

"Me too."

About five years passed. I occasionally heard from Carpenter and Debbie and was grateful they were doing well. Bill was attending graduate school and was about to receive a PhD in English. He was doing his thesis on, of course, James Joyce. The boys were also doing well—tall, handsome, and bright.

Then, one night, Hastie called with terrible news. He sounded like he was holding back sobs. Bill Carpenter was dead. He'd drowned. He was gone.

Carpenter loved to write lyrics that said a lot of things, and I thought his forte, lyrically, was his ability to play on words. In a song that I wrote, "Out on the Road too Long," Carpenter had added just two words that made the verse, in my mind, so incredible. It came in the third verse.

In the dead of night,
There's a blinking light,
That is the town you just passed through;
And your only fear,
is that you'll disappear,
Like all the others that you knew, you know.

Chorus:

The big wheels keep on rolling;
Your only friend is a song;
For years you've been rolling;
But you've been out on the road too long.

Carpenter had added the words "you know" after the words "you knew," so that the meaning could either be "you know, the big wheels keep on rolling" or "like all the others that you knew, you know," like all those people you currently know. Like him. Because he was essentially, by going to Seattle, disappearing, and his song "Out to See" was so fitting, because that's what happened. That's what really happened.

Fifteen years earlier, Ruth, our two kids, and I had gone out to Seattle for a week to visit, and one day during that visit, we'd all driven down the Oregon coast to spend the day on the beach. So I knew which beach. I remembered the coastline, the mammoth rock formations that stood out in the ocean; I remembered the tug of the undertow, and because I was not a good swimmer, I remembered being afraid of it.

Carpenter had laughed. "Hell, it's mild today."

"Jesus," I'd said, looking around. The beach was crowded, but there was no lifeguard.

"Look," he'd said, "there's nothing to worry about. You just go with the flow. Don't fight it; go with it." He turned toward the sea. "Come on!" he'd yelled as he dove into the deep blue water.

"Nah, today I'm a landlubber," I'd yelled after him.

I snorted aloud, remembering.

"You say something?" Hastie had asked, buckling his seat belt.

I shook my head. "No. Just thinking."

"We'll be landing soon."

"Yeah."

The water had been quite chilly that day. The beach, rather crowded. It was Labor Day and, as usual, there was no lifeguard.

The entire Carpenter family was there, save James, their eldest. He was in New York going to the university. Classes were about to start. All three of their boys were handsome, tall, athletic, and extremely bright. Ridge, the middle son, was a senior in high school. Tallest of the three, Ridge had been modeling since he was twelve; he had movie star looks, and department stores loved him. The youngest son was Kai—charming and enthusiastic, with a candy-cane smile. All three boys were musicians, though Kai really had his father's gift. At fifteen, he was an extraordinary pianist.

That day at the beach was sunny. Debbie was asking if anyone was hungry, and she wondered if it was too early to open the picnic basket and start preparing the lunch she'd put together that morning. She sat cross-legged on the blanket, watching her boys—her two youngest sons and her big-boy husband—tossing a baseball around.

"Is anyone hungry?" she yelled. They'd been running around for forty-five minutes. Debbie shouted again, this time a little louder, and Bill finally held up his hand to acknowledge her and brought the catch to a halt. The three of them trotted over to the blanket.

"It's time for lunch," she said. "Aren't you guys hungry?"

Bill smiled down at her. "I'd like to jump in the water first. How about you guys?" And before she could say anything, the three of them took off for the water.

Like porpoises, they dove into the surf in unison and swam out about a hundred yards, where they momentarily frolicked until the three of them, almost simultaneously, felt the water suddenly pulling them. The force was strong and totally unexpected, and it had come from out of nowhere. They were all strong swimmers, but this was an undertow much stronger than they were.

Kai looked at his father with a worried expression. Bill fought the current to reach his son.

"Relax!" he yelled. It was as if they were in a trough—the water in front of them and behind them were like canyon walls. Bill looked around for Ridge and saw him five feet away trying to swim back to shore. But the harder he swam, the more he got sucked back. Bill knew they had to get up and over the wall of water. So he dove down, came up under Kai, and threw him over the edge. Then he swam for Ridge. He was past exhaustion, but he had to reach his middle son. He could see the fear in his boy's eyes, the panic in his face.

"Relax!" he said. "I got you. We've got to work together. All we got to do is get up over the top. When I say three, give it everything you got."

"Okay, Dad."

On the count of three, they each put every bit of energy they had left into the uplifting surge—Ridge lifting upward, Bill pushing him. The effort got Ridge over the top, but Bill was swept back into the trough. By now, he was weary, spent. His arms ached, and he knew he no longer possessed the energy to get over the top, so he did what he'd read about when caught in an undertow, did what he'd told me years before to do: He threw himself backwards into the cliff of water and … let himself be swept away, swept … out to sea.

Struggling, the boys had miraculously made it to the beach,

and Debbie had come running to the water's edge. The three of them stood there for an hour, staring out into the ocean. A crowd had gathered. People prayed aloud, but the prayers went unanswered. Bill Carpenter was gone.

Late that afternoon, a Coast Guard plane had spotted his body floating face down about two and a half miles off the coast.

* * *

Hastie and I arrived in Seattle two days after the tragedy, and we took a cab to Dick and Mary's house, where the family was initially gathering. They lived not ten minutes away from Debbie and Bill's. Bill had been the youngest of four brothers, and the two eldest and their wives were there. The oldest, Ken, had flown in from Connecticut, where he was the pastor of New Haven's largest church. Next in terms of age was Ross, a retired army major now living in South Carolina. These two men had no idea who I was or why I'd traveled from Philadelphia to mourn their youngest brother, and when I began to tell them, I realized that neither of them had any idea who Bill had been either.

It had started off easy enough. They all sat in the kitchen, a sunny room, around a chrome table. Ken smiled at me, but I saw a look of curiosity on the minister's face.

"So what do you do, Mr. Fink?"

"Please, call me Ted."

"Okay, Ted. What do you do?"

"Well, right now, I'm in the real estate business."

"I see. That's nice. You've come a long way."

I read what they were thinking, but I hid my annoyance. I was probably older than they were. "Yeah." I smiled. "I could have sent a card, but your brother meant a lot to me."

Ross, who was drinking coffee, put his cup down carefully onto the saucer. "Really?" he said. "How so?"

"The music."

"The music? What do you mean? Did you play music with

him?"

"No, not really. It was just Bill, Steve, and Dick. They were the trio. I managed them for a while, but we never really played out together."

"You must have been very close," said the minister, his voice had almost a sarcastic edge.

"At times we were," I replied, "but ... well, I guess you know what kind of musician your brother was. He was a fantastic guitar player. But as good as he was on guitar, it was the music he wrote that set him apart. I mean, I cared for your brother as a person, but it was his music that I loved. He wrote some of the best music I've ever heard."

The two older brothers looked at each other as if they had no idea what I was talking about. They'd heard their brothers had been playing music in some local bars, but here was a grown man, having flown three thousand miles because of it and choking up talking about it. If the music had been so good, then why didn't the world know about it?

Once again, I surmised what they were thinking and forced a smile. I could have tried to explain how hard it was, how it wasn't enough to be a good or even a great musician, how you had to be in the right place at the right time, how so much depended on luck. I could have said those things, but I didn't. Instead, I just shrugged.

"That's how it goes," is what I'd finally said, assuming they understood what I meant. "And that's why I'm here. To thank him for what he gave me."

And sitting there, I wanted to say to ask: Why are you here? What made you come? Was it just the label "family" that made you fly all this way? What do you remember about him? What did he give you?

But I didn't ask any of those questions. I wasn't looking for a fight, and I didn't want to embarrass anyone.

Hastie and I stayed for two days. We stayed with Debbie and the kids, played a little music, went to the memorial, then sat around and talked—not about Bill; just made conversation.

I thought it strange. Two months before Bill's accident, I'd lost a dog, a beloved family pet. When the end came, the big boy, a curly coated retriever named Wally, collapsed in the kitchen. He was twelve years old and weighed one hundred and twenty pounds.

I'd helped him up and the big guy had made it into the bedroom where he slept at the foot of our bed. The vet had prepared me, saying that the end could be that quick. I called my son and daughter and told them I was planning to put the big dog down the next day, and they both said they wanted to be there when I did.

Actually, I needed them. I couldn't think of how I would get Wally to the vet's office alone. I told Ruth that in all likelihood, Wally was liable to have an accident since he couldn't stand, and Ruth told me not to worry.

That was at eight p.m.

The next morning, nothing had changed—the dog still couldn't get up. I went to work, then picked up my son at four p.m. We reached the house at 4:30, and when we opened the door, Wally was waiting for us—he was standing, and he needed to go out. He stumbled out into the yard, urinated, then collapsed again. As sick as he was, he refused to pee inside.

It took the entire family to lift him onto a blanket, and then into the back of the station wagon. We carried him into the vet's office, and then into a small room, where they put him on a white metal table, and with Wally breathing hard, we began to tell Wally stories. The telling went on, with him listening and blinking his eyes as if he understood, for a good twenty-five minutes. The dog was an absolute character and we loved him. Several times we were laughing so loud, people in the waiting room were probably wondering what was going on.

There was none of that with Bill. There were no stories. There was only the music. And unfortunately ... that would soon be forgotten.

As Steve had said, "Who will know?"

* * *

The lights were dim, the place was packed. As I came on stage, there was a smattering of applause. No one really knew me. I sat on a high stool, and a spotlight cast me in a circle of radiance. I briefly tuned my guitar and began to play a soft introduction. I talked over it.

"This song," I said, smiling, "was written by a friend of mine, a great songwriter who died much too early. His name was Bill Carpenter.

"He and his best friend, Steve Hastie, also a great songwriter, had just finished college and were planning to take a trip around the country, so of course they had to write a song about it. This is that song. It's called 'Out to See/Sea.' You'll never know how appropriate that title is."

Mural: A Screenplay

FADE IN

INT. POSH CENTER CITY OFFICE - DAY

FOCUS ON
An eraser on the end of a pencil. The eraser is being used to remove the smile from a simply drawn round face. The hand flips the pencil around and replaces the smile with a curved line representing a frown.

WIDER SHOT
The pencil is being held by SAMUEL SHUNDER, psychiatrist. Behind him is a huge picture window and a panoramic view of Philadelphia, with City Hall and the statue of William Penn as the focus.

FOCUS ON

CLOSE SHOT
The face of Samuel Shunder, nodding and listening. He looks down at his pad and considers his doodling.

O.S. MARVIN SCHWARTZBERG
He is dressed in an expensive suit and lying on a leather divan.

SCHWARTZBERG
My brother is coming back to town.

SHUNDER
Mmm-hmm.

SCHWARTZBERG
It's been ten years since I've seen him.

SHUNDER
And how do you feel about that?

SCHWARTZBERG
I'm worried.

SHUNDER
About you or him?

SCHWARTZBERG (O.S.)
Him. When it happened, he withdrew, went into himself. I handle things differently. I seek people. I get involved. I hide behind flamboyance. I needed help, so I came to you. I believe if something happens, you have to get it out. You need to have an outpouring, a catharsis. But Jay is different. Always was. Always did things solo. That's how he got his name. See what I mean? He held it in.

SHUNDER
How do you know that he hasn't been getting help, seeing a psychiatrist?

SCHWARTZBERG (O.S.)
He never stayed put long enough to see one. He's all over the world, painting it out. Paint therapy, is what you might call it.

SHUNDER
But in our previous session, you said his last letters and work were positive, that he was excited about the new project at the Center.

SCHWARTZBERG
Yes, miraculously, from what I can judge of his work, he seems to have come out of it. There's a brightness of color

that gives me hope. Still, I'm worried. There's so much at stake. It's been so long. I don't know....

SHUNDER

Let's start there. What worries you the most?

CUT TO:
MOVING SHOT

The camera moves out the window of Shunder's office, swirls around the hat of the statue of William Penn atop City Hall, then up the Ben Franklin Parkway to the art museum, then right, past the old prison, through many North Philadelphia neighborhoods, passing billboards, vacant lots, boarded houses, small corner stores, then down a long, narrow street at the third or fourth floor level. At the end of the street is the Frankford El. A train goes ROARING through. But the rattle of the train gives way to the even more BOISTEROUS NOISE beneath the El. A gang of kids, mostly pre-teens, has cornered an ugly old dog. Several of the boys have raised stones as if to pelt the animal, OLD BLOOD. One of them is about to unleash a pit bull.

CUT TO:
EXT. ACROSS THE STREET

The door of a neighborhood tavern bangs open. JASON (JAY/JAKE) SOLO, a rather eccentric-looking character steps out onto the pavement and waves good-bye to those unseen in the bar, and then turns around, looking for something. He is slightly intoxicated. He is a man in his early fifties, dressed in timberland work boots, denim overalls, and a long, flowing black topcoat. Unable to find what he is looking for, his attention is directed to the gang on the other side of the street. He makes his way, ignoring traffic, across the street to the kids. When he reaches them and sees what's going on, he immediately smacks the kid, who is about to release the pit bull, on the back of the head.

SOLO
(sarcastically)
Oh, excuse me.

SOLO pats the kid on the head where he had just hit him. The gang angrily turns toward him. He is now bent over, his face in theirs.

SOLO (cont.)
(continues, not intimidated)
In some parts of the world, m' boys, they eats dogs 'cause the people are starvin'. In other parts, they love 'em because the dogs get 'em places they couldn't get to without 'em.

He has their attention now. He puts his face close to theirs.

SOLO (cont.)
It was winter. The Alaskan snows were so high and the food so low, we thought for sure we were going to die. I tell ye...

He suddenly starts reciting the lyrics to an old, obscure folk song.

SOLO (cont.)
...it was early in October-o....

FLASH TO:

EXT. ALASKAN TUNDRA - LATE DAY

The back of a man in a sled, whipping a team of dogs, heading across a white tundra to the mountains beyond.

SOLO (O.S.)
I hitched my team in order-o,
to ride the hills of Saladio;
to me road to me road to,
My rideo....

END FLASH

SOLO (cont.)
It was that team, I tell ye, that got us through, and do you know who was leading the fuckin' pack? Why, it was that mangy cur that you see right there who, by the way, would rip the livin' shit out of that piece of crap you're about to unleash. I don't calls him Ol' Blood for nothin'.

The boy with the pit bull is about to protest, but Solo, without looking, smacks him again on the back of the head, and the pit bull whimpers.

SOLO (cont.)
I pop my whip,
I bring the blood...

He feels a hand in his back pocket, trying to lift his wallet. Without looking around, Solo grabs the hand, holds it, and goes on as if nothing is more important than finishing the verse.

SOLO (cont.)
I make my leaders take the mud;
I grab that wheel,
I turn it round,One wrong turn and we're on hard ground
To me rol to me rol to,
My rideo.

Now get the hell out of here, and don't let me see you tryin' to kill no dogs.

As they disperse:

FIRST KID
Hey, m'man: What was it, snow or mud?

SECOND KID
(to first kid)
It was bullshit, stupid.

Solo has not let go of the hand and slowly turns to see whose hand it is. It belongs to SUSANNA (ZANA) RAINES. Fourteen years old. Hispanic. She is dressed in jeans and a sweatshirt. He smiles with surprise and studies her. He brings his hand, still clasping hers, to his chest and smells her. He breathes in heavily. He closes his eyes, relishing the scent of her.

FLASH TO:

EXT. A CITY ALLEY - DUSK

A teenage boy is making love to Susanna. The boy has her against a wooden fence and they are kissing passionately.

END FLASH

ZANA
Let me go, you dirty pervert! I'll scream.

SOLO
Go ahead.

ZANA
I mean it!

SOLO
Go on. I'll help you. Police! Police!

Old Blood shows his teeth and growls at Zana.

ZANA
(Softer, pleading)
Let me go.

SOLO
And why should I?

ZANA
Because … because I'm not a thief.

SOLO
Wasn't that my wallet you were trying to take out of m' pocket or were you tryin' to caress me ass?

ZANA
I didn't mean it. I'm sorry.

SOLO
You didn't mean it! Was it an accident? In other words your hand Accidentally fell into my back pocket and, finding a strange Wallet, you decided to lift it?

ZANA
You know what I mean.

SOLO
No, I don't. How could I?

ZANA
I won't do it again. I promise.

SOLO

Why should I believe you? I think I should take you to your mother. Is she as pretty as you are?

ZANA

(Tears well up in her eyes)
Please....

SOLO

It's either that, or the police.

Solo studies the wrist he is holding.

SOLO

Now I'm goin' to let go of your hand and we're goin' to walk. Together. Pleasantly. If you try to run away, that dog...

Old Blood curls his lip and snarls.

SOLO (cont.)

...will bring you back.

He releases her hand.

ZANA

What do you call it?

Zana cautiously reaches her hand down to pet the dog. The dog now licks her hand.

SOLO

That there is Old Blood.

ZANA

Hi, Old Blood. Why do you call him that?

SOLO

Once he reached a certain point he went from Young Blood to Old Blood. It was an automatic thing. What should I call you?

ZANA

Well, my friends call me Zana. Want me to tell you what that's short for?

SOLO

Oh, ZANAdu.

MOVING SHOT

They begin walking.

ZANA

(not getting his pun)
Susanna.

SOLO

Susanna, what, pray tell?

ZANA

Raines. Susanna Raines.

SOLO

Zana Raines. That's a name a movie star would be proud to own.

ZANA

What do they call you?

SOLO

If you called me Jake, that would be Jake with me.

He extends his hand as if to shake hers.

ZANA

You know, Jake, you're about as corny as an old bum can get. First, you're talkin' Irish, and then fancy English … I don't know about you.

SOLO

Actually, I'm just a runaway Jewish kid from the Northeast.

She looks at his hand suspiciously, then finally takes it.

ZANA

Does this mean we're friends? 'Cause if it does, there is an unwritten law that says friends don't tell on one another.

SOLO

Well, I never heard of that law, but let's sit down and discuss it. You know, you're a pretty smart kid. I'm impressed.

EXT. TRANSIT BENCH AT A BUS STOP

Across the street is a vacant lot full of trash and weeds. The lot has been created by the demolition of several tenements. The windowless brick walls of the surrounding buildings are covered with graffiti. Solo and Zana sit down on the transit bench.

FOCUS ON
SOLO studying ZANA'S face closely, fascinated.

FLASH TO:

EXT. THE BEACH - MIDDAY

Solo, ten years younger, and his four-year-old daughter setting up a beach umbrella. A happy scene.

END FLASH

SOLO

Listen, "Z," (she likes the way he has shortened her name) I won't take this any further if you tell me the truth. But you've got to trust me. That's what friends do; they trust each other. Tell me the truth, and I'll let you go. Lie to me, and I'll know it. And then we won't be friends. Deal?

ZANA

Deal.

SOLO

Okay. Where do you live?

ZANA

Right around the corner. 1857 Clementine. Second Floor. Rear.

SOLO

With whom?

ZANA

My mama. You were right about that.

SOLO

And where do you go to school?

ZANA

Conwell Junior High

SOLO

Why did you try to lift my wallet? Don't lie to me.

ZANA

Money. I need money.

SOLO

Drugs?

ZANA

(raises her eyebrows at the stupidity of the question)
Yeah, right.

SOLO

Okay then, you tell me.

ZANA

Well, I was walkin' down the street and saw the fuss, so I came over. I was standing behind you, just chillin', mindin' my own business, when you flipped back your coat and I saw the wallet stickin' out of your pocket, looking at me with a happy face, sayin' "Take me, I'm yours." And you were so caught up in that story, talkin' with that stupid Irish accent that I could absolutely, positively, not resist.

SOLO

That doesn't tell me why you tried to take my wallet.

ZANA

I told you. Money. I need money. I'm poor.

SOLO

You know, you're quite a thespian.

ZANA

I am not. I like boys, and I have a boyfriend to prove it.

SOLO

(laughs out loud)

Tell me, why you need the money? I mean, you can get a job. Why try to pick a pocket?

ZANA

(rolls her eyes in frustration at his apparent stupidity)

I don't know. I never did it before, I swear. But I needed it fast.

SOLO

Why? Why, is what I want to know.

ZANA

Okay, and this is the truth. (She lets out a puff of breath) You'll never understand this, but okay, this is the perfect spot to say it. This is my favorite bench; I sit here a lot. You know why?

SOLO

I haven't the faintest.

ZANA

Okay, here it is: You see that vacant lot? You see those walls? I want to paint those walls.

Solo stares at her intently, almost in disbelief. He follows her eyes, which are now shining, back to the walls.

SOLO

When did you decide you wanted to do that?

ZANA

Off and on for over a year now. But lately it's been real intense, because ... well, would you believe that I just found out, last week at school, that the city just hired somebody to paint a mural on those walls? With all the walls in this stinkin' city, they had to pick my wall.

SOLO

Your wall. I see.

ZANA

And that's the truth. Hand to God.

SOLO

I believe you. I understand.

ZANA

You can't possibly. You see, I want to paint something in that space that is, well ... like, 3D. A huge mural where the perspective is only in the painting, but in the walls themselves.

SOLO

Of course.

ZANA

Did you know that Philadelphia is the Mural Capital of the world?

SOLO

I did not know that.

ZANA

It is. It really is. And some of them are so amazin' that even the "taggers" won't spray on 'em. I swear. Did you ever see Dr. J? Not the guy, the mural.

SOLO

No, I haven't.

ZANA

It is high grit. Awesome.

SOLO

Wow!

ZANA

And worst of all, I can't tell no one that I had the idea first. I can't say it. They wouldn't believe me. Now, I'd just sound stupid. Don't you see?

SOLO

I do. So you were going to steal my money to buy paints to paint your mural.

ZANA

That's the God's honest truth, I swear it. Well, it seemed better than tryin' to rob a bank. Although it sounds stupid now, since it's obvious that you wouldn't have that much money in your wallet.

SOLO

Or my pocket, which is where I usually carry my money. (He puts his hands behind his head and stretches out his legs) Oh, irony, how sweet is thy scent!

(Zana rolls her eyes)

You know, Z, you could have told me any cock and bull story and I wouldn't have believed it.

But this one is so unique and so strange and so eerie and so truly astounding, that I am overwhelmed with charity and leniency You are free to go, Zana Raines.

ZANA

Really?

SOLO

Don't let me catch you with your hand in anyone else's back pocket.

ZANA

(gets up.)
Thanks. I won't. Good-bye, Old Blood.

She rubs the dog's head.

ZANA

I'm glad they didn't hurt you.

She starts walking away.

ZANA

Good-bye, Jake.

Still looking at the walls, Solo waves good-bye

SOLO

Good-bye Zanadu.

He sits there a while, thinking
And now, He slaps his knees
To see the stately pleasure dome.

CUT TO:

EXT. RITTENHOUSE SQUARE - EVENING

Solo walking with Old Blood.

INT. LOBBY - A VERY POSH APARTMENT BUILDING - MOMENTS LATER

The DOORMAN opens the door for Solo, greets him coldly, suspiciously.

DOORMAN
May I help you?

SOLO
I'm here to see Marvin Schwartzberg.

DOORMAN
Really? And who should I say is calling?

SOLO
His brother.

DOORMAN
(rings up to the apartment)
Mr. Schwartzberg, there is a gentleman down here to see you. He ... he says he's your brother. (he seems startled by the response and takes the phone away from his ear) He says, "Solo, man"?

SOLO
Captain Marvel!

DOORMAN
(into phone) Captain Marvel.
(to SOLO) He says to go right up.

The doorman is recalcitrant as he holds the door to the elevator for him.

DOORMAN (cont.)
Mr. Schwartzberg, I'm sorry, it's...

SOLO
No problem, amigo.

INT. ELEVATOR TO PENTHOUSE

Opens to a totally white apartment: white rugs, white trim, white furniture. But the walls are solid art. Standing there, waiting for the doors to open, is Marvin Schwartzberg. He is dressed in white. There is a huge smile of anticipation on his face.

MARVIN
Solo!

SOLO
Marv!

Hesitant at first, they embrace warmly. Marvin grabs Solo's face between his hands, then jokingly...

MARVIN
Jesus Christ, you're starting to look as old as me.

SOLO
But you're looking great!

MARVIN
That's what I mean! God, you are a sight for sore eyes. I've missed you.

MOVING SHOT

They walk down a hall to a sunken living room. Marvin has his arm around Solo.

MARVIN
(pointing to paintings as they walk)
Sold. Sold. Sold. All Solos!

SOLO
Then we're doing well.

MARVIN
Bro, I'm doing well. But you're doing fabulous. Financially, that is I have it all socked away for you. All you've got to do is write the checks.

As they step down into the living room, toward a bank of windows overlooking the city, a woman stands and turns to them.

FOCUS ON:

CLAUDIA SCHWARTZBERG. She is striking. She is in her late thirties. She has a warm, sincere smile.

MARVIN (cont.)
My latest. Formerly the fabulous Claudia Corelli, now the very fabulous Claudia Schwartzberg.

SOLO
Number four.

MARVIN
Yes!

SOLO
When did this happen?

MARVIN

Two years ago. I would have invited you to the wedding, but I had no fucking idea where you were, and since you didn't show up for numbers two and three, I figured you wouldn't come in for number four, so we got married without you. Two years ago next month.

SOLO

Marvin, Marvin, Marvin. I am overwhelmed. The doorman was a knight of the round table…

MARVIN

I must be protected.

SOLO

The ride in the elevator to this height was exhilarating; the apartment itself is … is brighter than the sun, the view is astonishing; but Claudia … Claudia is the most beautiful woman I have ever seen.

He waves his finger in the air like Tevya.

SOLO (cont.)

This is a wedding I would have come in for!

He goes to her, kisses her cheek, breathes in her scent. He closes his eyes to relish her, then opens them and looks into Claudia's eyes affectionately.

SOLO (cont.)

This is a woman!

CLAUDIA

Thank you, kind sir.

MARVIN

And remember, if you don't mind my reminding you, your sister-in-law.

SOLO

And that is what makes it all the more astonishing.

CLAUDIA

Yes, you are definitely brothers. Hi, Solo.
(she kisses him on the cheek)
I've heard so much about you. Solo this. Solo that. Are you as crazy as Marvin?

SOLO

I taught him everything he knows about crazy.

CLAUDIA

Oh God, this is going to be an exciting visit. Sit. Tell. We want to hear everything.

MARVIN

Ten years! It's marvelous. Are you excited to be back? God, you're a sight for sore eyes.

SOLO

(good naturedly, still looking at Claudia)
How can your eyes be sore?

MARVIN

It's an expression.

SOLO

But yes, I think, I am ... (he settles back into the sofa. His expression momentarily tightens.) ... happy to be back.

MARVIN
You think? Jake, this is the most exciting thing that has happened to an artist in the last twenty, thirty years...

CLAUDIA
It was the pictures you sent in from the quarries in Yugoslavia. They were unbelievable!

MARVIN
They sold like hot cakes but they were so unbelievably depressing.

CLAUDIA
It started something. Concern. Committees. Charities. The faces.

SOLO
You know, I was never good with faces until that trip. I learned something there.

MARVIN
They were from the soul.

SOLO
They were, and you know why?

FLASH TO:

EXT. BEACH - LATE AFTERNOON

Solo is intently arguing with someone not in the camera. His daughter building castles in the sand.

END FLASH

MARVIN

I do. But I thought that, by the end of your stay in Yugoslavia, you had worked a lot of that out. There was suddenly a brightness in your work, and your last letters were so positive.

SOLO

I thought I had. But then yesterday, something happened that made me wonder.

MARVIN

Wait a minute. Yesterday? When did you get into town?

SOLO

About week ago.

MARVIN

You son of a bitch! That's a bummer. I mean it. Okay, so what happened yesterday?

SOLO

It's a long story. I'll get to it in a minute, I promise. But, Marv, believe me, it had nothing to do with you. That part of it is all past. I love you. I came in last week to case out the Art Center, unencumbered.

MARVIN

No one recognized you?

SOLO

No one has seen me without a beard in over thirty years. You, you would know me with my head cut off. I'm your brother. Remember?

MARVIN

Jay, this is the biggest thing that has happened in arts in the last fifty years. For an artist, this would be like painting the Sistine Chapel. I mean, just to be considered for this is monumental. But to be given the entire project is … the fee is astronomical. The Art Center is the building on the Avenue of the Arts. People, important people, people who buy art, will fly in from all over the world to see theater here. The Avenue of the Arts is a multi-billion dollar project. And you are going to be the artist everyone will see, the one everyone will talk about. The one everyone will buy. This is better than making weapons in wartime. As Dad used to say … (he waved his finger in the air, speaking with a thick Jewish accent) … you buy for a nickel, you sell for a dollar, that's a good business.

Are you ready to start?

SOLO

Well, that's the problem.

MARVIN

The problem? The problem? What are you talking about? Ten years! I haven't seen the guy in ten years, and suddenly I have an ache in the pit of my stomach.

SOLO

We have to push it back.

MARVIN

Back? Are you crazy? What are you talking about? Why?

SOLO

There's another project that has to come first.

MARVIN

What?

SOLO

A mural.

MARVIN

Where?

SOLO

Kensington Avenue, at Front.

MARVIN

Front and Kensington? Oh, shit. I can't stand this. Are you crazy? No. You're kidding. Tell me, please tell me you're kidding.

(he turns to Claudia) Please tell me he's kidding.

CLAUDIA

I think it's time to eat.

INT. HALLWAY TO DINING ROOM

MOVING SHOT

They pass by an oil painting of a young, dirty-faced girl squatting in an Afghanistan stone quarry, looking up. The viewer sees right into her eyes.

MARVIN

(stops in front of the painting)
I will never sell this one. If you don't mind, I bought it. It's become my favorite thing.

INT. DINING ROOM

FOCUS ON:

An elegant table. Claudia is coming from the kitchen with a tray.

MARVIN

Would you believe she cooks? And wait 'til you taste this stuff. Okay, let's get serious about this project. I don't know whether the Art Center can wait. Why should they? What's this new project all about? What's it pay? Who commissioned it?

SOLO

I don't know. I don't have it yet.

MARVIN

Jay, do you know how long I've been working on this? Do you have any idea what this could mean? How it would be remembered? Do you? Aren't you excited about the idea?

SOLO

I do, and I am. I am very excited about the Center. Believe me, want to do the Center. But this other thing, I really believe, can't wait.

MARVIN

But you really don't have the walls, and to make the Arts Center wait is ridiculous!

SOLO

That's your job. You can do it. Look, I haven't asked a lot of you in the last ten years. Now I need two big favors: I need you to push the Center back, and I need you to get me those walls.

MARVIN

It's probably a city job, The Mural Arts Project.

SOLO

Now you're thinking.

MARVIN

Since you've been away, Philadelphia has become the "mural capital" of the world.

SOLO

(laughs)
I just found that out.

MARVIN

Our city walls now run the gamut from Frank Sinatra and Mario Lanza to Frank Rizzo, as well as scores of other scenes. Waterfalls, flowers, you get the idea. (thinking aloud) But, you know, the publicity might do us good. I could probably convince the Art Center of the civic...

SOLO

That's the other problem. No publicity. I'm not going to do it as Solo.

MARVIN

Why must you make everything difficult? (he turns to Claudia in disbelief) You know what a fucking mushig-gina is? It's a pain in the ass stubborn mule!

Later over coffee...

MARVIN
I guess if you have been here for a week and you don't have any bags, you won't be staying with us.

CLAUDIA
Aww ... why not? We were counting on it.

SOLO
Well, I have the dog...

MARVIN
You still got Blood?

SOLO
Well, he's Old Blood now.

MARVIN
I bet ... why he must be...

SOLO
Fourteen.

MARVIN
(sadly)
Yes, of course. Well, where the hell is he?

SOLO
Outside. Waiting.

CLAUDIA
Outside? Well, bring him up. We don't mind.

SOLO
He won't come. He's not used to posh, and he can't stand Marvin.

MARVIN

That's not true.

SOLO

Didn't he almost try to take your hand off?

MARVIN

Well, that was...

SOLO

A long time ago.

CUT TO:

EXT. CITY STREET - NIGHT

Solo leaves the building. Old Blood, who has been waiting, joins him, and together they walk off.

CUT TO:

INT. SCHWARTZBERG APT. - BEDROOM

Getting ready for bed.

MARVIN

I love him. I love him. We were so close. What happened? Okay, I know what happened. But it's insane. This Center thing is so big. You know how hard I've worked on it. Jesus Christ!

CLAUDIA

You can push them back.

MARVIN

I don't know. But now I have to get the city to give me

Front and Kensington.

CLAUDIA

You knew about those walls.

MARVIN

Of course. I'm in the business. There is nothing that goes on in this city, or any city for that matter, concerning art that I don't know about. It's my job. Put a fucking mural in the ghetto. Normally, I'm all for it. But not now. It pays five thousand dollars and takes two months. Not fucking now. (pacing) Of course, I know the piece. It's a coveted piece. Many people want to do it.

CLAUDIA

The city would die to have Jay do it.

MARVIN

But he doesn't want publicity. That means I can't use his name.

CLAUDIA

He didn't say forever. Make a deal that they won't say it's a Solo until after he finishes the Arts Center.

MARVIN

Well, we'll see.

CLAUDIA

And what was all that about the dog. I thought you were good with dogs?

MARVIN

I am. But Jay bought that hound as a puppy when Asta was born. He trained that dog to take care of her. One day,

I picked her up too suddenly, and the dog freaked.

He rolls up his sleeve to show her the bite marks.

MARVIN (cont.)

I'll tell you one thing, nothing would have happened had he taken Blood to the beach. That dog loved that little girl. She could lie all over him, and ride him, and ... I think the only reason he's still with Jay, is because Jay is the last link to the girl, and the dog, like Jay, thinks the girl is coming back.

Marvin pulls back the covers and gets into bed.

CLAUDIA

Get some sleep. You'll fix everything in the morning.

Marvin turns out the light.

MARVIN

What a pain in the ass.

CUT TO:

MOVING SHOT

INT. CHESTNUT STREET - THE MARVIN SCHWARTZBERG GALLERY - MORNING

Enter Marvin, walking briskly. A perturbed look is on his face. He waves to one of his salespeople, opens a door in the back of the gallery.

INT. OFFICE - JANET WRIGHT, MARVIN'S SECRETARY

Behind her desk. Black. Attractive. In her forties.

MARVIN

Janet, get me Howard Sparks down at City Hall on the phone.

JANET

Yes, sir. There are some messages...

MARVIN

Nothing until I talk to Sparks. And I need to talk to him immediately, if not sooner.

Marvin walks straight to a door to the right of Janet's desk and disappears into his office.

INT. MARVIN'S OFFICE - TWENTY MINUTES LATER

BUZZ of the intercom. Marvin flips the switch.

JANET

I have Mr. Sparks on the line, sir.

MARVIN

Put him through on line one.

He flips another switch on the intercom.

MARVIN (cont.)

Howie, how are you?

CUT SCREEN

HOWARD SPARKS. Black. In his forties. Head of City Municipal Artistic Projects.

SPARKS

Marvin! So good to hear your voice. To what do I owe the honor of this call so early on a Monday morning?

MARVIN

Howard, I won't beat around the bush. I need a favor.

SPARKS

Of course. (laughs) Why is it people always need favors first thing Monday mornings? It's uncanny. Only kidding. Marvin, if it's in my power, I'll consider it. What's going on?

MARVIN

Okay, you know the city mural project we were talking about a couple of months ago?

SPARKS

Yes, of course. I asked you if you could find me an artist for one of the walls, and you said you couldn't be bothered ... I mean, you said you didn't have time to get involved...

MARVIN

But I did make a sizable contribution to the fund.

SPARKS

Yes, you did. And we are eternally grateful, but—

MARVIN

And the truth is, I never stopped regretting my lack of "personal" support. I was overwhelmed at the time and wasn't thinking clearly. I feel guilty as hell, and now I want to do something for the community.

SPARKS
Marvin, you are so full of shit, it's pathetic.

MARVIN
That's why I need the favor. Are you listening?

SPARKS
I'm still on the phone.

MARVIN
You know that piece at Front and Kensington?

SPARKS
Of course.

MARVIN
Has it been assigned?

SPARKS
I think so.

MARVIN
Has the artist been notified?

SPARKS
Not yet. I think that goes out at the end of the month.

MARVIN
Then I need a big favor. Can we do lunch?

CUT TO:

EXT. TERRACE RESTAURANT - ROUGE ON THE SQUARE - AFTERNOON

Marvin and Howard. Sparks is heavyset, well spoken, convivial.

SPARKS

(cutting into a capon)

It won't be easy, Marvin, believe me. Getting that project reassigned at this date is going to be difficult. The person in charge of the Mural Arts Project is Toni Bishop, and believe me, the lady is a royal pain in the ass. A very righteous woman. The last of the "Just," if you know what I mean.

MARVIN

Would she do it if it would benefit the program?

SPARKS

Maybe. But how could it benefit the program?

MARVIN

Because the artist who wants to do this is a pretty famous guy.

SPARKS

And who might that be?

MARVIN

You've got to trust me on this.

SPARKS

No, my friend, you've got to trust me on this.

MARVIN

Okay, here it is. But you can't say a word to anyone.

Schwartzberg raises his hand in a Boy Scout salute and crosses his heart.

MARVIN

Jay Solo.

SPARKS

Marvin, you are the biggest wad of crap that ever rolled down the mountain! Why would a guy who has just been hired to do the Center want to do a couple of walls at K&A?

MARVIN

Believe me, I don't know.

SPARKS

Is this on the level?

MARVIN

Absolutely.

SPARKS

You're not just hyping me so I stick my neck out and get you the walls, and next week you tell me that Solo broke a leg and can't do it so you can put in some other nincompoop, are you?

MARVIN

I swear.

SPARKS

Has he seen the walls? Does he know where they are? How much it pays?

MARVIN

I think so.

SPARKS

(leans forward, whispers)

Is he crazy? Will he actually do it?

MARVIN

Some people say he's definitely crazy. But once my brother gets something into his head...

SPARKS

Your brother? Jason Solo is your brother?

MARVIN

Howie, Goddamn it. You said I could trust you on this.

Sparks gives the Boy Scout salute, crosses his heart, and mockingly zips his lips.

MARVIN (cont.)

And if he gets the walls, there can't be any publicity until after he finishes the Center. That must be understood. Swear it. Swear it on your mother.

SPARKS

My mother died ten years ago, but if it'll make you feel better, I'll swear it on your mother. Marvin, you can trust me, but I'm afraid we're going to have to let Toni Bishop in on the idea. We can't get it done without her. If it's okay with you, I'll call her today.

CUT TO:

INSERT. PAPER - PRINTED ADDRESS - 1857 CLEMENTINE

EXT. CLEMENTINE STREET - TENEMENT FRONT - LATE MORNING

Solo and Old Blood. Solo is looking from the paper in his hand to the building address and realizes that the address Zana gave him doesn't exist. He smiles to himself, amused that he'd been taken in, and shakes his head knowingly.

Solo loses the smile and begins walking up the street. He sees a woman sitting on the steps, rocking a baby carriage. He stops to talk to her.

SOLO

Excuse me. What is the local junior high around here?

WOMAN

That would be Conwell.

SOLO

That's it. Where would that be?

WOMAN

That would be 'round the corner on Lippincott.

MOVING SHOT

Solo walks to Kensington Avenue and is approached by JEEPER JONES, a neighborhood panhandler.

JONES

(hat in hand)
'Scuse me, sir. Could you spare some change?
I'm hungry as hell and I need a cup of coffee, bad.

SOLO

You look like you could use a stiff one.

JONES

I'd be lyin' if I said I didn't, but right now, I need food

more. An' anythin' you give me will go for food, you got mah word.

SOLO

(reaching into his pocket)

What's your name?

JONES

Jeeper. Jeeper Jones.

SOLO

This here five is for food, Jeeper. Don't let me catch you lyin' to me. And the next time you ask me for money, you're gonna have to earn it.

JONES

You got mah word. Thank ya, thank ya.

Solo watches Jones as he hurriedly limps down Kensington Ave. Solo turns and continues walking up the road toward Allegheny Avenue.

CUT TO:

MOVING SHOT

EXT. CONWELL JUNIOR HIGH - HUGE - THREE-STORY BRICK - 11:00 AM

All the windows on the first floor are barred. The exterior walls are badly graffitied. Solo starts walking toward the school, then up the school steps as if he is going to enter. Suddenly, he thinks better of it, checks his watch, and walks away. Once again on Kensington Avenue, he sees Jeeper Jones across the street. Jones has a sandwich. He holds it up and points to it for Solo to see. Solo gives him a "thumbs up" and keeps walking.

CUT TO:

EXT. MUNICIPAL SERVICES BLDG. - LATER THAT DAY

Marvin and Solo walking up marble steps to the entrance. Old Blood is with them, but stops halfway and sits.

SOLO

Tell me again why I'm here, Marv.

MARVIN

You are here because you won't get the walls unless this lady approves it. I already told you, it won't be easy. She has already assigned them. You're good with ladies, or you used to be good with them. You want the walls, it's up to you. You've got to get them. I can't do it on my own. And if she turns you down, I want her to turn you down. Capiche?

INT. ELEVATOR

SOLO

Marvin, I have something to tell you.

MARVIN

(looks at him suspiciously)

SOLO

I haven't been good with ladies in a long time.

MARVIN

(checks his watch)

You got about two minutes to bone up.

INT. LOBBY - RECEPTIONIST'S DESK

MARVIN

Marvin Schwartzberg to see Toni Bishop.

RECEPTIONIST

It's that office there. Go in and take a seat; she'll be right with you.

INT. TONI BISHOP'S OFFICE

Solo and Marvin enter and sit down. Solo checks out the office artwork, and Marvin checks his watch with some annoyance. After several minutes, TONI BISHOP enters. She is tall, White, attractive, thirty-five, sophisticated. Upon her entrance, both men stand.

BISHOP

(forced smile)

Please sit.

They sit. There is an awkward moment of silence.

BISHOP (cont.)

Normally, I wouldn't even consider seeing you. I have spent an enormous amount of time selecting an artist for the walls at the Kensington and Front streets, and I reached a decision last week.

To be frank, I agonized over the decision. Right now, I don't think there is anything you can tell me that would make me change my mind, but at the request of Mr. Sparks, and because Mr. Schwartzberg is an important patron of the arts, I have agreed to see you on such short notice. Right now, I'm supposed to be somewhere else, another meeting. I'm hoping you can tell me why, in approximately ten minutes, I should give you those walls.

MARVIN

Ms. Bishop, I truly appreciate you seeing us, but this isn't about me, believe me. It's about the artist.

BISHOP

Who is the artist? And why does he have to have those particular walls?

MARVIN

Howard didn't tell you?

BISHOP

No. I assume it's this gentleman, but I haven't seen him around the Philadelphia art community, so I have no idea who he is.

Marvin is about to say something, but Solo stops him.

SOLO

Ms. Bishop, excuse me, I've been away, out of the country for many years, and things got started here in such a way, you were in such a rush, and because of the short notice, we haven't had a chance to introduce ourselves...

SOLO (cont.)

Hi, I'm Jay Solo.

Bishop takes his hand, then turns to Marvin.

BISHOP

The...

Marvin nods. Bishop lets go of Solo's hand, sits back in her chair, and bites her lip.

BISHOP

Mr. Solo, I have only had this job for a short time, and you'd better believe it is very important to me for reasons you could never in a million years understand. I would do anything for this program, and your name would be so important. To be frank, right up until this very moment, you were one of my favorite people. I admire your work. But right now, I am extremely disappointed—no, I am outraged that you would come here at the last minute, use your influence to get a wall that someone else needs and would literally die to have. I mean, you could have all the important walls you want. You are doing the Center aren't you? Isn't that enough?

Both Solo and Marvin are stunned, mouths agape at her fervor and anger. Suddenly Solo begins to laugh.

BISHOP

What is so funny? What is so bloody funny?!

SOLO

(tries desperately to control his laughter)

The only reason he brought me along is because he said I have a way with women.

Solo is besieged once again with a fit of laughter. Bishop comes from behind her desk and orders them out.

BISHOP

Out! Get out! Get out of here immediately!

In bewilderment, Marvin begins to rise, but Solo is still convulsed. In frustration, Bishop leaves the room. On her desk is a handkerchief. Solo picks it up and wipes his eyes, then puts it into his pocket.

MARVIN
You are the biggest schmuck in the United States of America. Mom would be proud of you.

SOLO
(dries his eyes with his hands)
Did Mom think I had a way with women, too?

EXT. MUNICIPAL BLDG - MOMENTS LATER

They are coming down the steps and joined by Old Blood.

MARVIN
(checks his watch)
I haven't been kicked out of an interview that fast since the last time you were in town.

SOLO
That was truly one for the books. What time is it?

MARVIN
Almost two. Are you coming for dinner tonight?

SOLO
If I'm not there by seven, eat without me.

Solo hails a cab driven by CAB DRIVER, BOBBY DiCOUZA.

MARVIN
What's your plan?

SOLO
Right now, I have to buy a hat.

MARVIN
But you don't wear hats.

Solo gets into the cab. As he is about to close the door, Old Blood jumps in.

SOLO
That's right.

CAB DRIVER
Hey, what da fuck is dat! Is dat your dog? I don't drive no dogs.

SOLO
I don't own this dog.

CAB DRIVER
Really? Get him da fuck outta here!

SOLO
You get him da fuck outta here!

CAB DRIVER
(to Marvin)
Hey buddy, is dis your fuckin' dog?

MARVIN
(imitates the driver)
That ain't my fuckin' dog!

CAB DRIVER
Holy shit. Awright. (slams down the meter bar)
Dis here is a double fuckin' fare.

CUT TO:
EXT. CONWELL JUNIOR HIGH - 3:15 PM

Solo gets out of the cab.

SOLO

Wait here.

CAB DRIVER

I'm keepin' da meter runnin'

He walks up the steps of the school and opens the door.

INT. THE HALLS OF THE SCHOOL

INT. SCHOOL OFFICE

Solo finds the school office and approaches the SCHOOL SECRETARY.

SOLO

Do you have a student here named Susanna Raines?

SECRETARY

I don't think so. Why?

SOLO

Do you know most of the students in the school?

SECRETARY

Just about everyone. What's it about?

SOLO

(takes out a pad and pencil; draws the face of the girl)
This young lady is about so high. Has pigtails. Wears jeans. I think they call her Zana.

SECRETARY

(her face drops in recognition)
That would be Zita—now Zana, if you please—Ruiz. What's she done now?

SOLO

Not a thing. Who is her counselor, and is that person available?

SECRETARY

Mrs. Goldstein, there is a gentleman out here who wants to see you about Zana Ruiz.

INT. OFFICE OF SHELLY GOLDSTEIN

GOLDSTEIN is heavyset, over-worked, weary. Takes off her glasses and rubs her eyes.

GOLDSTEIN

Zana, Zana, Zana, what is it now? I think you're probably looking for our Rozita Ruiz.

SOLO

Nothing serious. She's applying for a job, and I wanted to find out about her.

GOLDSTEIN

Really? Well, well, well.

SOLO

Are those good wells or bad wells?

GOLDSTEIN

Our Zita, or Zana, as she has informed us she wants to be called, has had some problems.

SOLO

Is it possible to be more specific?

GOLDSTEIN

What kind of job is she applying for, Mr...

SOLO

Schwartz. I need an artist. Is she an artist?

GOLDSTEIN

(brightens)

As a matter of fact, she is. I, personally, think she is an extraordinary young artist. That's one of her paintings. She did that last year.

Solo turns and looks at the painting. An oil. (A GIRL SITTING PRECARIOUSLY IN A TREE) Goldstein comes from behind her desk and stands next to Solo.

GOLDSTEIN

Extraordinary, isn't it? It's one of my favorite things. She gave it to me. She says she can't hang them at home, so she might as well give them away. Can you imagine? I'll be honest, Mr. Schwartz, Zana has problems. Her mother tries, but she is definitely overpowered by a father who is extremely bitter. Who knows why? I believe he abuses the girl; not physically, of course, but mentally. He is very hard. An angry-man. The effect, I believe, has robbed her of her optimism early.

She is very street smart, if you know what I mean, and is very bright, but she is doing poorly in everything. I mean, everything but art. She's in trouble, so a job might be the perfect thing for her. But in all honesty, I can't vouch for her trustworthiness or, well...

SOLO

Thank you, Mrs. Goldstein. Seeing this painting has told

me what I needed to know. I appreciate your candor.

CUT TO:

EXT. IN FRONT OF CONWELL JUNIOR HIGH

Cab is running. Driver outside vehicle, leaning against the door, arms folded, annoyed.

CAB DRIVER

I got out of da fuckin' cab to grab a smoke, and now da dog won't let me in my own fuckin' cab. I don't know if you're gettin' in either!

SOLO

Jesus. That's bad. Let me see what I can do. I got a way with dogs.

CAB DRIVER

Will you stop pullin' my fuckin' leg and tell him to let me da fuck in?

Solo points to the dog, and Old Blood goes into the back seat.

CAB DRIVER (cont.)

You know, I got the meter runnin' da whole time. Dat dog better not ha' turned off da fuckin' meter.

SOLO

Will you stop worrying about the money? I have the money. Relax.

CAB DRIVER

You sure? No offense, but you ain't exactly dressed to kill. I mean, dis could amount to somethin' here.

SOLO

Relax. We have two more stops, then you're through.

CAB DRIVER

Okay, you're da boss. Where to?

SOLO

Take me to a hat shop. I want to buy a hat.

CAB DRIVER

You got it.

CUT TO:

INT. DEPARTMENT STORE - HAT SHOP - TWENTY MINUTES LATER

Solo selects a hat and pays for it. He leaves the shop.

EXT. OUTSIDE THE STORE - MOMENTS LATER

The cab driver is waiting outside the store, leaning against the cab. Old Blood is now next to him. He is petting the big dog on the head.

CAB DRIVER

He had to go. We're friends.

SOLO

That's good. What's your name?

CAB DRIVER

Bobby DiCouza.

SOLO

Bobby, get us to the Municipal building.

CUT TO:

EXT. THE PARKING LOT OF THE MUNICIPAL BUILDING - EARLY EVENING

Toni Bishop is walking to her car. She sees Solo and Old Blood standing by her car. She stops. Her first reaction is fear.

BISHOP

What are you doing here? How did you know this was my car?

SOLO

(he holds up the handkerchief he took from her desk)
The dog told me. He has special talents. He's a genius, in a way. Highly trained.

BISHOP

What (Old Blood growls) do you want?

SOLO

Ms. Bishop, I went out and bought a hat today so that I could come to you with hat in hand and tell you how sorry I am that ... that I laughed, and to ask you please, give me five minutes of your time. Hat in hand. I don't even wear a hat. Please!

BISHOP

Go ahead. If you must.

SOLO

Could we do it over coffee?

BISHOP

(looks at her watch)

I have ...

SOLO

I have a cab right there. He'll take us to a place close by and I'll tell you why and what, and then he'll take you right back here. One cup of coffee. Five minutes.

Toni Bishop, exasperated, nods her acceptance, and Solo waves for the cab. Old Blood jumps into the front seat.

SOLO

Bobby, we need a place to have coffee.

BOBBY

I know a nice Italian place close by.

CUT TO:

INT. NICE LITTLE ITALIAN PLACE

Waiting to be seated.

SOLO

I really want to apologize for what happened today. This whole thing has gotten off—

BISHOP

You're a very aggressive person. Do you always just bull in, expecting to have your way? Were you born that way, or is your attitude a result of fame?

SOLO

Ms. Bishop, could you please cut me just a little bit of slack? I'm trying, honest to God, to be a nice guy, and if you perceive me as being aggressive, it's because my wonderful little mother—may God rest her soul—always told me: You never know unless you ask.

Seated at the table.

SOLO (cont.)

I honestly don't know what happened to me. I'm so sorry I started laughing. Did you ever get into a laughing jag? Then you know how it can be. You don't know why. To anybody else, it isn't funny.

Waitress delivers coffee.

SOLO (cont.)

Anyway, what I'd like to tell you is what motivated me to want those walls, because, as of last Friday, I didn't even know they existed. Actually I came to town thrilled about doing the Center. As you said, it's ... the Center. Now, (rubs his hands and thinks) I've got to go back ten years.

FLASH TO:

EXT. BEACH

Solo spins around from the conversation and doesn't see his daughter. She is gone. He runs up and down the beach.

END FLASH

SOLO

My wife died in childbirth. That was bad. Real bad. But at least I had two things I loved. I had my art and I had my girl. I had Asta. I raised her, I nursed her and she became my life. But that day, that lousy day, we were on the beach and I was so caught up in a heated argument about money, fucking money! that I didn't see what happened. It was only a moment I swear, but when I turned she was gone. For all I know, someone might have taken her. I don't know. We searched. Everybody searched. The police. Everybody, I don't know what happened. If she drowned, they never found her body. I don't know. She probably drowned. It was my fault. I take full responsibility. I... I...

BISHOP

Oh my God, I'm so sorry. I...

SOLO

I'm not telling you this for sympathy. Believe me, you are the first person I've talked to about this in ten years. After the accident, I mourned, I truly mourned, for a long, long time. It took many years, and I thought I'd worked it out, until last Friday, when ... when a very strange thing occurred. This girl, this young girl showed me those walls. Why? Because she's been dreaming about those walls for two years, and in her mind, those walls were hers. She has no idea, absolutely no idea, as to who I am. No idea even that I'm an artist! There she is, fourteen, dreaming about putting paint somewhere. You probably can't understand this, but I used to have those dreams.

BISHOP

Mr. Solo...

SOLO

Please, call me Jake.

BISHOP

No. I can't. Let's not. Mr. Solo, my father was an artist. A painter. Not great, but good. Very good. He drove a school bus to support us. He wore a beret. He had one good pair of pants. He worked so hard, never got any recognition, and believe me, it killed him, little by little. I watched it happen. He spent everything he had on paints and canvas. Never took a vacation. He used to say: I'm not going to be able to leave you anything but the paintings, but when I die, you'll have them." Ironically, they were all lost in a fire. He was killed trying to save them. He would have cut off his arm for one of those walls, to have his name on one of those walls. You probably can't understand this, but there are a lot of struggling artists out there who still have those dreams. It's selfish of you to want to paint them.

SOLO

I don't want to paint them! I want the kid to paint them. They're her walls! Oh, I may be selfish in that she's fourteen—the same age my daughter would have been now, and maybe, psychologically, I'm still trying to work this out—but I don't want my name on those walls. This is not for me. This kid is in trouble, and we have a chance to save her. She is having those dreams right now! In a way, this is like some kind of dream. It seems all of the cosmic forces are at work here. The coincidence of my meeting her, of her trying to pick my pocket, of her being a painter … it's just too incredible to let pass!

BISHOP

So this is not a publicity stunt? You aren't doing this to hype the mural that you are going to do at the Center?

SOLO

I'm not even going to use my name. Swear to God, hope to die! I want this to be her project. And it's not just her. I've been thinking about this. There's a school, close by, that she goes to. We could use, or will probably need, a bunch of kids to make this happen. Whatever the project pays, give it to them. Let them work the summer to create the wall.

BISHOP
And you would teach them?

SOLO
I would coach them, yes.

BISHOP
Do you think it could work?

SOLO
I don't know. But what do we have to lose? If it doesn't work, we'll paint the walls white and give them to some other guy.

BISHOP
I don't know...

SOLO
Look, withhold your judgment for a day. Come with me to the school tomorrow. Let's meet this girl, together. If I'm wrong, I'll let it go. I swear.

BISHOP
Hope to die?

SOLO
Absolutely.

CUT TO:

INT. CONWELL SCHOOL OFFICE - LATE MORNING

Solo, Toni Bishop, and Mrs. Goldstein.

Enter Zana. Solo smiles. Zana sees him, stops. She rolls her eyes as if she's been caught, walks toward them with her head down.

Finally, she looks at Solo with defiance, hands on hips.

ZANA

You promised.

SOLO

(imitating her)

You lied.

ZANA

You squealed.

SOLO

Did not.

ZANA

Did too.

GOLDSTEIN

Look, I don't know what's going on here, and frankly, I don't have the time to play, but Zana, this might actually be some good news for you, so if I were you, I'd chill. Ms. Bishop is with the city and is actually in charge of selecting artists to paint the mural on the walls at Kensington and Front Streets. And for some ungodly reason, she's come to see you.

Zana's mouth drops open and looks from one adult to the other. Solo smiles and winks.

ZANA

You're kiddin' me.

SOLO

She's not kidding you.

BISHOP
I'm not making any promises, but Mr. ...

SOLO
Schwartz.

BISHOP
Schwartz, has convinced me you might have talent.

SOLO
I saw the Lady In The Tree. I liked it. Now, I want Ms. Bishop to see it and talk to you.

INT. MRS. GOLDSTEIN'S OFFICE - MOMENTS LATER

Everyone is looking at the painting of Lady In The Tree.

GOLDSTEIN
I am now going to let Zana take the two of you around and show you the rest of her work. I have an appointment.

SERIES OF SHOTS

INT. THE SCHOOL HALLS

Zana showing Toni Bishop and Solo her work.

INT. AN ART CLASS

Zana showing them more work. Whispering because there is a class in progress.

INT. THE SCHOOL HALLS

Sitting on a wooden bench.

BISHOP

Zana, I'm impressed. You have a raw talent that is quite astounding. But the walls in question … it's a huge job…

ZANA

I could do it. I know I could. I know I could.

BISHOP

The commitment, the work … it would be a big job for an adult, just carrying the paint to the wall …

ZANA

Please, please. I've never wanted anythin' more in my whole life.

BISHOP

Okay, I'll tell you what I'll do. I'll give you a week to work up an idea. Not just a proposal for the walls, but a plan of execution. If it's okay with Mrs. Goldstein and the principal, you will meet with Mr. … Schwartz here, who will serve as your advisor on the project.

ZANA

Are you an artist, Jake?

SOLO

I've done some painting.

BISHOP

Mr. Schwartz cannot do any painting. The idea and the execution of the proposal must be yours. Mr. Schwartz will be there to advise you, to help you formulate your ideas.

ZANA

If it's my idea, will it be my tag, my project?

BISHOP

It would. But I want to caution you: Don't get your hopes up. You may not get it. Other artists out there want those walls. And, I want you to know, if you get it, there will be plenty of restrictions on you. There would be many, many problems to overcome.

ZANA

I understand. I do.

CUT TO:

EXT. SCHOOL STEPS

Old Blood is waiting for Solo and Toni Bishop at the curb.

BISHOP

(reaches down, pets Old Blood)

You know, I didn't really believe you about just meeting that girl, her trying to take your wallet and all. What I find incredible is how you knew she had talent from that short conversation.

SOLO

When you're fourteen and dream of putting paint on a wall, you are an artist. Your entire soul is in the idea of creating. That's what you live for. She's a pistol, isn't she?

BISHOP

(smiles)

Like I told Zana, don't get your hopes up.

SOLO

I appreciate this, Toni. Thank you.

They shake hands. She gets in her car. He's about to say something, but she drives away.

CUT TO:

SERIES OF SHOTS:

EXT. LOCAL STREET

Solo walking up the street with Old Blood.
INT. NEIGHBORHOOD STORE

Solo having coffee. Old Blood waiting outside.

FOCUS ON:

Other people in the store.

EXT. TRANSIT BENCH
Sitting across from the walls.

EXT. CONWELL JUNIOR HIGH

Bell rings. Kids start pouring out. Solo and Old Blood are waiting. Zana comes out and sees them.

ZANA
Thank you, really. Thank you so much.

SOLO
Forget it. If you want this, there's a lot of work to be done. Getting the plan together is going to take every bit of the week she's given you.

Solo begins walking up the street. Zana and Old Blood fall in alongside him.

SOLO (cont.)

I can't do it for you, but I can advise you.

They reach Kensington Avenue.

ZANA

Where are we going?

SOLO

To the walls.

EXT. ON THE SIDEWALK THAT BORDERS THE LOT - MOMENTS LATER

ZANA

You are safe, right? I mean, you aren't a molester or anythin'?

SOLO

You are totally safe with me.

MOVING SHOT

OVER THE SHOULDER

Walking through the lot to the walls. Tall weeds. Trash. Tin cans. Ashes from various fires.

ANGLE ON WALLS

At the walls. Walking along them. Touching them.

SOLO

Remember, it has to be a whole plan. You must think about

the whole project. You're not going to get it if you don't.

ZANA
(looks up, head cranked back)
Do you really think I have a chance?

SOLO
A chance? Yes. But it'll be up to you. If you don't try, you'll never know. You only have a week. Remember, it's not just the drawings of what you're going to paint, but how you're going to paint them. For instance, the weeds and brush at this point are five feet high. That means there will be five feet of wall that people from the street won't be able to see.

ZANA
The weeds will have to be chopped down.

SOLO
Good. But who's gonna do it?

ZANA
I don't know. People?

SOLO
You've got to know. Before you start to draw one line, you've got to see the whole picture. For instance, how many feet are we talking here? How big are these walls? What do you think the square footage is?

ZANA
(lets out an exasperated puff of air)
I don't know.

Solo takes out a tape measure.

SOLO

Let's try to figure that out. You've got to know.

ZANA

Jake? Can I ask you a question?

SOLO

Shoot.

ZANA

Why are you doin' this?

SOLO

(Solo, imitating Zana, lets out an exasperated puff of air.)
I don't know. I'm tryin' to…

ZANA

(imitating Solo)
Figure that out.

EXT. OVER THE SHOULDER SHOT - TWENTY MINUTES LATER

Walking out of the lot. Walls behind them.

ZANA

I never knew the lot was so big.

SOLO

Now you're thinking.

ZANA

Or that painting was so much work.

SOLO

It ain't easy, Magee.

ZANA

Who's Magee?

SOLO

It's just an expression. You never heard of Fibber Magee and Molly? Yeah you're way to young.

SOLO laughs.

SOLO (continues)

It was an old radio show. Back in the day.Because once you start it, you've got to finish it. There's a lot of serious artists out there who want this thing. You've got to be committed. It's work—hard work. Think about how many gallons of paint you'll need, and then think about who's gonna carry all of it to the wall. Tonight, you've got to think about the whole project, what it entails. If you are serious about this project, we will meet for one half hour each day after school at Mrs. Goldstein's office. I'll give you my opinions on your plan as it progresses. If you are not into it, don't show up. I'll understand.

CUT TO:
INT. TONI BISHOP'S APT. - NIGHT

Toni Bishop is lying on a sofa, reading. Doorbell rings. She gets up and answers the door. Solo is at the door. She is not exactly pleased to see him.

SOLO

I would have called, but you were unlisted.

BISHOP

Then how did you get my address?

SOLO

My brother has a mailing list of everybody in town who is interested in art or ever went to an art show, and you were on it. I thought if you weren't busy we could have dinner...

BISHOP

I don't think that would be a ... a good idea.

SOLO

Are you busy? Because if you're not, how could it be a bad idea? It's dinner. I'm buying. I mean, I'm not totally uninteresting. I promise not to bore you. I know a great little Chinese place around the corner. Besides, I'm lonely as hell, I don't know a single person in town, and I need someone to talk to.

BISHOP

Come in out of the hall while I get my coat. And by the way, that great little Chinese place is really Vietnamese.

SOLO

Oh, yeah. I love Vietnamese.

CUT TO:

INT. GREAT LITTLE VIETNAMESE RESTAURANT

They are being handed menus by the waiter.

WAITER

The asparagus and lobster soup very good. Special. I will be right back.

Toni Bishop puts down the menu and sighs.

BISHOP

You've created quite a dilemma for me, Mr. Solo…

SOLO

Jay. Please. I mean, we are having dinner. By the way, how come you're not married?

BISHOP

How do you know I'm not?

SOLO

I … I just assumed…

BISHOP

You assume so much. You assume the walls are free. You assume the girl can paint. You assume no one else is involved. Could get hurt. Decisions weren't made. People aren't busy!

SOLO

I'm sorry.

Silence.

BISHOP

Just picky.

SOLO

What?

BISHOP

Why.

SOLO

Why what?

BISHOP

Why I'm not married. Isn't that what you were asking?

SOLO

Boy, was my brother wrong.

BISHOP

About what?

SOLO

About me having a way with women.

Toni smiles.

BISHOP

Well, you must have something. You've certainly got me thinking. Seriously thinking. In a way, I'm sorry I met Zana, gone along with it the decision you've got me thinking about would have disappeared. But she has talent, that's for sure.

SOLO

It's incredible how much. But one of the reasons I came over tonight is to tell you that whatever you decide is okay with me. And actually, I kind of felt your dilemma as you drove away this morning.

BISHOP

I appreciate that. Truth is, right now, I don't need the additional pressure.

SOLO

(looks inquisitive)

BISHOP

Just because I'm not married doesn't mean I'm not

engaged, or should I say, "un-engaged." We just broke up. So I'm a little edgy. The problem is, when I think about giving the walls to Zana, I feel so guilty, because I committed myself to someone else, and even though he hasn't been told, I still feel guilty. I can't help it, I just do.

SOLO

I don't want you to feel guilty. I want you to feel good.

BISHOP

Thank you.

SOLO

At least stop worrying about it for a couple of days. She may not do it. Today, after you left, I tried to talk her out of it.

BISHOP

What do you mean?

SOLO

I took steps to make sure that Zana understood how much work was involved. Let's see if she passes the first test and has what it really takes.

CUT TO:

EXT. CHESTNUT STREET - UPSCALE SHOPS

Toni Bishop and Solo walking. Solo stops. Toni Bishop turns toward him.

SOLO

Would you do me a favor?

BISHOP

What?

SOLO

Would you let me hold you?

BISHOP

What?!

SOLO

Stand close to you.

BISHOP

Are you totally insane? Why?

SOLO

Trust me. Please. (holds out his arms) Step into my office. Please.

BISHOP

I will not. I—

SOLO

What can it hurt? I'm not going to try to kiss you, I just want to breathe you in. Please.

BISHOP

(steps closer to him)
I can't believe...

SOLO

(closes his eyes and breathes her in)
You see, it's not enough to see you. I plan to paint you, and I believe, (he lifts her chin and stares into her eyes) in order to capture you completely, I must know your aroma.

BISHOP
But I'm wearing perfume.

SOLO
I know. (he breathes in again) But I'm way beyond that.

CUT TO:

INT. AN EMPTY CLASSROOM AT CONWELL JUNIOR HIGH

Solo sitting on the teacher's desk, waiting. He checks his watch.

INSERT:
FACE OF CLASSROOM CLOCK reading 3:15

Door suddenly bangs open, and in comes Zana carrying a bunch of papers and rolled up drawings. Behind her is a boy (about 15) dressed up like a super fly, EDGAR (SPRAY) JOHNSON. He is Black. He has long dreadlocks. Earrings. He is wearing a Homer Simpson T-shirt.

ZANA
Sorry I'm late. I had so much to get together. I have some preliminary sketches and a plan. And I had to use the school computer, and there are some other kids who could help.

SOLO
Who's your friend?

ZANA
Oh, sorry. This here is Edgar. He's a known "Tagger." You can call him Spray. That's what people call him. Next to me, he's the tops.

SPRAY

(laughs)

That's a matter of o-pin-ion. You see, when it comes to the can, Spray is the man, 'cause on the wall, I dos it all. You know what I'm sayin'?

ZANA

He does that all the time. You'll get used to it.

SOLO

Hey, Spray. What say?

Spray and Solo shake hands and bang fists.

ZANA

Please don't encourage him. I told him about the wall because after yesterday, I figured I couldn't do it alone and I needed a crew. Spray can get the crew.

SOLO

Good girl. Now you're thinking. But get one thing straight: Anybody that puts a brush on that wall will have his name on it as one of the artists.

SPRAY

Right on. Write on! You need a crew, that's something I do! I came to fame, by writin' my name.

ZANA

Just remember whose project this is.

SPRAY

Hey, Zana-girl. Be cool, woman. You the boss. I'm the ho'se.

Solo looks at some of her notes. He frowns. Zana sees his expression.

ZANA

What's the matter, Jake?

SOLO

This won't fly.

ZANA

Why not?

SOLO

There are more misspelled words here than paint on a drop cloth. Run-on sentences. It's unreadable.

SPRAY

She gots to know how to spell, too?!

SOLO

How can you expect to get the job, if people can't read your proposal? Being an artist is no excuse or license for being illiterate. This has to be rewritten. When you finish it, take it to your English teacher and have him or her look at it first. Let's see your drawings.

Zana's face drops.

SOLO (cont.)

You can't get discouraged.

Solo opens the drawings.

SOLO (cont.)

Hmm, this looks interesting. I love that face.

Zana smiles.

CUT TO:

INT. AN UPSCALE RESTAURANT - NOON

Toni Bishop and NANCY DORFMAN. Nancy Dorfman is Toni's best friend and confidante. She is showing Toni the latest pictures of her husband and her four-year-old son. Nancy is very upbeat.

NANCY

Do you believe I took that? Is that incredible?!

TONI

It's almost art.

NANCY

No. It's the camera. (she sits back, puts the pictures away and studies Toni.) So, what's up with you? Still thinking about Zeke?

TONI

No. Not as much lately.

NANCY

Then what is it? Something's bothering you.

TONI

You and my mother are the only people who can look at me and see what I'm thinking. It's amazing.

NANCY

Well, I have been your best friend for twenty-five years. Just because I'm not an artist, doesn't mean I can't read a face. What's the matter?

TONI

I don't know. It's just that for the first time in a long time I feel like I'm being manipulated.

NANCY
You're seeing Zeke again?

TONI
No. It's not a relationship; it's in my work. The thing that I have always loved about this job is that I've never been pressured politically, but now … I don't know.

Waiter arrives to take the order.

PULL BACK

Show the whole restaurant. Comes back in again as they are eating.

TONI (cont.)
It's almost like it's kismet, the way things are happening, falling into place. Had he not come back in town in time, had the girl not tried to pick his pocket, be an artist, want to paint those walls. A week later, and I would have told Pedro Sycks, the artist I originally chose, and it would have been over. I wouldn't be in this mess. I have a knot in my gut that won't go away.

NANCY
How did you let it get this far?

TONI
I overreacted. Didn't let him say anything. Kicked him out of my office. Then I felt like such a fool that I overcompensated. The problem is, the girl has talent. Real serious talent. Still, I just don't like the idea of it. I feel as if I'm being used. I can't explain it.

NANCY
Is it the publicity? Is that why he's doing it?

TONI

That's what I thought. But no. He doesn't want any publicity. At least that's what he says. He's doing it for this girl. I think it's because of his daughter that died. It's so involved.

CROSS CUT

EXT. SCHWARTZBERG GALLERY - NOON

Marvin Schwartzberg is on the sidewalk in front of his gallery, directing the placement of a painting by an employee who is working on the inside. Solo is with him.

MARVIN

Have you been thinking about the Center?

SOLO

I have.

MARVIN

Have you committed anything to paper?

SOLO

I have not.

MARVIN

(he turns to face Solo)
Why the hell not, Jay?

SOLO

I thought we agreed we were going to push that back.

MARVIN

The actual painting of the walls, okay. But I've got to have something to show them. I have to be able to say, "Here, look at this. Is this incredible?" I need something.

SOLO

When are you going to learn? The creative process is not like an instant camera. It takes time.

MARVIN

Bullshit. When are you going to learn that this is business? It's like any other job. You've got to perform.

SOLO

Actually, I have some preliminary sketches. Faces. Torsos.

MARVIN

Besides, you don't know that this girl is going to get the walls. I wouldn't count on it.

SOLO

This girl has huge talent.

MARVIN

So do thousands of others. Wake up. You and I know that the only reason you are doing this is because this girl is fourteen, and that's the age that ... that Asta would have been had she lived.

SOLO

Yeah. Maybe. It might have started out that way. But it's the way things have unfolded that has colored the waters. After years of wandering alone, punishing myself ... I can't explain it, Marvin, but I feel involved. I haven't been hiding in the dark of bars, drinking with a bunch of bums. You know what I mean?

MARVIN

I do, and I'm glad. I haven't seen you this excited in a long time. I just don't want you to be disappointed, is all.

SOLO

Marvin, I'm an artist. I know what disappointment is. Whatever happens, get it or not, this has already been a learning experience, and that's what I've told Toni...

SCHWARTZBERG

Toni? Toni. (he smiles) I like the familiarity of that. And what did Toni say?

CROSS CUT

Nancy Dorfman and Toni Bishop.

End of lunch. Over coffee. Waiter delivers check. Disappears.

NANCY

So, all kidding aside, who is the artist?

TONI

I can't tell you.

NANCY

Not even me? Who am I going to tell?

TONI

(she smiles)

Everybody. You know you would. Besides, I have to be absolutely sure. I just can't.

NANCY

You're right. Is he good looking?

TONI
You'd like him.

NANCY
So he's drop dead handsome!

TONI
Let's say … interesting.

CUT TO:
SERIES OF SHOTS

INT. SCHOOL AND CLASSROOMS

Solo working with Zana

1. He is leaning over a set of drawings, shaking his head as if the drawings won't do. Zana's face shows frustration.

2. The next day. A different set of drawings. Solo studying them. Points out something. Zana sees it, shakes her head in determination.

3. The next day. Solo alone. Checks his watch. Zana is obviously late. She comes in, banging the door, holding some drawings. She plops down at a desk, exhausted. He comes over and takes the drawings from under her arms. He opens them, studies them.

SOLO
Not bad. Almost.

Zana brightens. Solo hands the drawings back to her. She accepts them with renewed determination. It is obvious from the smile on his face he admires her grit.

4. The next day. Solo looking at the drawings. Smiles. Nods. Pats

Zana on the back.

CUT TO:

INT. TONI BISHOP'S OFFICE

Solo is there and has just presented Toni with the initial drawings of Zana's ideas. Toni opens them up. Solo moves his chair away from the desk to the corner of the room so that his presence will not detract her from her decision. As she studies the drawings and is about to comment, the door bursts open and in walks ZEKE MARCUS. Thirty-seven. He is obviously irate.

ZEKE

Toni, what the hell is going on? Am I getting the Kensington walls or what?

TONI

Zeke, this is the wrong time.

ZEKE

Wrong time, my ass! I just got word this morning that you're considering someone else.

TONI

Who told you that?

ZEKE

You promised me those walls.

TONI

That's a lie. I never did!

ZEKE

Does this have anything to do with us? Is it revenge? This

is exactly the kind of crap my ex-wife would have done. Goddamn it to hell, you promised me those fuckin' walls. You know you did.

SOLO

Excuse me, maybe I should come—

ZEKE

(startled that someone else is in the room)
Who the hell is this?

TONI

I would have introduced you, if you had not come in here like a maniac. But right now, it's none of your business! How dare you come into my office like that! How dare you assume that any walls are yours! I never, ever, gave you any reason to believe that they were. And how dare you assume that our … our … would have anything to do with my decision…

SOLO

Hey, maybe—

ZEKE

Shut up, old man, before I put you through the wall.

Toni reaches for the phone.

TONI

Maggie, get Officer Hare.

SOLO

Now, wait a minute. I don't mind keeping quiet. (he turns to Toni) It's the "old man" part I object to.

TONI

(to Zeke)
Get out of my office!

As Solo turns back to Zeke, Zeke suddenly hits him in the face. Solo is knocked into his chair. (angle on Solo). He smiles, is about to get up to fight Zeke, when OFFICER HARE comes in and grabs Zeke from behind. He locks Zeke's arms together at his sides.

OFFICER HARE

Should I lock up this bum, miss?

TONI

That's up to Mr.... (she gestures to SOLO)

SOLO

Schwartz.

TONI

Schwartz. I just want him out of here.

Officer Hare looks at Solo.

SOLO

No. Just get his address for me. I would like an opportunity to finish this.

ZEKE

(shakes loose; smiles viciously)
Any time, Pops.

SOLO

There you go again.

Zeke storms out of the office.

OFFICER HARE

I'll see him out of the building. Sorry, miss.

Solo and Toni stand there for several moments, breathing heavily, trying to compose themselves.

TONI

Nothing like a good fight to get your blood going.

SOLO

(rubbing his jaw.)

I don't call that a good fight. A good fight is where I get to hit the guy back.

TONI

Are you all right?

SOLO

Is this an office or a foxhole? I mean, the guy called me "pops"! Dems fightin' words, lady.

TONI

I'm sorry.

SOLO

And you. You should be a baseball umpire. I never saw anybody throw people out the way you do. You're outta here! (he gestures like a baseball umpire)

TONI

(she smiles)

I'm glad you can laugh about it.

SOLO

(he touches his jaw again)

I'm not laughing.

TONI

Zeke isn't normally like that. You probably wouldn't understand this but he's struggling.

SOLO

Toni, of all the things that happened here today, that comment disturbs me the most! It's the second time you've insinuated that I wouldn't understand what it means to be an artist, a struggling artist. I'm forty-five years old. I've been an artist all my life. I started making a living maybe as an artist twelve years ago. There was no overnight success! My overnight success came after a lot of years of struggling. I washed dishes in restaurants, swept out buildings, and cleaned urinals, just to buy canvas, so please don't tell me about struggling. Believe me, I understand what that guy is going through. But that's no excuse.

TONI

I'm sorry.

SOLO

Accepted. Hey, maybe my problem was that I never got angry. Maybe I should have.

TONI

Jay, would you do me a favor and let me look at this later? Right now I'm too frazzled.

SOLO

Of course, and look, whatever you decide, I'll understand. I mean that.

He walks to the door.

TONI

Thank you.

SOLO
And Toni, that guy must be crazy to have let you get away.

TONI
Call me at four. I'll know something then.

SOLO
You got it.

CUT TO:

EXT. ANY STREET. PUBLIC PHONE - LATE AFTERNOON

SOLO
Hello. It's Jay, and it's four o'clock.

CROSS CUT

Solo and Toni

INT. TONI BISHOP'S OFFICE

She is standing. Zana's drawings are spread out on her desk.

TONI
Jay! Congratulations. I'm giving it to you.

SOLO
Not to me.

TONI
No, you're right. To Zana. This stuff is so exciting...

SOLO
You're not doing it because your old boyfriend blew his

top at you and acted like a dope?

TONI

Not at all. As a matter of fact, I'm relieved. The truth is, he wasn't going to get it anyway. I had been bending over backwards to give him every break because I didn't want people to think that I wasn't giving it to him for all the wrong reasons. Trouble was, the idea for the other guy's proposal wasn't much better than his, so people would have thought it was sour grapes anyway. That was my fear. But now I'm prepared to take the heat.

SOLO

I understand.

TONI

But now that's all gone. I am actually relieved, because Zana's stuff would have easily won and should be done. I'm excited.

SOLO

So am I.

TONI

Oh, I just talked to our legal department. Her mother and father will have to come in and sign a waiver.

SOLO

For what?

TONI

A release. She's a minor and it's dangerous work. Being on a scaffold three stories high?

SOLO

Gee … I never even thought of that. I'll pick up the waiver

and go over there tonight.

CUT TO:

EXT. TENEMENT SUBSIDIZED HIGH RISE – NIGHT

Solo walks through the gates of the courtyard of a tenement high-rise project. It is a gruesome concrete building. He passes by two groups of teenagers, one mostly Black, the other Latino. Both groups look at him suspiciously, coldly.

INT. SMALL SQUARE HALLWAY

Graffiti everywhere. Flight of stairs leading up five floors.

ANGLE ON Solo looking up.

Blows out a puff of breath. Looks at a small scrap of paper.

ANGLE ON PAPER (4-B)

He begins to climb.

INT. SMALL HALLWAY

Four doors.

Solo, slightly out of breath, knocks on 4-B. Zana answers the door and is surprised to see him.

ZANA

Jake!

She sticks her head out into the hall and looks both ways as if she expects to see someone else, or Old Blood.

ZANA (cont.)

You by yourself?

SOLO

I am.

ZANA

Weren't there any guys out there?

SOLO

There were.

ZANA

Man! They must have thought you were some kinda cop or somethin'.

SOLO

It takes a cop to find you, 'cause (heavy sarcasm) we're just a couple of blocks from Clementine Street. Are you going to invite me in, or what?

From behind the door, we hear the voice of Zana's mother, MRS. RUIZ. She is coming to the door.

MRS. RUIZ (O.S.)

What is it Zita?

ZANA

(rolls her eyes)

It's Zana, Ma. Zana.

Mrs. Ruiz comes to the door. She is stocky, wearing an apron, wiping her hands.

MRS. RUIZ

To me, you'll always be Zita, which is short for Rozita,

which is your name. Who is this?

ZANA

Ma, this is Jake. The man I told you about.

MRS. RUIZ

Oooh. The man with the paints and the dog.

Mrs. Ruiz looks out in the hall to see if Old Blood is there.

ZANA

The one and the same.

MRS. RUIZ

So, you invite him in.

Mrs. Ruiz opens the door. Solo extends his hand.

SOLO

Jake Schwartz.

Mrs. Ruiz wipes her hands on her apron again, then shakes his hand.

INT. LIVING ROOM

Clean, but worn. Enter Zana's FATHER, LUIS RUIZ, from the kitchen. He is five-foot-eight. Slender. He removes a dinner napkin from his shirt. His face is hard. He stares at Solo in confusion.

ZANA

Jake, this is my father, Lou.

LUIS

Lou? No, never Lou! It is Luis. Luis! That is the name I was born with and the only name I want.

Luis folds his arms proudly across his chest and stares at her, waiting for her to say his name. Zana breathes heavily and dramatically.

ZANA

Luis.

LUIS

And who is Jake?

ZANA

A friend.

LUIS

A friend? He looks old enough to be your grandfather.

ZANA

Friendship has no age limits.

SOLO

I'm sorry. I didn't think there would be a problem—

LUIS

Was I talking to you?

MRS. RUIZ

Luis!

LUIS

Mama, I will handle this! A stranger is standing in my house, disturbing my dinner, and he doesn't think it would be a problem!

MRS. RUIZ

I invited him in. He has something to tell us.

SOLO

Actually, I'm Zana's advisor. I'm going to advise her on a project that she is going to do for the community. I didn't think it would be a problem, because it happens to be a great honor.

ZANA

(puts her hands to her mouth)
Oh my God, did I get it!?

SOLO

You did.

ZANA

(jumping up and down)
Oh my God, oh my God!

LUIS

What project? What did she get?

SOLO

She is going to paint a mural on the walls at Front and Kensington.

ZANA

The walls! The empty lot!

LUIS

I am against it.

ZANA

Why?

LUIS

Why? Why wasn't I told? Why wasn't I informed?

ZANA

Because ... because I was afraid to tell you.

LUIS

Afraid? Why? Did I ever hit you? Did I ever once strike you?

ZANA

Not with your hands or your fists, but you've struck me often enough.

Luis looks from Zana to his wife in disbelief.

LUIS

What, what have I said?

ZANA

(crying)

I can't. It's too numerous. Too many.

Luis straightens up, takes a deep breath, addresses himself to Solo.

LUIS

So, she is going to paint a mural on the wall. And who is she doing this for?

SOLO

The community, and—

LUIS

The community! What community? (sarcasm) You think this community cares one way or the other if the walls are painted? You want them to have something nice to look at when they puff their crack, is that it, mister?

ZANA

See! See, how you go? That's what I mean. You make everything so ugly. Your anger kills everything! Steals the pleasure.

MRS. RUIZ

She is right, Luis.

LUIS

(ignoring his wife)

I'm only trying to teach you, Pepita. I'm only trying to make you see. They don't want you to paint those walls for the people of this community; you'll be painting those walls for the rich people, so when they drive down the street with their cars locked tight, they won't know there's a ghetto. They won't feel guilty. It's like blinders on a horse. They'll see a pretty little painting on a wall and they'll say, "Isn't this nice? There's no poverty here, there's no drugs here, there's no murder here!" Camouflage, Zita, camouflage.

SOLO

Mr. Ruiz. You may be right. At least you are entitled to your opinion. But whether you like it or not, your daughter is an artist. She needs to paint. And she has won the right to paint those walls. In fact, they're going to pay her to paint those walls! But in order to make that happen, you have got to sign this waiver, in case there is an accident, 'cause she'll be working on a scaffold and she's only fourteen.

MRS. RUIZ

(turns to SOLO, her back to her husband)

Is it dangerous?

SOLO

Not really. I'll be there, and she'll be in a harness. It's just a formality. This is a phenomenal opportunity, trust me.

Mrs. Ruiz looks at her husband, long and hard.

LUIS

I will not sign.

MRS. RUIZ

(turns her back to Luis)

Do you need us both to sign?

SOLO

One will do.

MRS. RUIZ

I will sign.

LUIS

You would sign it against my wishes?

SOLO

I don't want to start something...

LUIS

You have already started something.

SOLO

I could come back...

MRS. RUIZ

No. I will sign it now.

As Mrs. Ruiz signs the paper, Luis gets his coat and puts it on.

LUIS

I will walk you down.

ZANA

I will do it, Luis.

LUIS

(stares at her, coldly.)

I will do it.

CUT TO:

INT. STAIRWELL. DESCENDING

Solo and Luis walk in silence.

EXT. THE COURTYARD OF THE PROJECTS

They pass the two groups of teenagers. Bobby DiCouza and Old Blood are waiting in a running cab.

SOLO

(to Luis)

I'm fine. Don't worry. I have a cab and the dog. I'll be all right.

LUIS

I'm not worried about you. You may not think it, mister, but I love my Rozita.

SOLO

This is going to sound hard, but I'll tell it like it is. You say you love her, then act like you do.

LUIS

I'm just trying to teach her what I know, and … you may not understand this, but I am trying to protect her. You raise a boy, you send him into the street. You raise a girl, you worry all the time. I see what these girls become, standin' on the corner, selling their wares for a smoke of dope.

CUT TO:

EXT. STREET

Across the street from where Solo and Luis are standing, another group of teenagers are seen coming around the corner. They are sauntering and posturing with attitude, but fall silent when they see the two groups of boys that Solo and Luis have just passed in the courtyard of the projects. As they turn the corner, one member of the gang stops and, pretending his finger is a gun, points it at one of the boys in the courtyard. He pretends to pull the trigger. The boy he is aiming at sees him, forces a smile, stands a little straighter, turns to face him and gestures with his hands as if to say, "bring it on." Momentarily, the two gangs glare at each other. A tense few seconds ensue, but finally the boy and the gang on the other side of the street move on.

LUIS

You see that? You see what I mean? That, right there, is what this neighborhood is all about. You think those punks give a shit about some kids painting on some stinkin' broken down wall? I worry all the time. That's why I am hard. I want her to get out of here. You think she's gonna get out of here being an artist?

SOLO

I don't know. But I do know this, Luis, your tactics aren't working. If you really care about her, you may have to change them. We all have dreams. Remember that. Let her dream.

LUIS

Hey, man, nothin' hurts worse than broken dreams. You remember that! So don't you hurt her.

SOLO

I was going to say the same to you.

ANGLE ON Luis as he steps back. He points to Solo, wags his finger at him, and turns away.

CUT TO:

INT. CAB

CAB DRIVER

You awright?

SOLO

Yeah, I guess. I just may have gotten in over my head, is all.

CAB DRIVER

That's what involvem'nt is. Always over da head. And da worst thing of all is that it's people who get you in over your head. Ain't that always da way?

SOLO

So what do you do? Not get involved?

CAB DRIVER

Listen. That's what it's coming to. In some parts of the city, they hide behind the houses, you know, decks and shit. You never see nobody on the street. Down here, after a certain hour, da good people don't come out. They're hidin', too, you know what I mean?

CUT TO:

SERIES OF SHOTS

1. INT. MRS. GOLDSTEIN'S OFFICE - DAY

Solo talking to Mrs. Goldstein. She seems surprised, interested, delighted.

2. INT. SCHOOL LUNCHROOM

Zana talking to a bunch of kids, showing them the drawings.

3. INT. SCHOOL BULLETIN BOARD

Zana putting up a notice on the bulletin board.

INSERT ANNOUNCEMENT: Attention all artists. Meeting After School.

4. INT. CLASSROOM

Zana, Spray, and about fifteen other kids. Enter Solo, who is holding a cardboard box, and Mrs. Goldstein. Solo puts the box on the desk. Kids still talking.

SOLO

(holds up his hands to get their attention.)

My name is Jake Schwartz, and I am here because your classmate Zana—

FOCUS ON: EDWARDO JIMENEZ, a student noted for his pranks, interrupting, poor grades, and dissension.

EDWARDO

You mean Zita, man?

There is some laughter.

SOLO

That's right.

EDWARDO

Hey, Zita—

ZANA

Zana.

EDWARDO

Zana, Zita. Whatever. If you ma classmate, does that mean I get special privileges?

More laughter.

GOLDSTEIN

That'll be enough of that, Edwardo.

EDWARDO

(hurt, offended)

I just askin', Mrs. G. I heard this was a career opportunity, and I just wanted to know if a piece o' Zita/Zana was a benny of o' d' business.

More laughter.

SPRAY

Will you chill, man! Listen up. This is serious.

GOLDSTEIN

(glaring at Edwardo)

Maybe Edwardo shouldn't be a part of this. He has a problem with self-control.

SOLO

Edwardo, can you paint?

EDWARDO

You ask any of them. They'll tell you who Edwardo is. My tag is known far and wide!

SOLO

Then shut up and listen up, because this concerns you. I won't tolerate any bull. Zana here was awarded a commission by the city to paint a mural on the walls at Front and Kensington.

The students are surprised and interested.

SOLO (cont.)

Not only is it a tremendous honor, but they are also paying a sum of money to have it done. Her ideas have moved them to give the project to a student rather than to a professional artist. In order to do this, she will need a crew. She could hire people outside the community to help her do this work—it is a big job, an enormous responsibility—but she would prefer that you be part of it. Personally, I think that's a great idea; however, if you agree to work on this project, you will be paid for the work you do, providing—

Groans. The students are not surprised there are conditions; they expected something.

SOLO (cont.)

There are certain conditions, yes. First of all: you can't goof off. You will be assigned certain tasks, and you've got to do them. Goof off, and you're out. You don't get paid until the project is finished, and here's the big one: in order to get paid, you've got to be passing in school.

EDWARDO

Everything?

SOLO

Yes.

GOLDSTEIN

Good-bye, Edwardo.

EDWARDO

Now, you see, Mrs. G., that ain't fair. Based on my past history, you ruled me out, and based on what I've done this year, you've made it impossible!

SOLO

What are you flunking, Edwardo?

EDWARDO

Everything!

More laughter.

SOLO

That's the condition. Think about it carefully. If you stay

and work, you will get ten dollars an hour for every hour you work. But you won't get a single dime if you are not passing.

EDWARDO
(this time raising his hand)
What about the tag? Whose name will go on it?

SOLO
Everybody's.

EDWARDO
Even if we still flunkin'?

SOLO
That is correct. Listen, what we are putting together here is a team. This is just like any school sport. You got to pass to play.

SPRAY
And to get the pay.

SOLO
But whether you pass or not, you are part of this team, and your name will go on that wall.

FOCUS ON:

Another student: A.J. STILES. Black.

STILES
Hey, ma man, Mr. Jake, suppose we don't want to put our name on the thin', 'cause it t'aint our thin'.

SOLO

Okay, that's a good question. Inside this box is a diorama.

STILES

A who?

SOLO

(looks around the room; no one is offering to answer the question and he is taken aback.) Okay, that, as I said, is a good question. Diorama. Rhymes with Alabama, and I took my camera… (points to Spray)

SPRAY

…to add to the drama.

PAN SHOT

Camera rises to capture the whole group tuned in to Solo as he begins teaching them, moving around the room, writing on the blackboard.

CLOSE SHOT

FOCUS ON: Solo now standing by the diorama.

SOLO

This, then, is a diorama. What I did was to take Zana's drawings and shoot them down with a camera so that they would fit into this box. And so, to answer your question, A. J., if any of you don't like what you see here, don't stay. But if you do stay, you have to stick. Stick like glue to the end. Be part of this team to the finish off this project.

Solo takes the top and the front off of the box, revealing the diorama.

FOCUS ON:

Faces of the students. They are interested, impressed. They study it, some very seriously. Some laugh with renewed respect for Zana.

PAN SHOT

Camera rises again as a discussion of the proposed project begins. Goldstein leaves the room. Solo does something to make them laugh. They pat Zana on the back.

FOCUS ON:

A.J. Stiles

STILES

Hey, what is that empty square box in the corner? How come that ain't got no paint?

SPRAY

That is our space, man. That is incorporated in the whole theme, but it's for sprayers, and we can spray anything we want in it, dig? Show our own particular art right in there. Ya know what I'm sayin'? Zana did it for us.

STILES

A.J. likes it! I'm in. Zita, this is the best thin' I've seen since the anti-graffiti police got on ma case. It's high grit, girl!

A.J. "high fives" Zana. One by one, they all do the same.

SOLO

How did they find you, A.J.?

STILES

By my tag. If you don't sign it, it ain't art, Mr. S. It's just scribble. You should know that. My tag is known far and wide. It was like they were looking for Picasso.

SERIES OF SHOTS

1. EXT. THE EMPTY LOT

Solo is with the whole group, stepping over mounds of trash to get to the wall. He looks around as if to say "This has got to be cleaned up." Old Blood is there.

2. EXT. Putting up the scaffolding.

3. EXT. Solo is instructing a group of kids about the harness.

4. EXT. Patching the wall with cement.

5. EXT. Raking the trash. Bagging stuff and carrying tires and refrigerators, etc., to the curb.

6. EXT. White washing the walls.

7. EXT. Solo in the empty lot, explaining something to Toni Bishop. She is nodding and smiling.

8. EXT. JAMES BEASLEY, an elderly Black man, seen previously in some of the neighborhood shots, comes onto the lot with a chair and sits facing the walls. The next day, he is joined by another man, WILSON HOOD. It becomes routine to see them sitting there watching the kids. The next day, Old Blood is sitting by them.

9. EXT. Solo explaining something to Marvin Schwartzberg. Marvin is impressed. Solo introduces him to Zana. Marvin shakes Zana's hand. Beasley and Hood in background.

10. EXT. An enormous pile of trash (twenty old tires, fifty trash bags, a bunch of wood, couple of refrigerators, a gas range etc.) is on the sidewalk waiting for the trash men. Solo and several kids are waiting. FOCUS ON:

Trash truck and men. They are not happy that the trash is there. Solo and the kids help them throw it into the truck.

11. EXT. Focus on the lot. It is rough, but has been cut and is clean. There is a look of satisfaction on the faces of the students who are there.

INT. CLASSROOM - NEXT DAY

Solo at the blackboard. The team of students listening.

SOLO

A lot of you of you are wondering: How are we going to put this mural up? How can we make something so small into something so big? Anybody know? (he looks around the room for someone to come up with the answer.) It's simple. We create a grid. We transfer our drawings to graph paper. Each square here is a half-inch. We then paint a grid on the walls. Each square there will be one foot. That's what we're going to do today: paint our grid on our new walls.

Door flies open and in comes Spray. He has been running and is out of breath.

SPRAY

Hey, you guys won't believe this!

CUT TO:

EXT. THE EMPTY LOT - MOMENTS LATER

Someone has dumped another huge pile of trash in the previously clean lot.

FOCUS ON:

Kids and Solo. Anger, disappointment, dismay.

SPRAY

And that ain't all, Mr. S. While they were at it, they stole some of the planks off of the scaffolding.

STILES

They probably gettin' ready to steal the fuckin' scaffoldin', too.

FOCUS ON:

Kids, frustrated, picking up and bagging the new trash.

CUT TO:

EXT. A CITY STREET - MIDDAY

Solo and Jeeper Jones. Solo is pointing. Jones nods. Solo hands him a piece of paper. Jones nods and walks away, looking at the paper.

EXT. THE SCAFFOLDING - NEXT DAY

New planks are being put in place.

EXT. The grid is starting to be put on the walls.

EXT. Zana is starting to put some color on the walls.

CUT TO:

SERIES OF SHOTS

1. EXT. A CITY STREET - MIDNIGHT

A two-ton truck filled with junk is rolling quietly down the street.

2. EXT. ANOTHER STREET - MOMENTS LATER

Jeeper Jones at a pay phone looking at the paper Solo gave him.

3. INT. HOTEL ROOM. Solo in bed, answering the phone. He gets up and begins to dress, then he and Old Blood leave the room.

4. EXT. THE LOT - SHORTLY AFTER MIDNIGHT
The truck has backed onto the lot. There is a new pile of trash. Two men are seen carrying several pieces of the new planking to their truck. They are interrupted by Solo and Old Blood.

SOLO

Gentlemen.

The two men look at each other. They do not seem intimidated by Solo and Old Blood. They are still holding the plank.

FIRST MAN

(startled)
What the fuck!

SECOND MAN

Who the fuck are you?

SOLO

The trash police.

FIRST MAN

The what?

SECOND MAN
Get out of here, old man, before you get hurt.

SOLO
I was about to tell you to do the same fucking thing.

FIRST MAN
What are you looking for, a handout, or what? You ain't no trash police.

SOLO
Well, I don't know what you'd call it. You see, I consider the both of you pieces of trash, and I'm about to police the area!

The first man drops his end of the plank. He is a very large man. Suddenly, Solo and the huge man are nose to nose.

FIRST MAN
Get the fuck out of here, cocksucker, before I rip off your head and jam it down your fucking' neck. I ain't playing!

SOLO
Neither am I. And before you do some rippin', how about doin' some pickin'. Pick up all that fuckin' shit you dropped here, you sleaze, and put it back on your fuckin' truck.

FIRST MAN
(turns to the second man, who is still holding his end of the plank)
Is this fuckin' cocksucker dizzy, or what?

SECOND MAN
Just get rid of him, will ya?

Suddenly, the huge man picks Solo up and throws him into the pile of trash. Solo grits his teeth, gets up, runs over, and head butts the big man. The man is backed up, but remains on his feet, regains control of the fight, and once again throws Solo into the pile of trash.

FIRST MAN

(slightly out of breath)

You get back up, cocksucker, I'll kill you.

He stares at Solo, then turns back to pick up his end of the plank. As he does this, Solo jumps on his back. The big man spins around as if to shake him off. Solo begins to punch the guy in the side of the head, and it seems the big man is getting the worst of it. The second man now drops his end of the plank and picks up a nailed two-by-four from the pile of trash. Old Blood growls and is on him immediately. The big man now has the upper hand, has displaced Solo, has him down and is about to punch him in the mouth, when a light is shined into his face. It is Luis Ruiz and five or six men from the neighborhood.

FOCUS ON:

Luis shaking his finger and his head as if to say that wouldn't be a good idea.

SOUND of sirens.

LIGHTS of police cars.

POLICE CARS crash onto the scene.

The huge man looks up, sees the cops running toward them and, despite Luis' warning, punches Solo anyway. The men from the neighborhood jump on him and a melee results, ending with the police breaking it up.

CUT TO:

INT. CITY HOLDING TANK

Solo, Luis, the men from the neighborhood, as well as the two dumpers, have all been locked up in the same cell. Solo, with a black eye and cut lip, and Luis are sitting together on a bench, shoulder to shoulder, their arms folded across their chests, feet stretched out.

SOLO

Thanks.

LUIS

(without anger)

You're crazy, you know that? You are the only person I ever met from outside the 'neighborhood' that walks around like he's part of it. I think from now on they will call you "El Tigre."

SOLO

I learned a long time ago that if you walk without fear, you belong, you are part of it.

LUIS

(smiles, nods)

And crazy.

SOLO

I don't get you, Luis. You are so against this mural, but you come to my rescue? Why?

LUIS

One thing has nothing to do with the other.

SOLO

Luis, I've been thinking about what you said that night in

your apartment. I truly believe this mural is good for the neighborhood. This is a starting point, a rallying point. A thing you build off of. If you don't like the neighborhood, work to change it.

LUIS

Change it? Change it! That's so easy for you to say. You come here to live, work all day washing dishes, then you tell me that. You are a true gringo. Why? Because you just don't get it. You're the only one who doesn't understand that this is the ghetto! That mural is not gonna change anything.

SOLO

Then see it as an honor for Zana. It's an achievement!

LUIS

(he stares at Solo, softens)
I have a little Diego Rivera, huh?

SOLO

You should be very proud of her.

LUIS

I know. I am. I don't mean to be so pessimistic, so angry with her. I don't know. I just don't know. I try, but things just come out all wrong. She's slipping through my fingers. I'm losing her. Do you know what that's like? She hates me and who I am and who she is. She calls herself Susanna. Her name is Rozita. She calls me by my first name. I'm her father!

SOLO

Then act like you are. Give her a chance. She may surprise you. Lighten up.

LUIS

I can't.

SOLO

Luis, what happened to you to make you this way?

LUIS

It's a long story. Maybe some day, when I know you better, we will sit and have a drink and I will tell you, and you will help me figure it out.

CUT TO:

INT. THE OTHER SIDE OF THE BARS

Marvin and a police officer standing outside cell. Solo sees him and smiles.

SOLO

Captain Marvel, to the rescue!

MARVIN

So low, man. Brawling. Impersonating an officer. Are you crazy? (sighs heavily, shakes his head.) I posted your bail. Let's go.

SOLO

What about my friends? These guys (pointing to the men from the neighborhood) are with me.

MARVIN

Jesus Christ! (exasperated) Anything else?

FIRST MAN (dumper)

Hey, Jake, what about us?

Solo turns and stares at him in disbelief.

SOLO

You?

FIRST MAN (dumper)

Hey, man, don't be like that. Come on. I mean, what did we know? We didn't know the kids were doin' it. Had we known, believe me, we would'na. Ya beat the shit outta us, the fuckin' dog bit the shit outta me, we're gonna get fined, we may go to jail. What the fuck? We learned our lesson. I swear, we'll never do it again. Come on, whatdaya say? Me and Charlie, we'll clean the whole thing up in the morning, hand to God.

SECOND MAN (dumper)

Hand to God!

Solo turns to Marvin and shakes his head, indicating that Marvin should post bail for the two dumpers also. Marvin smiles, shakes his head in disbelief, and walks off.

CUT TO:

EXT. OUTSIDE POLICE STATION - EARLY MORNING

Solo is shaking hands with Luis.

SOLO

Thank you, Luis. Don't worry, I'm sure these charges will be dismissed.

LUIS

(smiles)
I'm not worried. You know, it felt good.

Solo and Marvin begin walking away.

MARVIN

(sarcastically)

Are you having a good time?

SOLO

(imitating Luis)

Like Luis said, "You know, it felt good!"

MARVIN

And you're looking pretty good.

Solo rubs his chin and tries to smile.

MARVIN

No, I mean it. It's strange, but true. You're excited. It's good to see. That mischievous look is back in your eye.

SOLO

It must be my old "getting involved" look. I never knew how important it was.

MARVIN

(hangs head)

You know, Jay...

FLASH TO:

EXT. THE BEACH - DAY

Same scene as before with the baby digging in the sand, Solo arguing with someone. Camera pulls back and reveals that the person Solo was arguing with was his brother Marvin. They are totally involved in their debate. Then they discover the baby is gone. Both men are seen running frantically up and down the beach.

SOLO

It's over, Marv. I realized a long time ago shit happens. It happened to us. I'll never forget her, but the self-exile and flagellation has come to an end. We've both got to stop feeling guilty. I love you, man. You'll always be my bro.

MARVIN

(fighting back tears)

Thank you.

They embrace.

CUT TO:

INT. POLICE STATION. SERGEANTS DESK - LATER THAT MORNING

TY MASON, reporter for a local TV station, is looking over the time-sheets on a clipboard of Sergeant LEON NUTTER's desk. Nutter enters the scene with a paper cup of coffee that he has just filled.

NUTTER

Nothing for you, Ty.

MASON

(running his finger down a list of names)

Looks like you've had a little activity.

NUTTER

Just a squabble on an empty lot. Dumpers. I'd have called you if anybody got killed.

INSERT:

Clipboard. List of names. Nutter's finger stops at the name Jason Solo. He runs his finger across to see the time the arrest was made.

MASON
Was this guy, Solo, part of the fracas?

NUTTER
Yeah. He got smashed around pretty good.

MASON
You sure this name is right?

NUTTER
Hey, I took it off his driver's license.

MASON
All of them made bail. Who bailed these guys out?

NUTTER
(opens a drawer, takes out a piece of paper)
Marvin Schwartzberg.

MASON
(makes the connection)
Son of a bitch!

INSERT:

TV monitor. Morning news. Two days later.

ANNOUNCER
Here's a juicy tidbit: it seems Jason Solo is back in town. The reclusive and internationally famous artist was bailed out of the city jail last night by his brother, noted art dealer, Marvin Schwartzberg...

INSERT:

OLD PICTURE of Solo

ANNOUNCER (O.S)

Seems there was a brawl on a vacant lot at Front and…

CUT TO:

EXT. VACANT LOT. WALLS - AFTERNOON

Solo is on the ground, directing several kids on the scaffolding. Zana is high up on the scaffolding, painting. The mural is starting to come together. The sky and top work have been painted in.

A TV camera crew's van pulls up onto the lot. The reporter, a woman, BLAKE BARRIE, exits the van. She has a hand-held microphone, approaches Solo. Behind her, another TV station's van pulls up, and a reporter jumps out. Suddenly, Solo is surrounded by a group of reporters.

BARRIE

Mr. Solo?

Solo turns to her.

SECOND NEWSMAN

Aren't you Jason Solo, the famous painter?

Solo looks around. There is nowhere to run. He is being filmed. He can't lie.

SOLO

What do you want? What are you doing here?

BARRIE

That seems to be the question. Mr. Solo, what are you doing here? We heard you got into a fight. Aren't you supposed to be working on the mural at The Arts Center? Is this some sort of publicity stunt to kick off the start of that mural?

SOLO

I'm just trying to help some kids...

THIRD REPORTER

Really? Aren't you the one who lost his daughter and has been in hiding for the last decade? Is this what you've been doing? Are the Chilean paintings real? Were you there?

FOURTH REPORTER

Did they ever find your daughter?

ZOOM OUT:

SKY SHOT

The reporters are surrounding him. Cameras and microphones in his face. The kids have stopped working. Solo puts his hands to his ears, then finally, in desperation, he throws his hands in the air and stalks off. The reporters follow him and Old Blood off the lot.

FOCUS ON:

Spray trying to find out what is going on. He catches up with Barrie, who can't run after Solo as fast as the others because she is in high heels.

SPRAY

Hey, what's happenin'?

BARRIE

Do you know who that is?

SPRAY

Yeah, that's Mr. Schwartz. He's an advisor, helpin' Zana with the paintin'. He's supervisin' the crew.

BARRIE

Zana? Who is Zana?

Spray points to the top of the scaffolding. Zana is looking down over the railing.

CUT TO:

EXT. CITY STREET - LATE IN DAY

Barrie interviewing Zeke Marcus.

ZEKE

That's the problem with the city and this whole mural arts thing. It's who you know and who you are. Those walls were mine. I had been told by Toni Bishop they were mine. But even with an insignificant wall like the one on Front and Kensington, it's who you know and who you are...

BARRIE

Are you saying that Zana Raines wouldn't have gotten the commission, that she isn't the artist?

ZEKE

Get real, will you? Do you really think the Mural Arts Committee would have given it to some little girl? It's Solo's wall.

CUT TO:

INT. KITCHEN - RUIZ APARTMENT

Mrs. Ruiz and Luis are watching the interview on TV. Zeke Marcus appears on their screen. It is the end of the interview.

ZEKE (cont.)

...He's the artist. That's why they took it away from me. In the end, he'll be the one to sign it. Just you wait and see.

SOUND. Slamming of door.

CUT TO:

INT. RUIZ APARTMENT. LIVING ROOM

Zana storms into the apartment. Walks angrily to her room. Slams the door.

CUT TO:

EXT. PARKING LOT. MUNICIPAL BUILDING - 7 PM

Solo and Old Blood are waiting by Toni Bishop's car. Toni sees him and stops in her tracks.

TONI

You bastard, you promised!

SOLO

Toni, I swear I never said a word. Hand to God, hope to die.

TONI

You look terrible.

INT. TONI BISHOP'S CAR - MOMENTS LATER

Old Blood in back seat.

SOLO

They were carrying the planks to their truck…

EXT. MOVING SHOT. CAR. Driving through city.

SOLO (O.S.)

The guy was huge…

EXT. CITY SIDEWALK. Getting out of the car in front of a restaurant.

SOLO (cont.)

…so by then, the cops came and threw us all in jail…

INT. A RESTAURANT - MOMENTS LATER

At a table.

SOLO

…I had to tell them who I was. And of course, Marvin came down to bail us out!

TONI

You see how it looks.

SOLO

I know, I was stupid. I should have never given them my name. Somebody figured it out. It was just dumb.

TONI

You know, one of your problems is that you don't think

about the consequences. You just jump in, create a mess, and assume you can fix things.

SOLO

I didn't know that getting involved again would be so damned complicated. I'm in over my head.

TONI

And talk about stupid. To go there in the middle of the night, alone?

SOLO

I was with Old Blood.

TONI

They could have killed you. The both of you. And then to call Marvin to bail you out? That was a dead giveaway. Everybody knows his name. Why didn't you call me?

SOLO

It was three o'clock in the morning.

TONI

I would have come down.

SOLO

Really?

TONI

Not for you … so much, as for the program.

SOLO

Oh, of course, are … are you in trouble? I mean, program-wise.

TONI

I'll live. I can handle it. No matter what they say, and I'm sure Zeke will have plenty to say. But, in my mind, I know I chose the best artist for the project. And I don't mean you.

SOLO

(takes her hand and leans forward)

I know.

TONI

(puts her other hand over his and leans forward)

I mean Zana.

SOLO

I know.

CUT TO:

INT. CLASSROOM. CONWELL JUNIOR HIGH - LATE IN THE DAY

Except for Solo, the room is empty. He is sitting on the edge of the teacher's desk. He looks at his watch. It is obvious the kids aren't showing up.

Enter Spray and A.J.

SPRAY

Ain't nobody comin', man. Jus' thought I'd stop by and tell ya.

SOLO

Why not?

STILES

It's what the fuck you did?

SOLO

To put it in your own vernacular, A.J.: What the fuck did I fuckin' do?

STILES

You bullshitted us, captin'. You said this was our wall. This was Zana's thin'. Our job. You got us workin' our butts off, an' this ain't our job at t'all.

SPRAY

It's just a big publicity stunt for somethin' else. That's what everybody says. Just bullshit.

They begin to leave.

STILES

An' no matter what us "taggers" do, it'll always be your wall.

CUT TO:

SERIES OF SHOTS:

EXT. THE EMPTY LOT.

Solo is there, alone. The kids are not there. He shakes his head knowingly.

INT. MRS. GOLDSTEIN'S OFFICE - DAY

Solo talking to Mrs. Goldstein.

INT. SOLO'S HOTEL ROOM - NIGHT

Solo sitting on the bed talking on the phone.

INT. KITCHEN. RUIZ'S APARTMENT - NIGHT

Luis, sitting at the kitchen table, hangs up the phone. He folds his hands in front of him and thinks. His wife comes over and puts her hand on his shoulder. Luis gets up and goes into their bedroom and disappears, comes out moments later holding a scrapbook. He knocks on Zana's door.

ZANA (O.S.)
Who is it?

LUIS
Luis, your father.

ZANA
What is it?

LUIS
I would like to come in.

ZANA
Why?

LUIS
I would like to talk to you.

INT. ZANA'S ROOM

Luis sits on her bed.

ZANA
Did you come to gloat?

LUIS
(sighs heavily)
Rozi ... Zana ... let me show you something.

He opens the scrapbook.

INSERT:

PICTURES of the Ruiz family.

FOCUS ON:

Luis and Zana through the years as she grows up. The love between father and daughter is evident.

LUIS (cont.)

I don't know what happened to me, to us. How I became so angry and … I am so sorry I let it affect you. Infect you. I let my bitterness come between us, and I don't want my anger to rob you of your dreams.

ZANA

But you were right.

LUIS

No, I was wrong. I wanted to keep you from getting hurt. But now I understand that getting hurt is part of the process.

ZANA

Why are you so angry?

LUIS

Why? It seems so silly now. But I left the country I love, the people I love, to come here to be something I am not, could never be. Now, I am ashamed of the place where I am, the place we live. The failures. I came here because I thought I could do better. That's why people come to America, isn't it? I was once an artist, an actor. I thought all I had to do was to be here; that someone would find me, recognize who I was, what I could do. (he laughs) I was so stupid, I thought someone would fall out of the trees or sky or somethin' and make me a movie star. You know, every life is like a painting. Each experience is like adding a little color. If we are not careful, the painting can get away from us. Now, in my painting, I am afraid, always regretting not doin' this or that, the turn not taken. And now I'm too old to dream.

ZANA

You are not old. That old.

LUIS

(smiles wryly)

Now my dreams are for you. No one ever fell out of the sky for me, but Zana ... someone did for you. You can't afford to let it slip away. I don't want you to be another one of my failures. And maybe you don't know how much I care for you. Maybe I was at fault for not sayin' it. But you are my daughter, and I love you now as much as I did then (he points to the pictures in the album) and you can see from the pictures how much that was.

CUT TO:

INT. TV STUDIO

Commentator RUSS LEWIS is interviewing Solo. The set is two swivel chairs on a carpeted platform. The show is called WHAT'S THE STORY?

LEWIS

(into the camera)

Good afternoon. I have with me today the internationally

known artist, Jay Solo, who recently made the headlines by getting into a fight with persons dumping trash on a vacant lot at Front and Kensington. Most notably, Mr. Solo has been chosen to paint the Mural for the new Arts Center, which everyone is aware is the focal point of the Avenue of the Arts. But a night in the city jail, and stories regarding his painting a mural at the sight of the riot, have raised some eyebrows. (turning to SOLO) What's the story, Mr. Solo?

SOLO

Russ, first let me say that I came here today to correct some misconceptions. The press has once again gotten the facts a little wrong.

LEWIS

So let me get this straight: You came back into town after, what, ten years or so to do a big important job, a job that is going to pay you a big pile of dough, and suddenly you see this wall and decide that is what you want to paint? I mean, what can the city be paying you?

SOLO

Okay, let's stop right there. First of all, I am not taking one dime to do what I am doing at Front and Kensington because, and let me make this perfectly clear: I am not doing the painting. What is going up on that wall is not my work.

LEWIS

Really? Then whose is it?

SOLO

It is the work of a brilliant young artist, and a bunch of very talented inner city kids.

LEWIS

You mean, the city gave that wall, designated for a mural, to a bunch of inner city kids? I mean, while it's not the Arts Center, it's still an important commission for a painter to get. And you have nothing to do with it? What, then, is your involvement?

SOLO

I'm just the coach.

LEWIS

Just a coach. So this is like inter-mural-sports?

SOLO

(forced smile)

Yes. I am teaching them how. And yes, I had something to do with the city looking at their work. But the young lady's work won on merit. Wait until you see this thing. It's incredible!

LEWIS

I can't wait. But it's still kind of hard to believe. So, you're just a nice guy. You're just helping them out, out of the goodness of your heart.

SOLO

My God, why is that so hard to believe? Have we become so cynical that every time we try to do something good, we are looked on with suspicion? The reason I'm working with these kids is obvious: I'm doing it not out of the goodness of my heart, but for the goodness of my heart. It makes me feel good! And I don't want any recognition for doing something that makes me feel good. My name—or as they say, "my tag"—will not go on that wall. That is reserved for the artist, Zana Raines. She's the head of the team. I'm just the coach.

LEWIS

Well, coach, from what you've told me, it seems you got a pretty angry team on your hands.

SOLO

I know. Unfortunately, this is the classic example of no good deed going unpunished. I made some stupid mistakes. I should have told them right up front who I was, but in truth, I didn't want to use my name because I knew it would detract from the recognition due the real artists. I thought I could get in there, help them out, and slip away quietly. But it didn't work out that way. (into the camera) I'm sorry. What happened was totally unintentional. I want everybody who worked on the project so far to know that. I don't care about what the papers say, what the press says, I want you guys to know how I feel and what the truth is.

LEWIS

So what happens now, coach?

SOLO

I don't know. That's up to them. I can't lay a brush on that wall. I won't lay a brush on that wall. But I'll be there, and all they have to do is show up.

CUT TO:

EXT. KENSINGTON and FRONT. THE LOT - AFTERNOON

It's a bright day.

SKY SHOT

The lot is empty except for Solo. He is sitting on a rock in the middle of the field and looking at the wall. Across the street, on Ridge, a couple of the kids see him there and watch him. Shortly, they are joined by a couple more kids. Walking onto the lot with his fold-up beach chair is Beasley. He places it near Solo and Old Blood.

CLOSE SHOT:

Beasley and Solo silently studying the wall.

BEASLEY
So where is everybody?

SOLO
I don't know.

BEASLEY
They don't want to be artists no more?

SOLO
That's the way it looks.

BEASLEY
Ain't that the way. All my life, I dug ditches.

SOLO
Really? So you were an impressionist.

BEASLEY
(he chuckles)
That's right! You got it. I'da given anythin' to ha' been an artist. Every "impression" I ever did was covered back up and over.

SOLO
(laughs)

SPRAY
Hey, coach what's goin' on?

CUT TO:

SKY SHOT

The entire bunch of kids standing behind him. Solo looks over his shoulder to see them there. He turns back to the wall. Zana kneels next to the rock Solo is sitting on and studies the entire wall.

ZANA
Do you think that sky's blue enough, coach?

SOLO
I don't know. What do you think, Spray?

SPRAY
Deeper. Deeper. I want them to see it in China.

STILES
Hey coach, they say you're a great painter. How do you get to be a great painter, man?

SOLO
Well, you can't be like my Aunt Sally, who could have been a great painter, or so she said, if it wasn't for the rash she got every time she picked up a paint brush. Consequently, she never painted. So remember, you can't be a saint... (he points to Spray)

SPRAY
...if you don't paint.

SOLO

You can't even be good. Remember: anything worth knowing takes practice. Nobody gets good overnight. And nobody gets great. It takes work. (he stands up, turns to them and smiles) Work. Work. Work. So... (points to Spray)

SPRAY

So ... if you got the rash, you can't make the cash.

SOLO

Correct. Anybody here got that rash? No? Good. Okay, let's get some paint up on that wall.

CRANE SHOT

Solo walking and pointing to the wall. The kids following.

ZANA

And what's up with that phony name?

SOLO

I was about to ask you the same question. Maybe it's time for the both of us to be proud of who we are.

CUT TO:

SKY SHOT

MOVING SHOT

Around the neighborhood, giving the impression of time elapsed.

SUNNY DAY - TWO MONTHS HENCE

Beasley is carrying his chair onto the now-manicured lot. People are placing folding chairs in rows. A stage has been erected in front of the walls, and the walls have been covered by canvas. People start arriving. People are now seated in the audience and dignitaries are on the platform. Solo is behind the dais. He has been speaking and is about to finish. Zana is seated next to him.

SOLO

And now, ladies and gentlemen, I am proud, very, very proud to introduce to you this project's real artist. I give you Za—

Zana pulls at his sleeve. He leans over to talk to her. Smiles and nods.

SOLO (cont.)

Correction. I give you the artist, Ms. Rozita Ruiz

She stands, they shake hands. The canvas drops, revealing the walls. Thunderous applause.

FADE OUT

THE SHORT OF IT

Family Stories

The Other Side of the Bridge

I would like you to shut your eyes and think about your home, the place you live. I want you to visualize it. Picture all of your favorite things, your favorite books, your favorite pictures. Of course, your garden, your kitchen; the new range, your comfortable chair. Now, I want you to imagine needing to go, having to leave. Your life, your future, depends on it. What would you take with you? You say you'll pack the big car. No. Sorry. You don't have a car. You can only take what you can carry. And what you carry on your back will have to be, in addition to your most precious things, a change of clothes, some bedding, and food, because on the way to where you are going, there are no shops, no restaurants, no motels. You will sleep on the ground, you will eat what you have brought with you, and you will pray there is enough water along the way.

"Are you kidding me?"

Yeah, that's what I was thinking when my aunt Minnie told me the following story in 1985.

The year was 1898, and a lot was happening in Kiev, the place where my grandfather, Avrom Bisbolstiv, worked as a trolley-car conductor. In those days, trolleys were nothing more than covered carts powered by four horses. At that time, Ukraine was in turmoil. A lot was happening because the Cossacks and the Prussians were in their perpetual, ongoing battle over who would control the country. Every day, one or the other dominated the population, and the best you could hope for was not to get in the way of the constant skirmishes.

One dark November day, a group of Cossack soldiers entered the town of Kiev and dragged Avrom Bisbolstiv and several other young men out of a café, hauling them away to a nearby second-story room where about a hundred other men were waiting. Cossack soldiers guarded the door. Soon, an officer of rank entered the room and told the group they were about to do something honorable for their country—they were to be inducted into the great Russian army. The officer, a heavyset man with an enormous handlebar mustache, told them, "Not to worry, you will soon be home with your families. It is only a twenty-five-year commitment!"

Only the guards thought this was funny.

Every man there knew it was a death sentence.

Avrom stood in the back of the room. Behind him was a window. And while the others loudly protested, Avrom simply opened the window, climbed out, and dropped to the ground. He ran home. There, his wife, Bessa, and his three children listened as he told them what had happened and what he planned to do. He had to leave. If not, they would come for him, take him away, and make him a Cossack gun-bearer. If that happened, the chances were great he might never see them again. Instead, he would go to another land, save his money, and send for them.

"Where will you go?" Bessa asked him, trying not to show her fear. She was once again pregnant, but didn't dare tell him now.

"I will go to America."

"America!" she exclaimed, closing her eyes and clasping her hands together. "What a beautiful name."

"Yes, America. It ... it means freedom."

In a little more than one hundred years, the American dream had reached the far corners of the world, and Avrom had dreams.

Little is known of his journey. He was a man of few words. Yes, at immigration, Ellis Island, they'd changed his name from Bisbolstiv, which he couldn't spell, to Finkelstein, which he also couldn't spell. But he would learn, and he would work, and he would save, then send for his wife and children. It took a year and a half to save the seventy dollars they would need to make their journey.

And now it was my grandmother's turn. The only difference was, she now had four children. A son had been born. She looked about her home. What should she take? What would be of value? What could she carry? Of course the kids could carry; Jack was seven, Hymie was five, and Minnie was four. Each would have to carry something. It would be a long trek to the border. Many, many miles.

It was a time of tremendous upheaval when my grandmother and her children left Kyiv, the only home she'd ever known. The battling to see who'd take control of the land was incessant, the bombs frightening. Still, she had to go, and so she started out without looking back. Many days later, she found herself and her little ones on a road flooded with thousands of other people also trying to escape. Like the others, she was exhausted. She was carrying the baby in one arm, the family's only treasure—a brass samovar—under the other, and had a huge sack on her back. They all marched wearily to a bridge that served as the border. The bridge spanned a ravine, a steep gorge.

As she plodded along, a stranger came up beside her. He'd seen that she was struggling. He was a thin-faced man, bearded, with friendly eyes, and he was wearing a full-length woolen coat and a leather cap. He removed the cap, and stared compassionately at my grandmother.

"You seem to be struggling. Can I help you?"

My grandmother thanked him, and at first she refused, but the man smiled a soft, gentle smile, an understanding smile. She studied him as they trudged on.

"I could hold the baby for a while," he suggested.

So she gave him the baby to hold.

They continued to plod along, and finally they came to the bridge. But the bridge was closed. This caused great concern to the hundreds of people who'd come to cross. The guards seemed to be looking for someone. They started milling through the crowd.

The man holding the baby saw them coming and, with the infant still in his arms, he started to move away from the approaching soldiers. Then he started running. The guards saw him and started to push their way through the crowd to get to him. The man stopped momentarily at the edge of the ravine, then jumped, ran, slid, and tumbled down the gorge. The guards reached the edge of the ravine, readied their rifles, and started firing as the man, still holding the child, disappeared into the trees below!

Incredible! Dreadful! Horrible! Staggering!

Now, my grandmother was faced with a desperate choice. A Sophie's Choice, if you will. Should she wait, stay there, hoping the man would come back, or should she go on? The border/bridge had just reopened. Suppose it closed again?

With a heavy heart, she pushed on. She had to. There was nothing else she could do. Tears rolled down her cheeks as she led her three children across the bridge. She could barely breathe from all of the sobbing. But that was to soon end, for once they'd crossed, my grandmother noticed, sitting alone on the side of the road, was the baby ... my father. My grandmother wiped her eyes, quelled her deep breaths, then simply picked up her baby and continued on her way.

"So you see," my Aunt Minnie said, "if people ever ask you, you tell them you come from the other side of the bridge."

I was astonished. "What? Why haven't I heard this story before?"

"Well, so many other things had happened."

"Other things!" I couldn't imagine. "It must have been such a hard, arduous journey."

"It was. But it was worth it," she confessed looking up to the heavens, gratefully. "Because coming to America meant freedom!"

My Father Was a Cowboy

The Rabbi who was going to preside over my father's funeral asked my mother, my brother, and myself if we could give him some information about our father. As far as I knew, Dad wasn't a religious man or a man who believed in organized religion, so this rabbi, who'd never met my father, needed us to give him something to help make his sermon meaningful. I couldn't help myself.

"My father was a cowboy," I said matter-of-factly.

My brother guffawed. "Ted tends to romanticize him."

He wasn't a real cowboy, of course. Even though he had bowlegs, he'd never ridden a horse, never chased down a steer, never strapped on a gun. No, the only thing Dad had ever strapped on was a tool belt. He was the best electrician to have ever come down the pike. But I always saw him like he was riding into the wind.

The rabbi, whose name I can't remember, ignored my brother and asked me what I meant.

"Well," I said, "he loved cowboy movies. Every once in a while, he would take me to see triple cowboy feature movies at the Logan Theater on Broad Street. He once told me the only man he'd step aside for was John Wayne. And he'd pull up his pants when he said it, and laugh."

Wayne was six-foot-three, and Dad was five–foot-four. But as a kid, I never doubted it for a minute. He was tough. He was strong. So I'd sometimes picture him with his hat brim pulled down, coat collar pulled up, riding into a snowstorm and, as I think back now, it had actually happened.

"He was working in the Philadelphia Shipyard at the time," I explained. "It was a good fifteen miles from the neighborhood in which we lived, and it snowed. It snowed like crazy. It started coming down just after he got to work, and continued heavily for the rest of that day. By the time he left the yard, which was down below Packer Avenue, and got into his car, it was nearly fifteen inches deep.

"At that time, we lived in Mt. Airy. Like all the other cars on the expressway that night, nothing was moving. Dad's car stopped, completely snowed in, about twelve miles from home. The only thing he could do was walk. We were all plenty worried, especially Mom. But Dad finally walked in at ten that night. Mom fed him. He slept until three in the morning, got dressed, grabbed a shovel, walked back to his car, dug himself out, and drove to work. Was he tough? Was he strong? Oh, yeah!"

"What do you remember most about him?"

"I remember sitting with him in his favorite chair and watching the Friday night fights. I remember his smile, the way he put his arm around me. I remember how warm he was and how much I loved him."

From a collection of old photos we have of him, I could see, as a young man, he dreamed. He was a dapper dresser and genuinely handsome. He had a blend of almost-blond hair, blue eyes, a naturally sparkling smile. And he had confidence. He had gone to trade school to learn electrical work, but loved music. In the early twenties, he led his own twenty-one-piece orchestra. He was the frontman; the guy people came to see. He played the guitar and banjo, but only occasionally. Most of the time, he smiled, waved his baton, and sang. For him, it was a business—a good business. But in his mind, it wasn't work. He loved it.

"In those days, there was work for musicians," I said. "Every hotel had its own house band, and those bands played in the hotel ballrooms. And those ballrooms made money, because people, in those days—the twenties—loved to dance, loved to be out, so consequently those ballrooms were packed.

"My father's band was the house orchestra for the Penn Sherwood Hotel, at Thirty-ninth and Chestnut Streets. That band played seven nights a week, and on Sunday afternoons, Dad would hold a musicians gathering on his family's porch. Great musicians from all over the city would come to play. Legend had it that hundreds of people would come with chairs, crowd the street to sit and listen.

"I am told he reached the peak of his *almost* success in nineteen-twenty-nine. He was twenty-eight years old. He was on his way. He had a car—a roadster—a lot of cool clothes, a great job; he was making real good money, and he had just met the hottest-looking girl in town: my mother. He loved her, and he loved what he was doing. Who wouldn't?

"But then ... it abruptly ended. The Stock Market collapsed. The last thing people were hiring were bands. Millions of people were out of work. People weren't going out. There was no money. Shhhiittt! Great musicians were standing on street corners, selling apples just to stay alive. Luckily, Dad had signed a contract in nineteen-twenty-seven through nineteen-thirty-one, with a provision that said, more or less, if times got hard, he had to cut the size of the band down to six. In nineteen-thirty-one, conditions were at their worst. Then, when things really looked grim, he was offered a job that would keep him playing, but would put him on the road. He and the band—not the whole band; only ten pieces—were going on a tour. Somebody had put together a bunch of Midwest towns and called it a tour. It was the marathon dance craze. A "crazy" month in any small town that would book them. He was the master of ceremonies. It was better than standing on a corner, selling apples.

"That gig lasted six years, and at the end of it, the handwriting was on the wall. His playin' days were over. His youthful shine was starting to fade. The marathon dances were a contest of endurance; the winner was the couple who could dance the longest. As long as there was a customer in the place, they danced, sometimes for fifteen, sixteen hours a day. That meant music had to be playin' for those hours, so Dad wasn't getting a lot of sleep. And Mom wasn't getting a lot of Dad. He was rarely home. Something had to give. Mom won. Dad put down his instrument, a Martin 21, and never played again. He gave the guitar to me. I still have it."

I took a breath. I was deep in thought. No one said anything, so I went on. It was like I owed it to him. You don't live a whole life and not have someone tell it like it was.

"And then, it was like everything went wrong. The depression was like a storm, blowing hard, making Dad fight for every inch of ground..."

He had saved some money from the marathons, and he had a plan. His younger brother, Sam, my favorite uncle, was a butcher. As a boy, he'd apprenticed in a neighborhood shop, and he had saved a little money. Uncle Sam had also made money by selecting beef at the major market for several small shops. Those shops paid a price for a man who could look at a side of beef and determine how it would taste when cooked. He also had an idea. He knew of a store they could turn into a moneymaking venture. Sam and Dad would run it, but Dad would have to learn how to cut meat.

Uncle Sam was going down to Ocean City to work for their brother-in-law, Dave Dorn, Aunt Minnie's husband. Dorn owned a very successful supermarket in Ocean City, New Jersey and he agreed to hire Dad as well as Sam, so that Sam could teach his brother the business. Sam and Dad were real brothers; they truly loved each other. All five brothers and two sisters in the family were close, but none like Sam and Dad. And for a short time, the store they built together did well. It was a pretty butcher shop; it gleamed. They were building a business. But then a major supermarket opened, right up the street, and put them right out of business.

"Uncle Sam was known in the beef business," I told the rabbi, "so he had no trouble finding a way to make money in the beef business. He went on to open a meat market on Sixty-first street, between Chestnut and Walnut, that employed five butchers. He delivered meats all over the city. Once a month, one of his men delivered T-bone steaks, lamb chops, and fillets to my apartment that filled up my freezer. My father, however, had to go into some other line of employ.

"Dad had learned electrical work as a boy. He'd gone to technical school, and after classes, he'd knock on doors, trying to sell his expertise. If you had a bell that didn't work, or a light that had a frayed cord, he was Johnny-on-the-spot, which was appropriate, because his name was Johnny. Johnny Fink.

"But he hated doing electrical work. He detested creeping into crawlspaces and milling through dank basements. It was hard, dirty work. But the main reason he detested working with wire was that it didn't pay. He couldn't make a living. Then he got lucky. World War Two broke out, and Dad got a job as an electrical foreman at the Philadelphia shipyard. During the war, he was the only electrician at the yard who could wire submarines. It was hard work, but he was happy; he was making a living wage and playing his part in the war effort. Once the war was over, though, he once again fell onto hard times. He couldn't get into the Electrical Union. And that just killed him inside, because the dichotomy between the wages of a union electrician and that of non-union men was huge and unfair. Despite his skill, Dad was barred from the union because it was a father-and-son shop; you could only get in if your father was in. It also didn't help that Dad was Jewish.

"It was a tough time. He was getting older, and the wind was blowing harder. He couldn't catch a break. He felt he had wasted so much time. In my eyes, he could do no wrong. I could see what he was going through; it was like he was running in perpetual motion and not getting anywhere. One time, when he was out of work, I saw him standing at the window, and I knew what he was thinking: What am I going to do now?"

The rabbi looked at my mother, who repeated what she'd already said several times: "He was a good man."

My brother nodded and whispered, "Yes, he was."

"He was a fighter."

My brother once again silently agreed.

"I never saw my father physically fight," I said, "although his temper was legendary. But he was so cool in the face of impending danger. Once, driving to our new house in the Oak Lane section of the city, a crazy drunken driver nearly hit us. Dad blasted his horn. Mom was in the front seat, I was in the back. We were about a hundred yards from our house. The other driver passed us, then came screeching to a stop. He didn't like the sound of Dad's horn, and when he saw we had pulled over in front of our house, the guy, thinking Dad wanted to fight, got out of his car and started cursing. 'Motherfuckin' Jew, motherfucker!' he yelled. 'Who the hell do you think you're beeping your fuckin' horn at!' He was one big son of a bitch; I mean, he was huge. Leaving his car in the middle of the street where he had stopped, he started lumbering drunkenly toward us. He had murder in his eye and was gonna kill him one bleepin' Jew bastard.

"Dad saw him coming. He told us to stay put. He took his keys out of the ignition and calmly walked to the rear of our car. The other guy saw how little Dad was, but he also saw that Dad had his hand in the trunk of our car. 'Motherfucker?' hissed the big man, coming to a stop. Dad just remained silent and stood there, staring unblinkingly at the monster. 'You got something in the trunk?' the drunk snarled, his fists balled up. Dad didn't say a word, didn't move a muscle. The big man looked back at his car and the woman now standing in the street. 'He's got somethin' in the trunk, Carrie.'

"'George,' she yelled at him, 'get the hell back here before he knocks your brains in!'

"The big man looked downcast, turned, went back to his car, and drove away.

"Dad waited a couple of minutes, took his hand out of the trunk, and opened the door for Mom. I got out of the car and immediately asked, 'What did you have in the trunk, Dad?'

"He forced a tight-lipped smile. 'Not a Goddamned thing. I was looking for the tire iron but couldn't find it. Wow, that guy would have killed me!'"

The rabbi laughed.

"I never heard that one." My brother smiled grimly.

"I remember that one, Ted. We had just bought the corner house on Middleton Street. I told you about it, Paul."

"Well, I was there," I said calmly. It was a matter of fact. "Do you remember that time, a couple of years later, when he almost got robbed?" I asked Mom. "It was in that second store, the one on Fifty-second Street, a couple weeks after he fired Mickey."

"Mickey was a thief," my mother said indignantly. "It nearly killed Dad. John was a good man, and he loved Mickey, treated him like he was a son. Taught him how to cut meat, gave him a key to the store. Paid him good. So good, it nearly broke us." Had it not been the rabbi's office, Mom would have spit on the floor.

"Because Dad could cut meat, he opened a couple of corner grocery stores. The first one was in a very poor neighborhood around the Girard College wall, a school to shelter poor homeless boys. It was almost like a prison. When the famous Steven Girard endowed the school in eighteen-forty-eight, he insisted that a thirty-six-foot-high wall surround the school. Prisons don't have walls that high."

Once again, the rabbi laughed.

"To get around the demands of the will, the executors dug an eighteen-foot trench and put one half of the wall in the ground. In the beginning, on Saturdays and Sundays, my brother would stock shelves and deliver orders, dragging bags of food in a little red wagon to customers' houses. Then it was me. I was eleven, and we were still living behind my mother's store, Essie's Specialty Shop. Dad would wake me up at five-thirty in the morning and say, 'Let's go,' and we would go.

"That's when he hired Mickey. Mickey was about my dad's height, and stocky. He was a light-complexioned African American, eager to learn, and Dad liked him. He taught him the business and trusted him. Mickey was an integral part of what was essentially a one-man store.

"Three days a week, he left Mickey alone in the store while he went down to the food distribution center to buy meat and produce. But one day he came back early, and as he walked into the store, a long-time customer was coming out. Mrs. Melber. She was carrying a large bag of groceries. Sticking out of the top of the bag was a loaf of bread. The bread sold for fifty-nine cents. When Dad went to the register, he saw that the sale read fifty-nine cents. He questioned Mickey about it, and the man told him that Mrs. Melber had come in with that bag, that she must have bought those goods up the street.

"But something about it didn't ring right. Dad had a suspicion that he couldn't shake. For the last several months, the new place had been losing money. So that night, Dad went to Mrs. Melber's home. She lived a couple of blocks away in a third-floor apartment. He knew her address because, on the weekends, I'd delivered orders there. Reluctantly, he climbed the stairs. The older woman was delighted to see him and invited him in. 'Hello, Johnny,' she said. 'Sit down. What can I do for you?'

"'I need to ask you what you bought at the store today. How much did you spend?'

"'Well, I spent twenty dollars and fifty-nine cents. I gave Mickey twenty-one dollars, and he gave me forty-one cents change.'

"It was a sad and depressed Dad who walked into the house that night. He'd liked Mickey, had trusted him, would have given him extra money if he'd needed it. He bitterly told my mother what had occurred. 'John,' she said, 'you've got to fire him.'

"Clenching his teeth, Dad said, 'I want to kill the sonofabitch.'

"'I know you do,' said Mom. 'I do, too, but you can't. Just let him go.'

"'But how can I run the store? Who's gonna open when I'm buying at the market? What am I going to do when I have to go to the bathroom, or eat lunch? How the hell can I run it alone?'

"'I don't know, but don't do anything that will get you in trouble. Promise me. We'll figure something out.'

"So Dad let Mickey go, but it weighed on him. He couldn't get the anger out of his system. It festered.

"Like the first store, the second store was small with a couple of rooms in the back. In the front of the place were the vegetables: pyramids of oranges and apples, with bins of potatoes and onions. The walls leading to the rear of the store were lined with shelves packed with canned goods. Across the back was a meat display case and a chopping block. Behind the display case was a huge walk-in refrigeration unit and the register. In the back of the store was another room where boxes of canned goods and other supplies were kept.

"As usual, I was there on a Saturday, stocking shelves and delivering orders. It was around ten o'clock in the morning, and I had gone into the back to get a crate of cabbage. When I left, Dad had gone into the walk-in box to get a side of beef. He was slicing the meat first, then using a cleaver to sever the bone. I came out of the rear with the crate on my shoulder just in time to see a guy trying to pull a holdup. He had an old large-brimmed hat pulled low and a worn gray topcoat with the collar turned up.

"Dad and the thief were staring at each other. The guy had his hand in the right-hand pocket of his topcoat and it looked like he had a gun. Dad had the cleaver, and he was so calm when he said, 'No, I'm not giving you any fuckin' thing 'cept this cleaver in your chest. Now get the fuck out of here.' I guess Dad was still pissed off and must have thought the guy looked a lot like Mickey.

"The thief looked up and momentarily saw me. He gave my father a cold stare, but turned on his heel and hurried out of the store. Dad never said a word about it, just kept on working, asked me if I knew where to put the cabbage."

The rabbi wrote this down on the pad in front of him and said aloud, "He was a hardworking man."

We all agreed. "It was really amazing how hard he worked, how long his daily hours were, how depressing his days were, and how little he complained. It was almost like he was punishing himself for all those years of doing what he loved, for playing music.

Now he was chopping meat, stocking shelves, and facing down thieves."

Now even my brother laughed. "Well, he did complain to O'Riley."

My mother smiled. "That was John."

"Yeah," I said. "Sure he did. Because he was pissed off. Yeah, as hard as he tried, the stores never worked out, and he eventually gave up on them, and for the next ten years, he went from electrical shop to electrical shop. He was always working, always bringing home a paycheck, and then he was diagnosed with prostate cancer. It was advanced. The doctors removed his prostate and removed his testicles. He was in bed for a few weeks, but then got up and went right back to work.

"Much to his disgust, and because of his medication, he grew breasts. He couldn't stand what was happening to him, to his body, and had them removed. Then in nineteen-sixty, he was working at Pangborne Electric. It was a large company that had both union and non-union electricians. The union men were making twenty-seven dollars an hour, while Dad and the rest of the non-union men were making a little over three dollars.

"One day, the shop foreman called Dad into his office and told him he needed him for a job in a large home in Lower Merion. 'As a special favor to me,' the foreman told him. 'Do your best.' Dad gave him a disparaging look. Whenever Dad did a job, whatever it was, he always did his best. Among the other non-union men at Pangborne, he was known as Lamont Cranston, the alter ego of the superhero, the Shadow. Dad could go into a house, rewire the whole place, and you'd never know he'd been there; you never saw a wire, no holes, no debris … he was immaculate.

"As usual, he did his work and finished up. Two months later, the foreman said he wanted him to go back to the same house, that they had some more work for him. Dad went back, did his work, and was packing up to leave, when in walked a huge man. This guy was at least six-foot-six. Dad was five-four. The guy stood in the archway of the living room where Dad had been working, looked down at my father, put his hands on his hips, and grinned from ear to ear. 'Are you Johnny the electrician?' he asked.

"'That's what they call me,' Dad said, not sure what to say.

"'Well, Johnny, I just wanted you to know I think you are the best electrician I ever saw.'

"Closing up his toolbox, Dad smiled graciously, and said, 'Thank you, but what do you know about electrical work?'

"'Johnny,' the big man said, still smiling, 'I'm O'Riley, the president of the Electrical Union.'

"My father's lower lip began to quiver and his mouth tightened. 'What did you say?'

O'Riley tilted his head as if surprised, then the big man repeated what he'd said. 'I'm James O'Riley, the president of the electrical union, local—'

"O'Riley never got the number of the local out, because Dad started jumping up and down in rage. 'Are you out of your freakin' mind? How dare you call me the best, when I'm making three stinkin' dollars an hour and your men are makin' close to thirty?' If Dad had been holding a meat cleaver, he would have chopped the big man down.

"He left his toolbox where he was loading it, pulled up his pants, and angrily strutted to the leader of the union. Standing on his toes, he shouted into O'Riley's face, and the big boss put out his arms to avoid the spittle as Dad went on, 'But, you're right, I am the best! None of your guys can do this kind of work. Not the way I do it. Because all they know is new construction. Jesus Christ, a kindergarten kid can do new construction. Three stinkin' dollars a fuckin' hour is all I'm fuckin' makin'. So, yeah, I'm pissed off! If I'm the best, then pay me like I am.'

"Dad snorted, came down off his toes and, in disgust, went back to get his toolbox. He pulled up on his britches, John Wayne style, feeling so much better. He let the big boss know what had been eating him up all these years. O'Riley! Heh!

"Dad only wanted to get the fuck out of that house when, as he bent over to get his box, he felt a hand on his shoulder. He spun around to protect himself, thinking O'Riley was going to punch him out, but to his surprise, the big man had a smile on his face. 'Johnny,' he said, 'you are one spunky little fella, ain't you? And you're right, you should be in the union and I'm gonna make sure you're a happy man.'

"And so at the age of sixty—Dad lied and told O'Riley he was only fifty—got into the union. And not only did O'Riley keep his word and get him into the union, he put him on the gravy shift—the shift that made the most money. It paid big, because it started at four in the afternoon and went until midnight, double pay. Dad went from three dollars an hour to fifty-four, and for the next ten years, until the cancer had finally worn him down, Dad was a happy man."

There was a moment of silence, and the rabbi ended that by folding his hands together in front of his mouth, shaking his head. "Well, I think I have enough. Thank you."

"Say he was a good man."

"I will, Mrs. Fink. I will."

My Mother

The first picture ever taken of my mother was in 1928, when she was sixteen, standing next to her mother who, in the picture, is seated in a wooden hard-backed chair, looking very, very old. I think her mother's name was Tessa. The old woman had had a hard life. As a young girl of thirteen, she'd been sent alone from Argentina to Germany to marry a man she'd been promised to but had never met. The man was cruel and beat her. She escaped to America with her eight-year-old son and married a man twenty-five years her senior, Philip Wexler. Philip was a huge man, a kind man—the proverbial gentle giant—a religious man, a good father, and a loyal and caring husband.

My mother, Esther, or Essie, was the youngest of three daughters whom Tessa had borne for Philip, and she was the most beautiful. Slender, yet voluptuous. Her hair was wild but luxurious, and everything about her was feminine.

She worked from the time she was five, sitting on a high stool, drying dishes in her mother's one-room restaurant. How her mother had gotten a restaurant was never explained.

Sixth grade was as far as she'd gotten in terms of formal schooling. Reluctantly, she never entered middle school; she left against her will to work full time in her oldest sister's husband's woman's bathing suit factory. Her family needed the money she earned.

The smartest thing my father ever did was to marry her.

THE LONG and SHORT OF IT

They met on a trolley car. He was seated near the front, when she stepped on and made her way to the rear. She walked right past him, and his head turned to watch her when she did. She was eighteen at the time, and she was beautiful. He got up, followed her to the back of the trolley, and told her so. She was not just gorgeous, she was movie star gorgeous—a cross between Claudia Colbert and Lana Turner—and she was ambitious. When she set her mind to something, nothing could stop her.

They'd married a year before the Great Depression. Little did they know that the Depression would change their lives. It made him hit the road, playing small towns to survive.

While he was away, she was constantly working, reading, thinking, and taking care of us kids. And though she greatly rued the fact that she'd never gone to high school, she never complained about the way things were. She was upbeat, cheerful, eager to get ahead. My earliest recollection of her was the night she became a businesswoman.

At that time, we all lived in a small second-floor apartment in a row-brownstone on 42nd Street between Viola and Parkside Streets. My father had returned from work exhausted, greeted us, then collapsed as usual in his easy chair. I was playing with something on the floor, and my brother was doing homework on the kitchen table. It was a serene setting, but from where I was playing, I could tell my mother was nervous about something. She was standing in front of the kitchen sink, preparing dinner, when she suddenly wiped her hands on her apron, took a deep breath, and turned toward my father.

"John," she said, "I did something today."

A half a block away was a small shopping center. It was really just a conglomeration of beat-up shops one after the other on both sides of the street. On the corner of Viola and 42nd was a worn-out store run by two older people who sold needles and thread and assorted shmatas.

I was only six, but I remember this incident so clearly.

He looked at her affectionately, and couldn't help smiling at her excitement.

"I'm listening," he said.

"I bought something today."

Quizzically, he tilted his head. "What'd you buy?"

"Well, you know that little store on the corner of the street?"

He had to think for a minute. It was only up the street from our apartment, but he had no idea what they sold and couldn't imagine her going in. He kinda looked at her funny. "What did you buy?"

"I bought the business," she said clapping her hands together. "I bought the whole business!"

The whole business? What? He had no idea what she was talking about and looked around like somebody else in the room might explain what she was saying. All that he eventually came up with was "Huh?"

"Yes," she went on gleefully, "and all I had to pay was a hundred dollars!" Her eyes sparkled.

"Wait a minute," he said, sitting up in his chair, "let me get this straight. Are you telling me you actually bought that piece-of-crap store on the corner of Forty-second and Viola?"

"Yes!"

"And you paid a hundred dollars for it?"

"Yes!"

His eyes started blinking. "Are you out of your freakin' mind? We don't have a hundred dollars!"

Well, that didn't matter to Mom. She planned to get the money she needed from her sister who'd married her second cousin, my Uncle Lou, and was now rich. Lou was still manufacturing woman's bathing suits and had sixty people working for him.

The rent for the building that housed the dingy store Mom bought was twenty-five dollars a month, but it included an apartment that was behind it.

It took a couple of days for Dad to calm down. He loved his wife and was willing, as he thought it was inevitable, go to debtor's prison for her. But Mom wouldn't let that happen. Mom sold every bit of merchandise in the old store, and what she didn't sell, she threw out. Dad ripped out the wavy, warped, decrepit shelves, lifted the ten layers of battered linoleum, and built beautiful blond cabinets with sliding glass doors and a countertop. When Dad had finished, the store was so stunning; people came from all over just to look at it. The highest compliment came from Otto Olsen who had a shoe repair shop two doors down and was considered by the entire neighborhood a real craftsman.

He walked into the shop as Dad was putting on the finishing touches. "It's beautiful," he said. "It almost matches your wife's beauty." There were tears in Olsen's eyes.

Mom called it Essie's Specialty Shop. And her specialty was "dressing woman." The store became an instant success, not because of the cabinets that Dad created, but because Mom was the greatest salesperson who'd ever come down the pike. If you came into the store, you didn't leave without something under your arm. Women came from all over and they'd tell her things they didn't tell anyone else. She'd listen to them, and cry with them and finally, with tears running down her face, she'd say, "That's the saddest story I've ever heard. You know what would make you feel better?" she'd say, taking a dress down from the rack. "This little number here, only nineteen ninety-five."

And she had a guiding rule: She made sure to compliment every woman who walked into the store. "What lovely eyes" or "Your hair is so attractive" or "You're so shapely." The women loved it. Once, a woman who was so ugly it was pathetic walked in, and my brother and I wondered what Mom would say. In my mind, the woman didn't have one redeeming feature. But Mom found something. "Your earlobes are so perfect!"

When the woman left, my brother and I made fun of her for finding the woman's earlobes to praise. But Mom didn't think it was funny. She put her hands on her hips and looked disappointed. "There is something beautiful in every living thing. Don't you ever forget it."

When she sold the store ten years later, she asked the buyer if she wanted to buy the "book." The new owner, a stocky woman who resembled a schoolteacher with glasses perched on the end of her nose, had purchased the business and had paid dollar for dollar for the merchandise, asked well before agreeing to the sale, "What book?" My mother held up a small, battered blue notebook and said, "This. It's the accounts book."

"What's it for?"

"Well, when a woman comes in and wants an item, but doesn't have quite enough money, I give them the item and write down the balance they owe here."

The woman laughed. "I don't think so. You keep it."

My mother was surprised. "Really? I think—"

"Look, all I'm interested in is the store and the merchandise. I don't want to be a debt collector."

My mother smiled. "Okay."

There was a little over eleven thousand dollars worth of collectible money in the book. In those days, that was a lot. Mom knew every woman who owed her money. At one time or another, they'd cried on her shoulder. Once a week, my mother took the bus back to the old neighborhood and collected every dime owed to her. The new buyer who'd taken over the business had lasted five months. After paying back my mother, there was little money left for new things.

Shortly after Mom had collected every penny owed to her, she was approached by the CEO of Blum's Department Store. His name was Martin Sosnow, and he'd heard of her from a New York ladies wear manufacturer. The particular store he was concerned with was located on the corner of Germantown and Chelten Avenues. A few days after he learned of Mom, he called her and asked to meet with her. At that meeting, he was impressed by her looks, her knowledge, and her style. He offered her a job.

"In what department?"

"I'll leave that up to you. You choose. I want you here."

"What department are you most worried about?"

"Well, to be honest, our millinery department is not doing well. We're thinking of closing it."

"Let me start there and see what I can do."

Blum's, with its failing millinery, was a beautiful store. It was pristine, spotless, with gleaming glass cases. In the middle of the store was a wide staircase that led extravagantly to the second floor. In a distant corner of that upstairs space was the millinery department. My mother cleared a path to it, and once every hour, Mom would put on a hat and descend the stairs. The whole place would stop as she came down. It was like the entrance of a movie star—regal, worldly, totally unexpected. As she went around the first floor, ladies would reach out and touch her, and she'd compliment them the way she always did. "Oh, you have the most beautiful cheeks," she'd say. "I have a hat upstairs that will be so perfect for you," and the shoppers would follow her up the stairs.

Blum's was so impressed with their increased sales; they asked her to work in their center city store.

"Where can I make the most money?" she asked.

"We have a fur coat department that needs you."

* * *

The manager of the downtown Blum's store had heard about my mother, but he had his doubts about her ability. He had three other salespeople in that department who'd been there for years and who he thought were professionals in every sense of the word. He had no high expectations as to what she could do, so he was flabbergasted at the end of the first month when she outsold all of those other salespersons put together. The problem was, my mother told me, they were men. When a woman puts on a coat, they couldn't touch her. They couldn't stand behind her as she looked in the mirror, run their hand down the sleeve of the coat she had on and whisper, "It's so beautiful. It makes you look gorgeous."

She worked at Blum's for three years, and at the end of every year, she led the whole store in sales. Then one day, she sadly walked into the office of the manager, Edward Krantz, and said,

"Eddie I have to leave, I'm sorry."

"What do you mean leave? You can't leave. I need you. Haven't we been good to you?"

"You have. I love working here. But my husband is sick and I have to take care of him. He doesn't know it, but he's dying."

Krantz sat down. You could tell he was touched. He'd come to love my mother, not just because of her sales record, but because she was good and kind and gentle. A tear rolled down his cheek. "Oh, Essie," he said, "I'm so sorry. Is there anything I can do?"

"Not really, Eddie, but thank you for offering."

"What are you going to do?"

"Well, he likes the shore, Atlantic City. I've taken an apartment there. My youngest son is going to go down there to fix it up for us. It's close to the boardwalk. We'll walk during the days, and sit in the rolling chairs at night to see our friends walk by."

"You have good boys. Isn't one of your sons a doctor?"

"Yes, my oldest. I'm so proud of him. I hope he comes to visit, but you know how doctors are. He's so busy."

At the end of the summer, I drove down the shore to bring them home. My father had always been a strong man, but the day I drove him back from the shore, he was diminished. He was as light as a feather. I had to carry him into the house. He kissed me when I set him down on the bed and he smiled. He was so thin, he was almost translucent. He weakly raised his hand and lifted his pointer finger. "You know Stuff when a man gets close to dy …"

"Dad …"

"No let me say this, please. Ted, listen. When a man gets…older he starts wondering about what he did in life that was worthwhile. I realize now that what I did was to be the father that helped raise you and Paul. I'm so proud of the two of you. I love you both so much."

My mother was standing at the door, and kissed me as I left. There were tears running down my cheeks. "I love you," she said.

My dad died two weeks later.

* * *

In 1951 we moved from living in the back rooms of Essie's Specialty Shop to a brand new house in the Oak Lane section of the city. This house was one of fifty row houses built on a street that curved. It was called an air-light—living room, dining room, kitchen, with three bedrooms and two baths upstairs. The total cost was twelve thousand dollars. My parents had put down a thousand dollars (mostly borrowed from her rich older sister) and they'd taken out a twenty-five year mortgage which cost them forty dollars a month. Forty dollars! And what's remarkable is that while working every day, they worried every month about meeting that monthly note.

A year before my father died, they moved to a one-bedroom apartment near the park. Shortly after his death, Mom moved to Florida, where she had many friends. Hard to be alone after your devoted mate of forty years passes on. As she once told me, with a twinkle in her eye, "I'm getting old waiting for my kids to come around once a week." I understood. She was a woman through and through and she needed friends nearby and a man to look after and share life with, and so, after a couple of years of adjusting to the Miami sun, she met a man whose love she accepted.

His name was Herb, and he had a condo in the same building. He'd been an accountant and had amassed a small fortune. Like my father, Herb had known the moment he saw her that she was special. The night they met, she'd just won the Official State of Florida's Senior Citizen Beauty Contest. She loved Herb, and he showered her with gifts. But Herb didn't tell her one very important thing. When Mom asked him about himself, he didn't tell her he had to be careful because he had suffered from leukemia and was in remission. Had he told her, he wouldn't have died shortly after they'd married. Mom would have made sure he was careful and had taken care of him.

Harry, on the other hand, was old when she met him at a condominium dance. He was bent over and bald, with glasses that sat on his pointed nose. He was very unlike my father and Herb, but a good man with one exceptional asset.

He could drive!

True, he could only make right-hand turns, but it got him to where he wanted to go. The first time I'd observed it, I had gone down to Florida on business. My mother said she wanted to take me to dinner, and that Harry would drive. He had to go four blocks out of his way to do it, because he only made rights. The other memorable thing about that night was the dinner. Of course, we arrived at four in the afternoon. It was a huge delicatessen—clean, bright, and crowded. My mother and Harry were not the only ones who ate dinner before dinnertime.

When the waitress delivered the menus, my mother indicated that she would order for all of us. I let her. She knew both the restaurant and what I loved to eat. This is what she ordered for each of us: Matzo-ball soup, gefilte fish, salad, roast beef with mashed potatoes and string beans, dessert, and non-alcoholic beverages. And anything she or Harry couldn't finish, they had wrapped to go.

When the check came, she insisted on paying. The total bill for the three of us, due to the early bird special—and we were definitely early birds—came to only twenty-three dollars! But wait! My mother had a fifteen dollar coupon! So the three of us ate for eight bucks, and Harry walked out of the place with three shopping bags of food. It was like we robbed the place.

When my mother was eighty-three, she moved back to Philadelphia and into a high-rise senior citizen facility that featured a nursing care center. The place was beautiful, clean, well maintained. The dining room was just as lovely, with a hostess and maître d'. She always entered for dinner with a flair. She still had it, and the people there loved her. By being with her, they, too, felt beautiful.

One day she called and said, "Teddy, there's a man trying to climb in through my window." I told her I'd be right down. I was worried, not about somebody creeping in, but about my mom's mind. My mother's apartment was on the twenty-third floor, so I doubted if anyone was trying to climb in. She was eighty-eight and I was afraid she was losing it.

I called my brother, the psychiatrist, who told me to bring her down to Belmont, a beautiful psychiatric facility he was the director of, and a place where she would stay a few days under a watchful eye. The staff would adjust her medications.

So we did. A few days later, I read in the *Inquirer* that the city, because of the extreme cold weather, was picking up the homeless and street people and housing them at Belmont. My wife and I became worried. I could only imagine my sweet little mother being intimidated by a horde of rough street people.

My wife and I immediately drove to Belmont and met Mom in the spacious lobby. We sat on a sofa and started talking. I could see the street people on the other side of the lobby. They were a raggedy bunch. Then, this one withered, toothless old guy staggered over to us, lip curled down, and said, "Ye got a smoke?" and before I could answer, my sweet little old mom said, "No," in a rough voice, "we don't got a smoke, and you don't need one, either. Now get the hell out of here!"

Geez, and I thought my father was tough.

She taught me a lot.

Back in the day, when I was in my twenties and going through a lot of shit—disappointed with what I was doing, where I perceived I was going—I would sometimes snap at her angrily, take my feelings out on her in a ranting rage, trying to verbally hurt her. I mean, I loved her with all my heart, but things just came out; I couldn't help it. And then I would feel guilty about the rage.

Then one day, she said, referring to an argument I had with her several days before, "I know you don't talk to your friends the way you did to me; I know that you didn't talk to your father that way. But you talk to me that way. Why? I'll tell you why. Because you know you can get away with it. You know I'll never stop loving you. You are my son; you'll always be my son. So let's not be belligerent. But if you have to vent, if you have to let it out, I'm here. I'll always be here for you. Just let me know in advance so I can be ready. 'Mom, I'm coming over to vent. I'll probably get angry and rant and rave, so be prepared.' That way, I'll be ready."

I would laugh, and so would she.

She never asked for much from me. She worked her fingers to the bone for our family. The only request she made of me during those late years, especially after she went into the nursing home, was that she didn't want to die alone. She wanted me to be holding her hand when she took her last breath. I promised her I would be there, but it was not to be. She died in her sleep at the age of ninety-two.

My Brother Paul

One of the reasons that I write is to examine the past. Most importantly, especially at this time in my life, is my past. I don't want to leave anybody behind, especially those I've loved, for as my mother has said: Everyone is beautiful, and everyone has a story.

Ninety-nine point nine percent of those who came before us lived a life and had stories to tell. Then they become drops of sand, never to be heard of again, and rarely, if ever, mentioned. Their memory fades like mist into the vastness of eternity. Soon after they die, no one will remember them or their accomplishments.

My big brother, Paul, had many accomplishments. Paul was a doctor, a Freudian psychoanalyst, a politician, a father, a husband, and a deep thinker. He was the chancellor of his college fraternity, the president of the American Psychiatric Association, the president of the National College of Psychiatry, the head of Jefferson University Dept of Psychiatry, wrote a monthly column for the American Journal of Psychiatry, and before he retired, he presided over no less than twenty-five special boards of city-wide importance.

Paul Jay Fink, born on the 26th day of June in the year 1933, the first child to Esther and John Fink, was six years older than me and so much wiser in many ways. But not in all ways. A perfectionist in some things, but hardly perfect. Like all of us, he had flaws. He'd been inflicted with tunnel vision in that, once he'd made up his mind concerning a certain thing or person, he was steadfast in his beliefs. Some of those things I could never understand. For instance, what was it that made my brother dislike my father so? I never understood it. My father was not a mean man. He worked hard, never struck us, always put food on the table, clothes on our backs, but still…

The 1930s were a tough time for our country as well as for my brother. Our mother worked a fifty-hour week in a shirt factory, and my father, a musician, was away most of the time, traveling as the master of ceremonies for a touring marathon dance troop. When the depression hit, it destroyed all of the big bands, so he took a small group on the road, hitting every one-horse town and playing for a fraction of what he'd been making. But what else could he do? He had a family; he had to make money somehow.

So, for the first four years of my brother's life, Paul never really knew his father. Dad would come back home for a few days, give Mom all the money he had, and then hit the highway for months at a time. Fortunately for my brother, our grandfather, Avrom, who had walked out of Kyiv in 1898, took care of him when my mother was at work. Avrom was a gentle and wise man and had taught my brother many things. By four years of age, Paul could read the Jewish Forward, a newspaper written in Yiddish. People in the neighborhood considered him a genius. When he was twelve, bearded, bent-over old men would ask him questions as if he knew the answers. A genius he was not. Very, very brilliant, he was. In high school, college, and medical school, he was always at the top of his class. But nothing came easy. He had to work extremely hard for everything he achieved. Like everyone in the family, though, work was not something that he was afraid of or shied away from. Paul loved and needed to be busy.

Dad had been playing in Chicago when my brother was born, and actually hadn't seen him until he was three weeks old. That time, he'd only stayed for two days before he had to hit the road again. The next time he returned home was after a four-month stint in Atlanta, Georgia. After that, Memphis, Altoona, and Biloxi. This went on for four years, until my mother couldn't stand it any longer and threatened divorce. "Get a regular job," she told him. "Come home. Stay home. Face reality. I need you. Your son needs you."

So my father, who loved my mother and wanted to do the right thing, left the music business that he loved. He and his brother, Sam, opened a beautiful little butcher shop instead, and for a year they did very nicely, until a supermarket opened up one block away and put them right out of business. It was a very arduous time. Not only had Dad lost a business, but he'd also lost his son.

My brother, who was only five at the time, resented my father, saw him as an interloper, a stranger who'd suddenly come into the house and was commanding the affection of our mother, the affection that, up until that time, my brother had monopolized, and for the rest of his life, Paul would resent our father. Years later, long after my father had died, I got into a fight with Paul because I was tired of hearing him say disparaging things about our dad. I'd never, ever heard him say one good thing about the man. Enough was enough.

I mean, it wasn't that our father didn't love my brother—he loved Paul with all his heart—it was simply that he didn't know how to show his affection, as if they didn't know where and how they fit into each other's lives. Then, what made matters worse for my brother and the relationship they might have had, I was born, and for the next couple of years, all attention was shifted to me. As I grew, all I wanted was my father, and he couldn't resist me. I was, so they say, one hell of a cute kid. Paul had our mother; I had our father.

The years passed.

Paul got his kudos from one and all for his seriousness, his intellect, and his brilliance. Unable to compete, I got my acclaim from singing, pretending to play the banjo, and making people laugh. He had the scholarship; I had the sportsmanship. He frowned on violence; I loved a good pitched battle. He walked the straight and narrow; I followed the mischievous path.

Initially, what had made it harder for us was the lack of space. In the early days, we shared a small room in the back of our mother's little store, Essie's Specialty Shop, purchased for one hundred dollars back in 1946. The store was only 12′ X 12′, but thanks to my mother's perseverance, it had always produced a profit. Together, with my father working as an electrician, they were able to get ahead.

And getting ahead was what they worked for.

They'd both lived through the Depression, they knew what it was not to have, but to struggle and to think about every penny. The goal was not to be rich, but to live comfortably.

Behind the store was the kitchen, followed by the living room, then our parents' bedroom, and our own tiny room and the bath. In order to get to the only bathroom in the apartment, our parents had to walk through our room.

Paul and I slept in bunk beds. The only other furniture in our room was a small desk, a single wooden chair, and a bureau with a lamp. We weren't poor, but there was little extra money; although, in 1948, my parents bought a fourteen-inch television, and Paul and I had a small radio in our room. And every night, my dad gave me a dime to buy an ice cream soda at Morton's ice cream parlor across the street.

Every Saturday, my mother gave my brother a quarter to take me to the movies at the Dell Theater at 40th and Girard. Paul hated it, but what could he do? Ten cartoon shorts and a Hopalong Cassidy cowboy movie wasn't his thing, but taking care of me on Saturday afternoons was his job and he reluctantly did it. I say reluctantly because, even though I idealized him and did everything I could to be around him, I couldn't help feeling, even in those early days, that my presence was an annoyance. We never talked. We never shared thoughts. As smart as he was, he never taught me anything, never took the time. Still, despite all of that, I loved him. Loved him then, love him now.

When I look back all those years ago, I realize he had some problems that I initially was too young to recognize. Maybe my father saw them but didn't quite know how to change them or help him. Maybe he didn't understand. Supposedly, in his youth, Paul had some feminine mannerisms. Nothing totally obvious. Nothing flamboyant. Sometimes they revealed themselves in the way he stood, bit his lower lip, ran his hand through his hair. Things he'd changed later in life. But, maybe that's why my father was so standoffish. Were those mannerisms the result of our father not being a part of Paul's early life, his not having been around during those formative years? Playing music hundreds of miles away left my brother without a father figure to emulate. Maybe being so close to our mother...? Maybe she smothered him? Who knows. Maybe Paul thought it was a way to attract our father's attention.

Personally, I was totally oblivious to them, and only became aware of them one afternoon when I was ten.

I was at a friend's house. We were outside on the porch just shooting the breeze, horsing around. My friend's name was Arnie Brush. Eddie Brush, his older brother, had come out onto the porch, saw me, and said something derogatory about Paul. I wasn't sure what he meant, and I don't remember exactly what he said, but I didn't like the way it came out. Eddie was about Paul's age, and husky. A big guy.

"What?" I'd said, sitting up. Until that moment, I'd only heard words of praise about my brother. Older Jewish men would stop him on the street and ask him questions as if his opinion mattered. Sometimes they consulted him about Jewish history and Torah interpretations. Back then, it was an extraordinary thing. But the thing Eddie Brush had said was different. The way he'd said it had made it an insulting, degrading remark.

"What?" I'd asked again. Eddie Brush looked away, but I'd persisted. Finally, he spit it out.

"Your brother's a faggot." He glared at me. "He's a sissy, a girl. He likes boys!"

I was only ten, but I'd jumped on that sonofabitch. He was so startled, he fell back against the porch wall. I was able to get in one half-hearted punch before he recovered and kicked my butt, and by that I mean he'd grabbed me by the coat, held me in front of him, and whacked me a couple of times across the back of the head, then threw me off of the porch.

I'd stormed away and never told anybody.

But I suddenly took notice.

Years later, I found out what had happened, and why Brush had said what he did. My mother told me that Paul's best friend, Moishe Rabinowitz, had spread an untrue story, and suddenly everyone in the neighborhood thought my brother was gay. This bunch of gossip had gotten back to our father. There was never any mention of it, but thinking back I remember how worried and concerned he was. At that time, my father was no longer working as an electrician. World War II had ended and the electrical union wouldn't accept him. So in order to survive, our dad bought a small grocery store in a neighborhood worse than the one we lived in and struggled to eke out a few bucks. On Saturdays and Sunday afternoons, Paul would work with him stocking shelves and delivering orders. I don't know how that worked out, or how they got along; it was never talked about. When I was eleven, I took Paul's place.

* * *

One summer evening, Paul came staggering into the kitchen from the street through the side door. His nose was bleeding, and he was holding his hand against the left side of his face. My mother saw him, shrieked, and immediately yelled for my father, who came running into the room.

"What the hell happened?"

"I got beat up."

My father's fist balled up. "Who? Who did it?"

"I don't know."

"What the hell do you mean you don't know?"

"There was a gang of them. They cornered me. And one of them started hitting me. I don't know who it was."

My father gritted his teeth. He started to put on his coat.

"When, where?"

"They're gone now."

"Why? What did you do?"

"Nothing. I didn't do anything. They just got around me, and this one guy started hitting me."

"Your hands. Couldn't you use your hands?" Meaning: Couldn't you fight back?

"No."

"Why not?"

"You never taught me how!"

I'd seen my father under pressure and he'd always been cool, but the night my brother got roughed up, I saw his hands shaking as a result of his anger, frustration, and inability to do anything.

"You're right, Paulie," he'd said, "I should have taught you how to use your hands."

The next day I heard Paul tell a friend, "What good would using my hands have done, it was the Faust gang." The Fausts, were a clan, a huge family that lived and controlled a neighborhood from thirty-ninth and Girard to fortieth. They were big, tough and mean. Every once in a while ten or twelve of them would march through our neighborhood and beat up some kid. Paul was unlucky enough to be in the path of their march. It was almost like a pogrom. All that ended a couple of years later when the whole bunch of them, for one crime or another, went to jail.

There might have been other reasons why my brother had disliked our father, but I was unaware of them. In their whole lives, they'd never had a conversation of any consequence. I never saw him put his arm around our dad. I never heard him say thank you.

Thank you.

Thank you for putting food on the table, for keeping a roof over our heads, for being proud of me. And yes, my dad was extremely proud of my brother.

* * *

After my brother was married and in medical school, he lived in a small apartment on Juniper Street in Center City. My dad was working twelve hours a day trying to make a go at another small Mom-and-Pop grocery store. Every two weeks we would deliver boxes of foodstuffs to Paul's apartment. The bi-monthly shipment was huge, consisting of canned goods, vegetables, steaks, chops and, because Shirley, his wife, was a smoker, cartons of cigarettes. And it was, of course, all free. The apartment was in one of the buildings that Shirley's father owned. Al Katz was his name, and he was a fairly successful real estate investor. I guess he was successful because he was making Paul and his daughter pay for the apartment. Our dad knew. Still, he delivered the goods with nary a thank you, nary a hug.

When my dad died of prostate cancer, we were all called into the hospital when the doctors thought his passing was close. I was thirty-two, Paul was thirty-nine. I was holding my dad's hand. Paul was standing at the foot of the bed. Our mother was there, crying. We were all watching the old guy fade. He seemed to be in a daze. Momentarily, he shut his eyes, took in a few gasps of air. His chest seemed to fall.

"Well," my brother said, void of emotion, "he's dead." And without saying anything else, he walked out of the room.

But our dad wasn't dead. Just as my brother left, our dad opened his eyes, turned his head, looked at my mother and me. A tear rolled down his face, and then he passed.

I wonder if he'd heard the almost disgusted tone in Paul's voice. I wonder if he knew he'd left.

My father and Paul hold special places in my heart, I wish I could have brought them closer together.

Eulogy for Paul aka Fink of Philadelphia

The Big Ben alarm clock that sat on the night table next to my brother's bed never, ever went off. Before he'd go to sleep at night, he'd set it and wind it; however, the next morning, thirty seconds before it was scheduled to start making noise, his eyes would pop open, and he'd reach out, push down the button, and jump out of bed, ready to start the day. There was so much to do, so much to think about.

I can say, unequivocally, that no one knew him longer and, in the early years, no one had known him better. He was my big brother, older by six years. I followed him around—I knew every nuance: every shrug of the shoulders, every lifted brow, every twinkle of his eye. I idolized him. In my eyes, he could do no wrong.

In those very early years, our family lived in three rooms in the back of my mother's store. We slept in bunk beds—me, on top; him, on the bottom. On Sunday nights, we listened to the old great radio programs. We sang songs together. He always had a song in his heart. No one, save Mario Lanza, sang the "Bluebird of Happiness" better. Of course, they were the only two I'd ever heard sing that classic.

Back then, we lived in an old neighborhood that was like a shtetl—close knit, everyone knew your name. And everyone knew Paul, knew he was special. Old men with bent shoulders used to come by, hands clasped behind their backs, and ask him questions.

They would walk away, one finger in the air, saying, "A gift, he has a gift."

And he did.

But, it was one he didn't take for granted. He worked at it, studied hard. New facts delighted him, and he earned every accolade he received.

And he wasn't afraid of physical work. At that time, in our family, everybody worked. By the time he was sixteen, he was an experienced waiter, working summers down at the shore and in the mountains. He wasn't into sports, but he was built like an athlete and was incredibly strong. He always walked around like he was six-foot-three. He could lift a huge tray of dishes up over his head, balance it on his fingertips, and navigate a crowded ballroom dance floor like he was Fred Astaire.

When I was fourteen, my mother said he had to take me down to the shore, get me a job, and look out for me. I could see him and Herbie Wartenberg singing as they poured coffee and served tipsy patrons late at night at the Pines Coffee Shop on the boardwalk.

His first true love in those early years was TEP. It embodied everything that made him feel good: the friendships that lasted a lifetime, the first chance to be an administrator of an organization and to make it into the great fraternity, the good times, the parties, the romance. He was an incredible romantic. I loved TEP, too, and knew all of its songs long before I became a brother.

Legend has it, he'd gotten a nickname at TEP that lasted for years. Actually, it was a title so fitting. Some fraternity brothers wanted to work in the Catskill Mountains. They'd gotten the name and number of an agent who booked summer help—basically college kids—into that area's kosher resorts. The guy was located in upstate New York, and the old Jewish man who answered the phone couldn't hear.

"Hello, this is Paul Fink calling from Philadelphia."

"Who?"

"Paul Fink. I'm calling from Philadelphia."

"Vhat?"

"Paul, Paul Fink from Philadelphia!"

"Who?"

Frustrated, Paul yelled, "Fink! Fink of Philadelphia."

Some other guy behind the old man yelled, "Moisha, who's that on the phone?"

Moisha yelled back, "It's Fink, Fink of Philadelphia."

"Oh, Fink of Philly? Okay, how many's he got?

* * *

When he was in college, Paul worked for a Jewish caterer named Harry Davis. Davis loved my brother, because Paul could get him help at the last minute.

One day, when I was sixteen, he came to me and said, "Ted, I can get you a job with Harry Davis, but you have to be in the union. Local 568. After school, go down to Twenty-second and Market. The union hall is on the second floor. Ask for Johnny Nicoletti."

So, I go down, and I open the front door. There's a wide flight of stairs leading up to the second floor. At the top of the stairs is a big, square- shaped guy staring down at me. He looks like he was in the movie *On The Waterfront.*

"Hey, kid, what you want?"

"I'm here to see Mr. Nicoletti."

He turns and yells, "Yo, Nick, there's a kid here to see you!"

Nicoletti is standing in the middle of a crowded floor, gathering guys to walk the picket line. The din was almost deafening. Nicoletti throws up his hands and yells, "All righta, shut up! I'ma talkin' to Paul Fink's abrother!" Then he puts his arm around my shoulder and says, "So tell me, little Fink, whata can I do for you?"

Gee, even the Mafia loved my brother!

He was indomitable. Nothing could stop him.

In his recent years, he started falling down, hurting himself, sometimes badly. But that didn't stop him. He had to be out there, had to be where the action was. Had to be involved.

About three months ago, we arranged a lunch. I was to pick

him up outside of his apartment building at twelve-thirty. At eleven on the day of the lunch, he calls me. "I'll have to meet you at one," he said. "I have two other lunches before you."

He loved being involved, loved being part of it. If a young person came up and asked him for advice on how to live a successful and productive life, this is what I think he'd say:

Feel the sun,
Touch the sky.
Live each day,
'Cause it flies by.
Put on your dancing feet.
Don't you know that life is sweet?

Go ahead,
Get on your way.
Don't you save it for a rainy day.

Live, love, learn, have a ball
And then, later, when you have it all,
Give back.

And that's what he did. That's what made him great.

I'm talking about Paul Fink of Philadelphia, and … the rest of the world.

My Darlin' Ru

The night we met was almost like the opening chapter of a Mickey Spillane novel. I was sitting at the long oval bar of The Venture Inn. It was a Friday night and the place was jammed. I had gone there with my longtime friend, S. Arthur (Art) Brown, a huge guy who was also the horniest S.O.B. I had ever known. On the way to the club, located at thirteenth & Juniper, he rubbed his hands gleefully and exclaimed, "This place has so many broads, it's unbelievable!"

It was a ten-minute walk from where he lived, and he was right -- the place was packed and the ladies were numerous. It took a while but I found myself a place at the bar and ordered a Dewar's Scotch on the rocks. I was not in a great mood that night. Hunting chicks was getting old. In the midst of the socializing chaos that surrounded me, I took to studying the cubes in my glass and contemplating my future. I was what you might call depressed. I was tired of the one-night stands, the dim witted, poufy, girls who had nothing to say. I studied the crowd on the other side of the bar. I considered the faces of the women, the forced smiles, the utter boredom. I was about to take another swig of my drink when I saw her. She was making her way thru the crowd swiftly, moving in and out. Looking behind her, she saw the guy she was running away from coming behind her. He was definitely chasing her. She picked up her pace. That's when our eyes met. Looking ahead, as she made her way around the bar, she was like a swimmer parting the people as she went. The guy doggedly following. Again, as she turned the corner of the bar our eyes met. I swiveled in my chair as she approached and she ran right into my arms. She put her arms around me and whispered in my ear, "Put your arms around me and pretend you love me."

Who was I to say, no?

The guy stopped short, and snorted something unintelligible and glared at me. Before he could say anything, I looked over at Art Brown. He had seen a lovely girl in my arms and was making his way thru the crowd to find out how I had gotten so lucky. "Do you know his guy?" I softly asked her as she clung to me?"

"I never saw him before in my life."

I held up a finger to the klutz before he could say anything. "You see the guy coming?"

The slug turned and saw Art making his way toward us. "He's gonna kick your fuckin' ass. Now get the hell outta here!"

Without hesitation the creep turned and disappeared.

Suddenly I felt better.

We still had our arms around each other by the time Art made it over to us, and the creep was long gone. Art looked at the girl and there was a recognition in his eye. "Oh, hi," he said. She nodded and smiled at him and then looked back at me.

"You two know each other?" I asked, never taking my eyes off of her.

"Yeah, she's one of the smart grad students that live upstairs in my complex on the third floor across the hall."

"Yeah. Really. I'm Ted. Can I buy you a drink?"

"I'd love one. I'm Ruth."

"Yeah, and I'm Art." There was a disgusted tone in his voice. She couldn't see it, but he frowned and shook his head, ran his finger across his neck and gave me the old umpire thumb. He was saying without verbalizing it, "This girl ain't gonna give you what you need."

I smiled at him. It was a, I'm-not-so-sure kind of smile. I just loved the way this girl was looking in my eyes.

I started to order her a drink. Art persisted. "What about that er… appointment we have to keep?"

"Nah. It's too late. I'm staying here. You go without me."

When the seat next to me opened up she took it. I liked the way she sat and nursed her drink. We talked for about an hour and then she said, "I have to get going, I have to review some papers for an exam I have coming up. Thanks for coming to my rescue."

"Can I walk you home, I know the way?"

There was no hesitation, just a smile. "Sure. I'd like that."

When we left, the slug was now chasing another girl around the bar. Art was leaning against a distant wall talking to a girl that was so drunk she was about to fall over. We waved to each other as Ruth and I walked out the door. "I don't think Art likes me," she said as I took her hand. I liked holding her hand.

"No. It's not that. He just thinks you're the wrong kinda girl for me."

"What kind of girl is that?"

"The marrying kind."

She squeezed my hand as I walked her home, and I started singing. In those days I thought I was Frank Sinatra, and right then and there I felt like him.

"You like to sing."

"Back in high school they use to call me, T the singer of G. I went to Germantown High. Does it bother you?"

"No. I love it."

Fifty-three years later I'm still writing and singing love songs to her.

I've been lucky in life. So far, I've survived many death-defying adventures, some paralyzing business failures and some hard times and managed somehow to outlast them. It took a lot of hard work, a love of life, and a fabulous woman by my side. I couldn't have accomplished anything without her.

Oh, we've had some fights, disagreements, who hasn't. For

instance, we almost didn't get married because the night before the ceremony we got into a feud inside a super market. We were there trying to stock up on the groceries we thought we needed for our honeymoon. We were going to go on a cross country trip dragging a pop-up tent behind my father's car. I got a shopping cart and we started loading it. Half way full we came to the tuna can section.

"I'll get four cans of tuna," I told her.

"Okay. Chicken of the Sea."

"Chicken of the Sea! No way. Three Diamonds."

"Don't be silly. Chicken of the Sea is best."

"Three Diamonds is the top of the line!"

"Don't be ridiculous!"

"What the hell do you know about tuna?"

"A hell of a lot more than you! My father use to make tuna salad and sell it in his store!"

"So did mine!"

We were now nose to nose and people were watching us.

I sneered and spit out, "Your father doesn't know diddly about TUNA!"

"What! Are you saying my father is a tuna dummy?"

"Yes!"

That's when she stormed out of the store. I watched her leave and started throwing cans of tuna in the cart. I was steamed and kept moving around the store loading the cart with crap, thinking she would come back in. But she didn't. So I went to the checkout counter, but the tab was so high, I didn't have enough cash to pay for it. "Excuse me but I'm a little short. My girl is outside and has our money, give me a sec."

The teller looked at me sarcastically. He had heard us fighting. "Yeah, sure. Good luck."

* * *

We had a wonderful wedding, a great dinner for fifty people at a restaurant called, The Steak Pit and a couple of days later we set out across country with our two Scotties, Buster and Banshee, on our honey moon. It was our goal to camp out in National Parks along the way and really see America. I almost lost her in Yellowstone.

We arrived at our campsite on the sixth night of our journey around seven o'clock. I set up the tent and asked Ruth to start gathering firewood for the fire we needed to make dinner. She agreed and walked off to collect the wood we needed. The dogs stayed with me. Luckily.

Because about ten minutes after my wife of eight days left, I saw Buster, my fearless male Scotty, tuck his tail between his hind legs and silently scoot under the car. Without a whimper Banshee was soon to follow. What the hell, I thought. I never saw him do that before. And then I turned and saw my darlin' Ru walking casually toward me with her arms full of firewood. Standing directly behind her on his two hind legs was an enormous, no-gigantic, Grizzly Bear.

"Ruth" I called softly.

"Yes?" She answered annoyed.

"Please come here."

"I will in a minute. Can't you see I'm collecting firewood."

"I can see that, but I really need you to come over here. Quickly."

"I'm almost done."

"Please do as I ask you."

"Why are you talking so softly …" And then she saw my face and turned her head, saw the bear, dropped the wood and we both ran for the car. The bear didn't even make a sound. He just shook his head bearishly, went down on all fours and headed for the nearest trashcan.

That night we held each other very closely.

* * *

Something else happened on our honeymoon that reflected the reality of those times. The plan was to drive to the coast and come back thru Canada, because Ruth's sister, Ann, was moving to Kitchener Ontario. Ann had been married for two years to Robert (Rob) Robinson who held a PhD in psychology and had just gotten a position at the local hospital. He told Ann he would go up three weeks ahead of her, secure a house and set everything up. Ann had just had a baby, a boy named, Jordon. So Ann packed up the house they were renting, put Jordon in a car seat and drove up to Canada to meet Rob. But Rob, he later changed the Rob to Bob, did something really stupid and cruel. After driving all day, and spending half the night unpacking, he told her, "I don't want to be married anymore." What an asshole RobBob was! What a completely rotten motherfucker! Because Ann is a fantastic woman. Beautiful, intelligent and charming, and like her sister, proud. She immediately packed up, put Jordon back in the car seat and drove back to the states. She had no place to go except to her parent's house.

When that happened Ruth and I were on the road driving toward Kitchener. In those days there were no cell phones, no credit cards, no ATM machines and we were almost broke. We weren't worried because we thought we could borrow cash from Ann and RobBob. But Ann had left for the states and RobBob, knowing we were coming was too much of a pussy to face us and tell us what had happened. The house that RobBob had rented was dark, deserted and void of the asshole who could now go bob on my dick. After waiting for three hours we found a payphone and made a collect call to Ruth's parents who told us what happened. "What are we going to do?" My Ru asked "We only have about eight dollars left." We had been away about three weeks. We were both exhausted, we had Buster and Banshee and were dragging a pop-up tent camper.

I studied a map. "If we take the back roads," I said, "I think we can make it. We can't afford to pay tolls."

"Okay. Let's go for it."

We drove out of Canada and were in Buffalo when we found ourselves going around in circles. We couldn't get out of the fucking town! It was like the old Abbott and Costello movie- bit, Slowly

I turn. All the signs pointed to the road we needed but there was a detour and following the arrows of that detour only led to another detour and then another, and another after that. I was now ready to kill RobBob, and started banging on the steering wheel like it was RobBob. Ruth started yelling at me for beating the steering wheel and we sat there for about fifteen minutes ranting and raving. What a way to end a fabulous honeymoon.

That went on until a cop came and directed us out of town. When he got us on the correct back road, the cop saw a 'just married' sticker on the back of our trailer. He pulled us over to make sure we knew the way. "Okay folks, sorry you had such a tough time getting here. I see you just got married. Well, I just want to say congrats and I hope you have many wonderful years ahead."

"So do we." We said in unison. And as we pulled away we started laughing. We were a team again, ready to face the future together.

* * *

"Five dollars!" I yelled.

"What is it, Babe?"

"What is it? It's this." I said handing Ru the notice.

I had been living in a beautiful apartment for about eight years before I met Ruth. It was a bi-level in an historic building on a large piece of land in the Germantown section of the city. The place had great amenities. A spacious living room with beamed ceiling, fireplace, and bay windows. At the time I was paying seventy dollars a month. What more could a bachelor ask. But then my landlord found out that I had married and as a wedding present raised my rent five fucking dollars.

"That son of a bitch." It was a half-hearted condemnation at best. "it's not that bad." It was almost like she laughed.

"Really? Well, we're moving."

"Really! Okay. Let's buy our own place."

"That's a great idea."

So we bought a place downtown at Twenty-first and Lombard Streets. It was a beautiful little trinity. The cost was thirty thousand dollars. The mortgage payments were sixty bucks a month. It was at that little house that we had our last major fight.

I was trying to get the fireplace going. Ruth was standing behind me acting as the director. "You've got to have paper."

"I know how to start a fire."

"You've got to pile the wood in a pyramid."

"Are you telling me how to start a fire!"

"You've got to put the paper inside the pyramid."

"Oh, Boy!"

"Be careful not to get dirt on the floor!"

Finally I couldn't take it anymore. I turned to her my teeth clamped tight. "God damn it to hell! GO UPSTAIRS!" I yelled pointing to the staircase on the other side of the room. She clamped her teeth together and furious she turned and marched to the staircase on the other side of the room. She was half way to the second floor when she stopped, her mouth dropped open and she yelled, "GO UPSTAIRS!" Suddenly she turned, ran back down the stairs and started, fists clinched, pounding on my chest. "I'LL GO UPSTAIRS YOU!"

I grabbed her wrists. "Maybe I should have said, go downstairs.

"We don't have a down stairs."

"Exactly."

"Let go of my wrists," she demanded.

"Only if you promise not to pound on my chest."

"Okay. I promise." Angrily, she snapped her arms down to her sides. "It's not funny."

"I'm not laughing. Listen, I didn't say, go the fuck upstairs you rotten motherfucker."

"It was your tone of voice. It was like you were ordering me."

"You were pestering me. It's not like I don't know how to make a fucking fire."

"And it's not like I'm a baby to be ordered to my room."

I hung my head. "You're right. I'm an asshole. I shouldn't have ordered you."

Suddenly she softened. She hung her head and whispered, "I hope I didn't hurt you. I love you."

"And I love you."

She came into my arms. "You know what? I think we should both go upstairs."

I smiled. "What a great idea!"

* * *

It was more than the physical attraction that kept us loving each other. It was more than her black hair, her warm smile, slim body, wonderful smile or the way she held my hand, touched my face, laid her head on my chest that filled my heart. It was the trust. She was and still is my best friend. I think about her and worry about her all the time.

We've had so many adventures. We've traveled to so many places and shared so many fabulous experiences.

Take the time that we went to England. Ann was with us on that trip. I got pneumonia from steaming off wallpaper in our new living room. I didn't know I was sick until we were half way there. I was moaning and groaning so much on the plane that the woman in the row ahead of us started yelling at me that I was going to make her sick too and ruin her vacation. Ruth and Ann literally carried me to the hotel where the house physician told me what I had and ordered me to stay in bed for the next four days. I was left alone while Ann and Ruth went shopping during the day and went to restaurants and the theater at night. They would come back to my room and tell me how much they didn't enjoy dinner or how lousy the shows were. What were they gonna say, "Oh, it was so great! You should have been there."

Anyway, once I got well we started traveling. I sat in the back of the car playing guitar while we toured England. Then we drove to Scotland. It was close to dinner time when we found a bed &

breakfast that had two adjoining rooms on the third floor. While we were unpacking we met a girl who was renting the other room on that floor. She was friendly, but a bit jittery. She seemed nervous. She asked if she could join us for dinner. "Sure," we said, "glad to have you."

As we were eating dinner I noticed her hand was shaking. "Are you okay?" I asked, I didn't want to catch anything else and that's when she told us the following story. "You see," she said tentatively, "I've been traveling alone, staying at youth hostels. Well a couple of nights ago I was at a place that consisted of two long stucco houses. Each one had about twenty beds. Well, the lights were turned off at eleven o'clock. Every bed was full. It was close to midnight when it happened. Suddenly, the girl about three cots up from me started screaming. And then another girl, on the other side of the room let out a horrible howl. Then someone switched on the lights and both of the girls were holding their throats and crying in fear. "Someone tried to choke me" they both said in unison. Then we heard screaming in the adjoining building. Two girls there experienced the same thing."

When we left the restaurant there was a full moon that pierced the misty streets. I can tell you we were all pretty shook up. We crept up the creaky stairs to our rooms, but the storyteller pleaded with Ruth, "Can I stay with you? I can sleep on the floor. I'm scared." She wasn't alone. Ann said she wanted to stay with us too. Ruth and I helped them drag mattresses into our room and we piled things against the door.

There I was with three beautiful girls in my bedroom piling shit up against the oak door, scared shitless. And for good reason, because that night about three in the morning, I heard, I swear to God, something out in the hall and I saw the doorknob being turned and tested.

The next morning we all thought that the way we acted was pretty funny. But then a guy walked out of the kitchen that looked exactly like Frankenstein's assistant. He was bent over, with a hunchback, and a face half covered with a Rorschach-like birthmark. Had he said, "Walk this way," we all would have run right the hell out of there.

We laugh about it now, and that's what's so important about love. Laughter. In tough times we hold each, work together and then laugh. Our humor, for us, is contagious and therapeutic.

Once, when our daughter had traveled to Paris for her third year college semester abroad, we went to visit her. Instead of staying in the dorms of Sorbonne University she had decided to search for a local French girl who wanted to share her living quarters. She found one who had a lovely apartment in a convenient, well maintained building. What she didn't know was that the girl had a boyfriend who sometimes lived there.

We met him when we went to visit her.

We had just arrived and were sitting in the girl's living room. Julie had just introduced us to the girl when suddenly the door to one of the bedrooms banged open and out came a black man with dreadlocks down to his shoulders. He stepped into the middle of the living room. His eyes intense, his head tilted toward us, his teeth clenched, his arms extended, and his fingers vibrating. What he said was, "Voodoo! Voodoo!"

Ruth and I stared at each other.

I guess what he was trying to do was scare the hell out of us, but it didn't work because Ruth, who was sitting next to me, grabbed my arm before I could respond and said, "Ted, you remind me of a man."

"What man?"

"The man with the power."

"What power?"

"The power of voodoo"

"Who Do?"

"You do?"

"I do what?"

"Remind me of a man."

Suddenly we were standing and doing the Cary Grant comedy

bit from the movie, The Bachelor and the Bobby-Soxer. Julie started laughing as Ruth and I started dancing in front of the Rastafarian and kept repeating the bit. The big man dropped his arms, his eyes were blinking furiously and he incredulously went back into the room from which he had emerged.

* * *

It wasn't just that my Ru was beautiful, or that she was caring, or a great mother, or that she loved me with all her heart that made her my Ru, it was her modesty. She was known all over the world. Really. She was a speech-Language pathologist that was recognized in her field as a teacher, an innovator and expert clinician and researcher. She created an Aphasia Center at MossRehab Hospital and was invited to present her work at Aphasia conferences nationally and internationally -in Austria, Denmark, Italy and Greece- to name a few. I always went along and was constantly amazed when strangers at those conferences would say, "Oh my God, you're Ruth Fink, I just read your new article!" or "Mrs. Fink you're one of my heroes!" She ran the MossRehab Aphasia Center, saw patients, wrote papers, created grants, was a founding member of a national aphasia organization called AphasiaAccess, and served as its president after her retirement.

Yeah, and in case I didn't mention it, I've been very Lucky.

Ruthie's Song

```
Cmaj7                          C
Let's go walking in the moonlight

Cmaj7                         C
Let's go walking by the shore
F
I want to hold you near
F
and whisper in your ear
                                     C
All those things I should have said before

Let's go talking in the moonlight
Let's go talking by the sea
There's so much I want to say
On this your special day
And that I'm so glad you're here with me

BRIDGE:

Em                           F
I know I should have told you long ago
Fm                         C
And listen babe, you know I tried
Em                      F
But you know how hard it is for me
Dm                   F
To tell you all those things I'm feeling
```

Dm   G
So deep down inside

So baby,
Let's go dancing in the moonlight
Let's go dancing with the tide
I guess all that's really left to say
Is I wouldn't have it any other way
And I'm so glad you're by my side

I'm so glad you're by my side

Juliet at Twenty-One

There is a Fink tradition that started long ago
When the Bisbolstivs left mother Kviv
And trudged thru the bleepin' snow
To settled in America and finally here in Philly
It's to write a poem about the ones we love even though the verse be silly
Yes, it's a chance to write a love song, it's a chance to be a poet
To say the things we feel inside and let the whole world know it.
And if this poem comes up short or if it's just a tad too small
Well, I didn't start the tradition blame it on your uncle Paul
No, the truth is it's impossible, absolutely impossible to say it all.

Today my friends I am very proud
As I'm sure you all can plainly see
For my daughter who was born this day
Has become the woman I hoped she'd be.
It's not just that she's beautiful and it's not just that she's smart
Or how she cares about the world at large that sets our Jul apart.
It's not just her sense of adventure, or her need to travel far
But that she wants to give something back that makes our Jewel a star
It's not just the songs she sings or the way she loves to dance
Or going to Cuba, or Peru, or Greece or living a while in France
Or the fact that she loves to party—she's the ultimate party girl
It's all those things and so much more that makes our Jul a pearl.

It's a rhapsody of romance, a chorus of compassion
a symphony of sensitivity, the honesty, the passion,
But most of all it's the music of the soul that sets our Jul apart
And keeps her here ever dear in the fires of our heart.

Jul/Julie/Juliet

The night before my daughter Juliet and Franklin Yates were married, Franklin's parents, Ernie and Jacqueline hosted a rehearsal dinner. Ernie, a highly regarded published poet said he planned to tell a story about Julie. He had once asked her if he could call her 'Jul' or 'Julie' and she said, "No. You have call me, Juliet." Well, Ernie told a wonderful, amusing story to a round of great applause. Then, as we had planned I stood up, pointing a finger and said "No, no no. I'm gonna tell you about my girl!" And I started to sing---

Hey, I'm gonna tell you about Julie;
I'm gonna tell you so you won't forget.
Yeah, I'm gonna tell you about my little Jul;
I mean Julie, I mean Juliet.

Now, I remember that girl as a precious little pearl,
And as shiny as a diamond ring.
When all of a sudden, she was off and runnin',
And into everything.
Sassy and spunky,
She could climb like a monkey,
And bounce on a trampoline.
Higher and higher, with a tiny pacifier;
Man, what a scene!

Hey, I'm gonna tell you about Julie;
And friends, I ain't finished yet.
Yeah, I'm gonna tell you about my Jul;
I mean Julie, I mean Juliet.

Smart and pretty, a girl of the city;
I mean, she's always out.

And let me tell you, cousin,
She has friends by the dozen;
And that's what it's all about.
I mean, she's so busy,
It'll make you dizzy,
The things that she gets done.
Yeah, love her at Fight, because she works day and night;
But she knows how to have some fun.

Whether she's out dinin' or trapeze flyin',
Or dancin' to that hip-hop;
(One thing is certain, her feet may be hurtin', but she ain't gonna stop.)
And let me tell you, Franklin, if you're looking for a rankin';
Well, she's right at the top.
She's one in a million, make that a trillion;
And I'm so proud to be her pop.
But there is this one little thing that you should know,
Before we get into tomorrow's big show;
Just this one little thing,
And, trust me, I'm trying to be nice,
So I hope you'll understand when I offer all of you this advice.

Hey, I'm gonna tell you about Julie;
I'm gonna tell you so you won't forget.
I'm the only one who can call her The Jul;
You and you and you have got to call her …
Juliet.

Julie's Balloon

Once upon a time and I don't know why
Julie's balloon flew in the sky
And when that balloon flew out of reach
We were all standing on the beach
Watching the clouds roll by
With a Mickey Mouse balloon in the sky
Singing higher and higher and higher I go
Goodbye , Goodbye, Goodbye … hello!

The years will come, the years will go
Where that balloon's headed we'll never know
Looking down from a sky so blue
Smiling at us as away it flew
Singing higher and higher and higher I go
Goodbye, goodbye, goodbye … hello

Matt at Twenty-One

It was blustery and cold that December day, in the winter of '83;
The storm had passed, but the snow held fast, and it was as slippery as could be.
Ruth's contractions were getting closer, and personally I was getting the jitters;
"What should we do?" I asked my darling Ru;
She said, "I'm hungry. Let's get us a Schmitter."
So that was how it all began,
The day another Fink of Philly came to grace the land.
So now, my friends, you can plainly see,
How another Fink from Philly came to be.
A tasty sandwich, a glass of brew,
A push and a squeeze from my darling Ru;
And voila my friends—the great Matthew.

Days fly by, years go fast;
Twenty-one winters have come to pass,
Each one filled with a memory,
That now, looking back, I can plainly see.

The day he first discovered his hand;
Playing violin in the high school band.
If you know him now, this may sound absurd,
But until he was three he spoke not a word.
He scampered about with no need for speech,
A bottle of orange juice clenched in his teeth.
It must have been something he did by choice,
Because he hasn't stopped talking since finding his voice.

I can see him clearly, playing second base;
Running to the finish of a cross-country race;

Watching him wrestle, the look of his nose out of place,
As some other kid tried to mangle his face.
He fought every match, unwilling to quit,
In spandex too large that just didn't fit.

He read Tolkien's trilogy when he was but ten,
And then he read them over and over and over again.
The novels he loves, the fiction he's read;
The hundreds of characters who collect in his head;
And he knows every line that Homer Simpson has said.
He finds adventure in every turn of a page;
Sees the beauty of writing, has a love for the phrase.

Golf, video games, scrabble, or football at school,
He has a passion for games and makes time for them all.
The light in his eye, the whimsical grin;
When he plays a game, he plays it to win.
And yet he's stoic like any true Philly fan:
If we lose we'll get by; we'll do what we can.
And that, my friends, is the sign of a man.

Now, don't get me wrong, perfect he ain't;
Unlike his mother, he isn't a saint.
At times, he can be a royal argumentative pain in the a$$,
But, despite it all, the kid does have class.

And on this day, when he's twenty-one,
I am proud, proud to say he is my son.

Sydney

I saw my cousin Sydney the other day. He of the deep-set narrow eyes and sagging, bell-shaped face. I saw him from my car as he plodded along. He moved, I thought, like a goose on land, shoulders back, head forward. I thought about stopping, but traffic would not allow. Instead, I honked. His head swiveled, but he did not recognize me. I've camouflaged my face with long hair and a full beard. So, without missing a step, nor ever losing his grim determination, Sydney once again became fixed on his mission. He seemed bent on getting somewhere.

I thought about giving him some money. His tweed topcoat seemed shabby and old, and he wore it open, set back on his shoulders. His stomach preceded him. His tightly knotted belt that accentuated his girth was too long, slightly out of position, and hung down to his crotch.

I worried about him as he went by, for it was not the greatest of neighborhoods, but before I knew it, traffic was moving, and he was gone.

Sydney, I calculated, was, perhaps, sixty-two. He was older, I knew, than my older brother who'd just turned sixty. My mother once told me that Sydney had not always been retarded. "When he was two years old," I remember her saying, "he was normal. Scarlet fever made him the way he was. Left him with the mind of a six-year-old. What a tragedy! What a shunda! What they"— (meaning my Aunt Eva and Uncle Hymie) — "had to go through!"

I know now that wasn't true. Scarlet Fever had nothing to do with it. Sydney suffered from Down syndrome. In those days people had to blame it on something other than the family gene pool.

He'd been a big kid; not in stature, but in bulk. To me, he always seemed like Humpty Dumpty: happy, pleasant, and ready to fall. My parents told me that was the way he always appeared. Maybe those had been happier times for him. Now, stress and concern had formed his lips into a tight, toothless line across his face.

Nothing had been easy for Sydney. When he was nine, he hugged a little girl too tightly, and the ignorant neighborhood grew nervous and demanded that Sydney be institutionalized. My aunt and uncle were not people of means who could afford a private care facility, so Sydney was sent to Pennhurst, a state mental hospital.

Pennhurst was a snake pit. Not only was it filled beyond capacity with the mentally handicapped, but it also housed deranged people of all types, including the criminally insane. Pennhurst had one of the worst reputations in the country for non-care and had been cited many times for staff who took advantage of, and were abusive to, its troubled inhabitants. Sydney grew up there and had remained in that environment as a patient until he was twenty-two. A cruel place to spend one's youth.

What sustained Sydney, however, was the undying devotion of his parents. Every weekend, for over twelve years, Hymie and Eva drove up to Pennhurst to take Sydney home. The three of them spent a lot of time in Atlantic City. In those days, before gambling, Atlantic City was a family resort. They rented an inexpensive room in one of those ubiquitous boarding houses that characterized the town, and walked the boardwalk. Often, they'd sit in the rolling chairs parked in front of the Chelsey and Ritz hotels. Sydney never tired of watching the hordes of humanity pass by.

When I was a kid, I worked in Atlantic City every summer, trying to make some extra money and, of course, I'd occasionally see them and say hello. I'd kiss my aunt, who'd smile and nod, and I'd shake my uncle's hand. "Where you working this year, Tedsilla?"

he'd always ask. But before I could tell him, Sydney would grab my hand and shake it vigorously. "Teddy," he'd say in his nasal monotone. He always knew my name. "How's your brother Paul?" And that was it. He'd nod profusely as I answered his solitary question, though I was never quite sure if it actually penetrated because, after the initial inquiry, he never responded verbally. From the time I was fourteen until I was out of college, this exchange occurred two, maybe three, times a summer—my name, and the name of some member of my immediate family. Nothing more. I know now he was letting me know he understood who I was and with whom I belonged.

When I graduated from college, I stopped going down to the shore, and I didn't see Sydney again for fifteen years. The death of his parents had brought us together again. I saw him at the funeral services, sitting with his two older sisters and their husbands. Once again, he knew my name: "Teddy," was all he said. But now, I was no one special. He knew everybody's names as they passed by to express their condolences.

At the funeral, people were all a-whisper, and there was much debate as to what would happen to Sydney. Eva and Hymie had always taken care of him, and his two sisters didn't want the burden. They both lived out of town; they both had husbands and children; they both had lives. They did not want Sydney.

Actually, Sydney had done something remarkable: When his father had his heart attack, Sydney had gotten him to the hospital and had taken care of Eva, who was bedridden at the time. He fed her and washed her down every morning, and then went to work. Since leaving Pennhurst, he'd worked steadily at a local supermarket as a clean-up boy. When he returned home from the store at six, he made his mother dinner and gave her her medicine. He also let the doctor into the apartment when he came by. He'd even contacted his sisters, but they hadn't come in to help.

Hymie died in the hospital fifteen days after he was admitted.

Eva died the exact same day, but in her own bed.

At the age of forty-five, in an eight hour period of time, Sydney had lost both of his parents, his guardians, and his only loved ones.

My father, who was Hymie's younger brother, debated the issue with my aunt Lucy. "Sure, he has a job, but he never really went anywhere without Hymie and Eva."

This was true. And they never went anywhere without him. If Sydney, no matter what the reason, wasn't invited to a family function, Hymie and Eva refused to go. Sydney, my aunt and uncle insisted, couldn't stay alone; they had this overriding fear that he might hurt himself, or hug some little girl.

"Sure," my father reasoned, "he goes back and forth to Acme, he cleans up there. He's been doing it for years. But what can they pay him? How can he survive? How's he gonna get around? They've got to institutionalize him. What's the alternative?"

In the minds of his sisters, there was no alternative. They planned to put him away. They swore it wouldn't be a Pennhurst. But how did they know what Pennhurst was like? In all the years he'd been institutionalized, they'd never once visited him.

They told him they'd find something nice. An institution in Scranton had a decent reputation. Wasn't huge, with a population of only twelve hundred mentally damaged people.

Sydney shuddered at the thought, and refused to go. "What's the alternative?" they said to him. "There is no alternative," they told him.

The next day, Sydney disappeared.

He'd walked out as his sisters were boxing up some mementos and family treasures. After a frantic search, the police were notified, but three days later, he returned on his own.

"I found a place to stay," he announced. And, much to their amazement, he had. Somehow he'd learned of and found a home designed for people with intellectual impairments—an assisted care residence for the mentally handicapped. A row house in Mount Airy that could effectively handle, and affectionately help, seven people. After searching for two days, Sydney, who'd gotten there on his own, pounded on the door. "I hear you take retarded people here," he said. "I don't want to go to no institution. Can I stay here?"

I didn't see him again until I saw him from my car as he walked down the street, and then, just today, I saw him at the bank. He'd just given a bunch of bankbooks to the teller and was attempting to find a comfortable way to lean on the writing bar of the counter. The position he'd settled on was a forty-five-degree angle. The writing bar was not something you'd normally lean on.

I tapped him on the shoulder. He stood up clumsily and looked at me. At the moment, I wasn't sure who looked more ragged. I'd just come off of supervising the demolition of a building, and as I said, I was full-bearded with hair down to my shoulders. My own mother wouldn't have recognized me.

But Sydney did.

"Teddy," he said, without hesitation. Then he turned away and thought for a moment. "How's Essie?"

"My mom is fine, Syd."

The teller gave him back the bankbooks, and he put them deeply into his pocket.

"Are you working, Sydney?" I asked.

"Still at Acme."

"Where you livin'?"

"Same place."

"Doin' a little banking, I see."

He patted his pocket. "For my friends."

"Sydney, do you need anything? Can I help you out in any way?"

He widened his stance and awkwardly put his hands on his hips, as though he were taking me in. He studied my bearded face, the long hair, the dusty jeans and declared, "No." How, he seemed to be thinking, could I help him?

We looked at each other for a couple of minutes, and then I smiled.

"Okay, Teddy," he said. There was work to be done. Tasks to accomplish. Bank books to distribute. We shook hands vigorously, and he was gone.

My Father Only Hit Me Once... er ...

My father only hit me once. It occurred at a time when he owned his second store, a small mom-and-pop grocery in what was then known as the 52nd and Parkside section of West Philadelphia. It was open seven days a week. The guy never had a day off, yet he never complained, almost as if he'd accepted his lot in life.

Every Saturday and every half day on Sunday, I worked with him as a stock boy and a delivery boy, filling shelves, stacking fruit, delivering orders ... and I did it all day. I never complained. For me, it was never work. If my dad needed me, I was there for him. I loved my father, and in my eyes, he could do no wrong.

On those work-days, he'd wake me up at six in the morning; he'd already been up for an hour. Breakfast would be on the table. It was always the same: cold cereal, milk, and orange juice. On the ride to the store in his old, broken-down car, we'd sing songs. He loved to sing, and I loved to sing with him. I loved being with him. I respected him.

The day he hit me had started out so brilliantly. The sky was clear. We sang, as usual, driving to work, and as soon as we opened, there was a nice flurry of business. But that afternoon was unusually quiet. During the lull, I asked if I could go to the corner drug store to make a phone call, and it was that phone call that had sent me into a depression. I came back to Johnny's with an expression my father had read immediately. I walked by him, biting my lip, went into the back storage room and carried out a case of canned beans. I began putting them up on the shelves. He carried out a slab of meat from the walk-in refrigerator, lifted it up off of his shoulder, and slammed it down onto the wooden chopping block, where he began to cut into it, but then he stopped.

"What's wrong?" he asked.

I needed to tell someone what an ass I'd been, so I told him. I'd always been able to talk to him. In the past, he'd always been sympathetic, understanding. This time, however, was different.

What happened was this: I would walk about three miles from our house to meet my buds at a place called the Hot Shoppe, located on the corner of Broad and Stenton. On Friday nights, the place was vibrating. I mean really jumping. Kids from all over the city came out there to hang. Maybe five hundred kids would be there to meet someone.

Well, one Friday, I'd met someone and we hooked up. That night, I walked her home and we made out. I unhooked her bra, fondled her breasts, licked her nipples, and put my hand up her dress. It was like we were so beautifully lost. When I got back to the Hot Shoppe, my guys asked me where I'd been, so I told them. And from the smile on my face, they knew I'd enjoyed myself. They pressed me, so I told them.

"You told them?" my father said.

"Yeah," I replied, "so I just called her, and she said that two of them had called, and..."

Dad never looked up from what he was doing as I related the details of why I was so distraught. He kept cutting the T-bone steaks until I finished my story, and when I did, I turned away from him and once again started grimly putting cans onto the shelves. I couldn't face him; I could see from his body language what he was thinking.

Calmly, he put the big knife down, walked to where I was working, and put his hand on my shoulder. When I turned around, he slapped me hard across the face.

My mouth dropped open. I was stunned. He'd never struck me before.

"I'm ashamed of you," he said, and I could see his lip quivering in anger. "What you do with a girl is between you and that girl. Do you understand me?"

Holding my cheek, I nodded that I understood.

He looked me hard in the eye, then let out a breath. "I know you do. The only other thing I want you to do is to somehow apologize to the young lady."

He never mentioned the incident again, but it stayed with me always.

* * *

Er...No. I was wrong.

I remember now that I was incorrect when I said my father only hit me once. There was a second time, but it was different. I guess I was eighteen at the time. I had just gotten off at work. It was a hot and humid Saturday night and I had spent the last five hours on the roof deck of the Bellevue Strafford Hotel in center Philadelphia serving wine and diners to members of a wedding party. As I drove back to the Mount Airy section I decided to stop at nearby Howard Johnson's, my favorite hang out at the time. On the weekends the place was jammed with kids and I knew everyone there. Walking up the steps I immediately saw two close friends, Art Solomon and Ross Fishman.

"Hey T," Art said, as I approached them.

"What's happening guys?"

"Nothin' man. This place is dead."

I hung with them, bullshitting, when Ross said this heat is killing me, and Solomon came up with a brilliant idea. "Hey guys, what say we go swimming. I know this street and there is a pool behind every house. I know this one place where it doesn't even have a gate into the back and the people are never home."

Art's father was in the real estate business and his father had told him so.

We all thought it was a stoke of genius and got into Ross' car and drove there.

At the end of Broad Street, the longest/straightest street in the world, there was an exclusive section called, Latham Park and that's where we headed. Just as Art had said, there was no gate leading to the pool. We parked in front of the path with no gate. Ross was content listening to the radio, Jean Shepherd the great storyteller was on and his car air-conditioner was working just fine. Art and I took off our cloths, totally naked we stealthily, walked, up the path, tiptoed to the pool and slid into the water. Don't ask me why, but Art had taken his wallet with him. Maybe he didn't trust Ross or had some girl's number tucked away in there. I don't know, but I didn't care. The water felt great.

Then everything went bluey.

It was the cops. We could see the lights flashing thru the bushes and we heard them coming up the ungated path. We immediately jumped out of the pool and hid behind a bush and made it into the next yard. We heard the cops cursing as we made our getaway. Like two jerks we started running. It was now one o'clock in the morning. "What the hell are we gonna do, now?" I moaned.

Art had a plan.

He had grabbed his wallet as he jumped out of the pool and in the wallet there was a change pocket. In that pouch was a coin, his lucky quarter. "Listen, T, I got this quarter." He held it up. "There's a phone booth on Old York Road. You know the one? We'll call Butch Segal and he'll come and get us."

"Are you crazy. We'd have to cross Old York Road." Old York Road was an extension of Broad Street and a major highway. "And it's at least three quarters of a mile down from where we are."

"What's the alternative?"

So that's what we did. We crossed the highway naked and walked bare ass behind bushes, and parked cars until was reached the phone booth. Luckily it was late at night. But it turned out to be just as unlucky, because when Butch answered the phone and Art blurted out, "Butch, Ted and I need you. We're both naked in a phone booth and we need..."

"Oh, get the fuck out of here, it's two thirty in the fuckin' morning!" And he hung up.

So much for great ideas.

We finally got home as the sun was coming up. We had recrossed Old York Road, grabbed some clothes off a clothesline and walked barefoot six miles to my house which was closer than Art's. Just as my house came into view, just as we were about to congratulate ourselves, we saw my father standing in the doorway. And he saw us when we saw him. He had been there since three o'clock in the morning and he was not smiling. He crooked his finger for us to approach and smacked us both on the back of the head as we entered, saying, "Schmuck one and Schmuck two." What the hell were we thinking? They had our clothes. They had my wallet. They had Ross who told them everything they wanted to know. "Oh yeah, Mr. Solomon your father will be here in about five minutes. Try to get some sleep, because in about five hours you'll be standing before a judge promising never to do it again. Me, your father and Ross' dad will have to be there too. I'll miss a half a day's work, promising you won't do it again. Oh yeah, and the fine will be fifty dollars." He walked away shaking his head, and cursing, but never said another word about it.

Good fathers: they let you know when you've done something really stupid, but they love you anyway.

The Fan

My wife thinks I'm an anomaly,
When it comes to my love for the Eagles;
But, in truth, I am not alone.
When they are playing, there are things I do,
That I thought would never be known.
But now the cat is out of the bag, and I'm exposed for what I am;
I'm proud to say I'm a freak with wings, and the ultimate Eagles fan.
You see, it's this ritual I go through, to help them win the game.
Everything must be exact; everything must be the same;
And it's this Sunday sacrament that she thinks is so inane;
And why she told her sister that she thought I was insane.

"He has to have his eggs by nine and take a walk at ten;
He has to step on certain stones—on that you can depend.
He'll cross the street at a certain place; it's all so so absurd!
And one hour before the game begins, he will not say a single word.
Everything has to be ready before the game can start;
His chair has to be just right, and next to him, a cart,
With his beer, his pretzels, his paper—everything must be just so.
What all this has to do with the Eagles, believe me, I don't know.
He sits there for the entire game, sits there all alone;
He will not answer the front door; he unplugs the telephone.
He yells and screams and hollers and gives me little peace;
He turns off the sound to the TV, he listens to Merrill Reese."

"That's so hilarious, and it's so unlike your husband Ted."
So, of course, she had to tell her friends exactly what my wife had said.
One was the wife of a rabbi; the other the wife of an attorney.
My sister-in-law retold the story, thinking it rather funny.
But the other two weren't laughing, their expressions far from sunny;

The rabbi's wife was the first to confess her personal tale of woe.

"He wraps himself in a blanket and sits twisted in his chair;
If you told him the house was afire, believe me, he wouldn't care.
Of course, he doesn't actually 'pray' for them to win;
That would be considered, in God's eyes, a moral sin;
It would be like a gambler praying to win a bet,
But sitting there in that blanket? It's about as close as you can get."

The attorney's wife just snorted and had her own tale to tell.
As far as she was concerned, the Eagles could go to hell.
For when it came to the Birds of Green, her husband turned into a louse;
"They scored once when I stepped outside, so he locked me out of the house."

So you see, I am not possessed; I'm not a deviate or worse.
Although my love for the Eagles might be considered by some a curse.
I will not stop my ritual; everything must be the same;
For without me, and Donovan, and Runyun, and Dawkins, they cannot win the game.

My sister-in-law was sympathetic, for now she understood;
In Philadelphia, football is an ill wind that cannot blow good.
It is the heartbreak, and the madness that turns a normal man into a goon.
"Well, be strong, dear, it won't be long, it will all be over soon."
"Oh, please, please ... please don't be silly;
Spring training starts in a couple of weeks, and that's when he becomes a Phillie!"

GALLERY

Leading his first big band

The Marathon Troupe

The Small Band

The Butcher Shop, 1938

My Mother and Her Mother, 1926

Mom and Dad, 1928

My Mother, 1948

My Brother, Paul ~ 1947

Me, 1947

Me, on stage at the Latin Casino ~ 1957

My Darlin' Ru

Ru in England

OTHER SHORT STORIES

Putski

Professional wrestling is a "sport" that never held my interest. I'd never been a fan, thinking it totally phony. Hell, they weren't hitting each other, anybody could see that; they were pulling their punches. No one could take a real beating like the ones they pretended to take, and survive, not bleed, and actually come back to beat on the other guy who, just moments before, had been pummeling them.

So when, fifteen years ago, my nephew Jordan had called me and told me I looked like Ivan Putski, I'd had no idea who he was talking about.

"Who's Ivan Putski?" I asked.

"Are you kidding me?" he shouted into the phone. "Uncle Ted, he's one of the most famous wrestlers of all time! His only loss was to Jesse Ventura. He's fifty-two and one, and Uncle Ted, you look just like him."

"I look like a professional wrestler?"

"Yes."

"Putski?"

"Yes."

I pretended to be aghast, then responded indignantly in my best Polish, "No. No Putski. Finkski." Of course, the kid laughed, and I enjoyed hearing him laugh. "No Putski," I reiterated emphatically. "Finkski."

A couple of days later, I had to go over to his house and I found a bunch of his friends waiting for me.

"He does look like Putski," one of them said, and I came right back with, "No Putski. Finkski!" and they all spontaneously shouted back, "No, Putski!" and once again I countered with, "No Putski. Finkski!" and joyously back and forth it went that day, and from then on every time I was in the neighborhood.

Then one day, Jordan called, and this time, he was really excited. "Uncle Ted, you won't believe this, but my school is having a fundraiser next month for the new gym. It's a wrestling match, and Ivan Putski is going to be there! He's going to be matched against Terrible Tim Maddigan. You've got to be there, too, Uncle Ted. Please!"

So, as much as I'd detested professional wrestling for the sham I thought it was, I told the kid I'd pay for a bunch of tickets for him and his friends and we'd watch the matches together.

Four matches were on the program, and Putski was the main event. The first three matches were just about what I'd expected, and didn't anticipate the Putski/Maddigan match to be any better, and even though the place was crowded and jumping, I was having a hard time staying awake. But then, I thought I'd gotten a reprieve. At the end of the third match, the announcer stepped into the ring and called for attention.

"Ladies and gentlemen," he said in a droning, nasal pitch, "I am sorry to announce that we have just been notified that Ivan Putski will not be fighting today. He is caught in a traffic jam and won't be able to get here in time for the scheduled bout. Taking his place will be..." But no one heard who would be taking Putski's place, the collective groan was so tremendous. At that point, I turned to my nephew and said, "No Putski, no Finkski. I'm outta here."

As I made my way out of the gymnasium, I couldn't help noticing people were actually heartbroken. Some kids were actually crying. I made my way up the aisle, out the main doors, and onto the street. Just as I'd gotten to the curb, a taxi came speeding up, and out jumped a guy who … who looked exactly like me! Same face, except the head was on a neck the size of a fire hydrant, with the fire hydrant on a body the size of a Sherman tank. Instantly, I knew who it was and, stunned, I said, "Putski?"

He looked at me and said, "Dah."

I slapped my chest and let out, "Finkski."

There was almost a glimmer of recognition in his eye before he said, "Finkski, do Putski a favor. Go inside, Finkski, and tell them Putski is here."

I don't know why, but suddenly, I was energized. I was delighted to do this for Putski. I went running back inside, ran right up the three steps to the ring and told the announcer that Putski was coming. He immediately smiled with delight and enthusiastically relayed my message to the crowd. An enormous cheer filled the auditorium, then got louder, rising to a deafening pitch, when Putski came running down the aisle, ripping his shirt off like Superman. I'd barely had time to get out of the way as he steamrolled by me, jumped over the ropes and into the ring.

But then, for some inexplicable reason—maybe he'd seen for the first time the resemblance between us—he turned to me and was about thank me, when Terrible Tim Maddigan barreled across the ring and clubbed Putski on the side of the head. Faster than Putski could say, "Thank you, Finkski," Putski was knocked completely out of the ring, landing on his head! He lay prostrate at my feet, a lump the size of an ostrich egg swelling up from his skull. I felt his pain, almost like we were the Corsican brothers. Suddenly, my head was killing me. Putski looked up, and I could see the birds and butterflies in his eyes flying amok as he tried to focus. Then he said, "He putzskied Putski, Finkski."

And I said, "Dah."

But I could feel my blood boiling. I looked at Terrible Tim Maddigan strutting around the ring, exalting that he'd knocked Putski through the ropes. His cheap shot had severely punished poor Putski. I clenched my teeth and tightened my belt. There was only one thing left for me to do. "Putski!" I shouted. "You can't let him do this to us! Get back in there and kick that bastard's ass."

And Putski said, "Dah."

So, with a head that looked like a surgeon had gone rogue by adding a kneecap above his eye, Ivan Putski climbed back into the ring and proceeded to kick the crap out of Terrible Tim Maddigan.

And that fight, ladies and gentlemen, I can tell you in all sincerity, was for real.

N.Y. Subway 1961

When the subway doors slide open, life's theater can be absurd.

Bluhluhluhbluh
Excuse me, sir, I don't mean to intrude,
and I hope you don't find what I say to be rude,
but could you spare me a dollar?
I would like to catch a train;
my English is so bad,
I really can't explain,
but I am lost, so very lost, I'm about to go insane!
Ah, thank you—on your head, may it never rain.

Bluhluhluhbluh
Pardon me, ma'am, but could you spare a five?
It is so very hard out here to survive.
Don't you see I'm hungry; I need something good to eat,
and food is so expensive out there upon the street.

Bluhluhluhbluh
Pardon me, my friend, but could you spare a twenty?
Now, why would you assume that I'm trying to be funny?
The truth is, I need a place to sleep;
I'm so very tired; I'm a dead man on my feet.
A cot, a bed, a mattress, a clean white sheet.
Oh, thank you, bless you, may your life be a wondrous treat.

Bluhluhluhbluh
Hmm, pardon me, m'lady, but you are a pretty lass,
and I could use, I must admit, a lovely piece of ass.
Do I have any money? Moi?
Why, yes, I have twenty-six bucks.

It was given to me, recently, by the nicest bunch of schmucks.
You do? You would? Ah, shucks!

Ah, America!

Elementary School

"You've got to go to kindergarten," is what my parents said;
You've got to learn to read and write; you've got to fill your head.
You're gonna have a good time, it'll be a lot of fun;
But you've got to go to kindergarten before you go to one.

You've got to go to first grade before you can get to two;
It's absolutely essential; it's what you've got to do.
You'll learn to print, you'll learn to draw, and when the year is through;
You'll feel so very good when you get to go to two.

Now you've got to get through second grade before you get to three;
You'll study plants and animals; you'll learn geography.
There'll be new things and old things and things you swore you knew;
But in order to get to third grade you got to pass grade two.

Now you've got to get through third grade in order to get to four;
You can't be playin' around all day; it just won't work no more.
All kinds of facts are important, and although it may sound absurd;
You cannot go to fourth grade unless you do well in third.

Now you've got to get through fourth grade in order to get to five;
The things you've learned are many; school's exciting, it's alive.
You're interested in many things, you're sure you know the score;
Because fifth grade is just one step up once you get through four.

Now when you get to fifth grade, you'll think life up there is sweet;
You'll tell everyone younger it was quite a dramatic feat.
But please try to remember, when you think you're hot and feelin' oh so cool;
That you've got to do well in fifth grade to get to middle school.

"So, you've got to go to kindergarten," is what my parents said;
You've got to learn to read and write; you've got to fill your head.
Oh, school can be a wonderful place, so kids, please don't forsake it;
It can be everything you want it to be for, in truth, it's what you make it.

An Epiphany on Patty's Day

Though it's been said before thousands of times, in thousands of ways, to the point where it is the cliché of clichés—the human mind is amazing! Mine won't let me waste it. Yesterday, I realized, once again, just how astounding a thing it is when, for an instant, it allowed me to be transported back to a time so long ago. In that split second, I was there—I could feel the warmth of the fires, hear the murmur of the sea, and smell the sweetness of her hair. And in that explicit moment, while relishing those succulent senses, it allowed me to understand and see something I actually never saw when I was there in the first place. Such a thing is an epiphany, and as the English would say, and Clive had come to repeatedly say, "It was brilliant, absolutely brilliant!"

Sometimes I feel like an archaeologist, excavating the nuggets in my past. Sometimes you dig and dig and turn up nothing but an empty shovel; other times, the artifact is —boom!— right there in front of you, waiting for you to examine it from afar. When such a rare, fleeting feeling and realization occurs, I feel like Indiana Jones examining century-old bones and saying, "So that's what happened."

What triggers such an epiphany, I wonder? What allows the mind to go back to a moment in time and recapture the exquisiteness so completely? Often, I am told, it's a trivial thing. For me, it was the movie *Return of the King*.

When I landed in Paris in 1961, I'd decided to make my way as a minstrel. I'd bought a guitar for twenty-five dollars and took to playing in the streets: in front of movie theatres, along the twisting cobblestone streets of Montmartre, on the marble steps of Sacre Coeur.

I'd been playing folk songs for about five years and was starting to get recognized as a regular at the Sundays jams at the Gilded Cage—now *Friday, Saturday, and Sunday*—a folk house that was established in 1935. It was out of the Gilded Cage that the Philadelphia Folk Festival was conceived. I actually sat in on the very first meeting to discuss the possibilities of such a festival, and left predicting that it would never fly. But what did I know? And what did I care? I was on my way to Europe to sing and play and have some fun; I was just twenty-one, and had nothing to get up for but the sun.

At that time my entire repertoire consisted of eight songs: Odetta's *Ox Driver* song; an old western tune called *Water:*; and the Irish ballads *Killgarie Mountain, The Shoals of Herring, The Wild Colonial Boy, Rothisea-o, Will Ye Go Lassie Go* and *the Claymond,* the last of which is really English, but I'd sung it as only an Irish/Jewish man might.

It was *Will Ye Go Lassie Go* that attracted Anita Longstrom to me. I'd been on French soil for less than a week when I found her and sang her that song. And she answered in that wonderful Swedish accent of hers: "Will you be my Jahnnie Guitar?" Truth be told, I was willing to be anything she wanted me to be, for she was absolutely gorgeous. What made her special was not only her spectacular body and fabulous face, but also that she was, in her stocking feet, six-foot-two! I felt like a munchkin when I stood next to her. But munch on her, I kin tell you, is what I did every opportunity that presented itself. She was indeed the most luscious lady—high cheekbones, the bluest eyes, golden blonde Viking hair, and a breast cup size of 44D.

But Anita was a sad case and suffered through periods of melancholy. Her lover, a Swedish diplomatic attaché, who'd taken her to Paris to be his secretary and sometimes lay, had spurned her. He'd put her up in a nice apartment and saw her, maybe, once a week. She was lonely when I sang to her. Hours before her hearing that first song, he'd told her in plain Swedish why she'd been brought along and that he would never leave his wife. She used me that night to forget about the attaché and, as I'd said previously, it was my pleasure.

She became my sexual partner, my business partner, and my good friend. In the beginning, we spent almost every night together and, of course, she became my performance collector and would pass the hat for me after I did my eight songs. With Anita collecting for me, we made lots of money. What made Anita sad was that she never fell out of love with the attaché and, realizing this, I would not allow myself to fall in love with her.

In fact, I was in love with somebody else: a Holland girl named Lidia. She was also a street performer. Picture a magnificent redhead with perfect skin and complexion. She was so beautiful that, despite her guitar never having had, at any one time, more than three strings, and that she could neither sing nor play the guitar, she made more money than any of the street singers. Sometimes more than all of them combined. Not a single tightfisted Frenchman didn't open his purse for her.

Yes, everyone loved Lidia, and I am happy to report, I was one of them. I loved her because, in addition to being a vision to look upon, she was so elated with the spirit of life, she uplifted all with whom she came in contact. As a matter of fact, she even made me feel good when she rejected me after I told her I loved her. She touched my cheek, kissed me, and told me she was flattered, but she was in love with an Englishman named Clive. She'd been waiting for his return for over a year, and she was soon leaving for the Riviera, where they'd planned, eleven months before, to meet.

"I wish you would come along," she said. "You and Clive would get along famously. We're supposed to meet on the beach in Saint Tropez. He said he'd get there sometime around the middle of the month. So that's where I have to go."

Two weeks later, as it turned out, I found myself in Saint Tropez. I had, in a moment of madness, bought a Zundapp motorcycle for forty dollars and took off for the coast. Anita was not with me. She couldn't leave Paris or the attaché, and although Lidia was in my thoughts, I never believed I would actually see her again. Still, when I reached the Riviera, the first thing I did was go to Saint Tropez and look for the beach fires around which she said she'd be. And, sure enough, there she was, her red hair almost the color of the flames. I'd found her! Who could miss her? Behind her, the sun was setting. It was twilight, and the beach fires had just been lit.

She was not as high-spirited, though, as she had been in Paris. No, Clive had not come, and she was worried.

"Where is he coming from?" I asked. "And why isn't he here with you?" *If I were he,* I thought…

"He's gone to the place all Englishmen must go. He's following an adventure. It's part of their history, their culture."

"And you're waiting for him?"

"Of course."

Oh, how that response made me love her all the more!

I was just about to tell her she was crazy when … when she looked past me, down the beach, and let out a sob. Tears rolled down her beautiful cheeks.

I followed her eyes to see a mangy, long-haired guy struggling up the beach under the weight of an enormous backpack.

Lidia wiped the tears from her cheeks; her eyes shone with admiration and love. And there, with the sun setting and the waves kissing the shore as gently as I knew she'd be kissing him, she said, "Clive, India?"

And Clive, smiling, looked up, stood up a little straighter, and replied, "There and back again."

Brilliant!

Over the years, I told this story many times, not really realizing what I was telling. I'd always told it because I thought it was astounding that Clive had taken a year to walk to India and back.

But the other night, when I saw the *Return of the King,* I had an epiphany.

Forty-four years later, I understood something about Clive and Lidia that I hadn't realized at the time. I guess the words were lost in the image of her running into his arms. They were both in love, and what I'd learned two nights ago was that they both were in love with Tolkien.

Del Ennis

Nothing is more pleasurable to me than lighting up a big fat doobie and walking the big dog through the woods. There, although leaves are crunching beneath my feet, I float as I walk, cast by the gentle whims of the wind to wherever my mind wants to take me. An escape of highs and lows. Sometimes, it can take you to places you don't want to go.

I sit on a rock that I have sat on many times before. This day in the amazing beauty of my woods, I think not of any successes I may have had, but of … of … Del Ennis.

Del Ennis?

Only if you are a baseball aficionado would you remember Del Ennis, who played left field for the Phillies and was part of the 1950s whiz kids. As I was growing up, he was one of my all-time favorite ballplayers. Baseball has always been a big part of my life; for nearly twenty-three years, I coached teams at many different levels and I actually got to meet Ennis when I went down to play ball in 1990 with the Phillies during Dream Week.

Dream Week is a portion of time where a bunch of over-the-hill guys get a chance to return to their youth and once again play the game they love. "There ain't nothin' like 'hardball'!" I'd heard Ennis yell to a bunch of his ballplayers. During Dream Week, famous ballplayers like Bowa and Unser are the team managers, and although Ennis was not my coach, one night, five of us over-the-hill ballplayers invited him out to dinner.

Since we were all new to town, Ennis suggested a place, and to our surprise, it wasn't what we'd expected. It wasn't a fancy place; Del Ennis was not a fancy guy. In fact, for the Clearwater area, it was moderately priced, but it was a place where baseball was the motif—pictures, mementos, memorabilia. Obviously, Ennis felt comfortable there, and the food was fantastic. We dined on superb T-bone steaks and crispy fries, and drank Scotch malt whiskey on the rocks. We talked baseball.

Ennis was no longer the svelte figure who once hit gigantic homers or who crashed fearlessly into fences trying to make a catch. He'd put on a lot of weight since his playing days; his frame fully occupied the captain's chair in which he sat and his double chin said all you needed to know. Now close to seventy, Ennis represented an era gone by. In today's world, with the numbers he put up in his rookie year alone, he'd be immediately signed to a multi-million-dollar contract. Back then, that first year in the majors he was paid eighteen grand. Eighteen grand! Completely laughable. He hit over three hundred, drove in well over one hundred RBI, and belted seventeen homers. He did get a raise that year, though ... of five hundred bucks!

I have always found it intoxicating talking baseball with people who know and love the game, and that night was no exception. Numbers and statistics and names of the great ones flew around the table like line drives, and throughout dinner, Ennis was upbeat and fascinating. But the thing I'll always remember was the story he told over dessert.

As we polished off our cheesecakes and sipped our coffees, Ennis began to tell us an amazing story about a game that took place in his second year in the majors. The recounting was, as I think back, startling, because it continued well beyond the coffee, the after-dinner drinks, and stogies.

I'm not quite sure why Ennis had begun the tale—maybe it was the booze—but he was serious as he recounted it, reflective you might say, and didn't seem to be telling it to us as much as reliving it for himself. He took us through inning after inning in that faraway, droning voice. They were playing the Cardinals…

"…When we got to the ninth," he said flatly, eyes glazed, "the score was tied at seven apiece. Those Cards had a man on second and third, and we had two outs. Musial was at the plate. We get two strikes on him, and then that son of a bitch hits a shot to the left. It was a hard-hit shot, a low liner, that just gets over the shortstop's glove. It's dyin' fast, see, but I got this great jump, see…" He grits his teeth, pauses. "But the ball," he said, "hits the heel of my glove. Hits the heel of my glove, see, and bounces away! They score two runs and win the game!"

He downed the last of his Courvoisier Cognac, then shuddered. None of us had said a word. What could we say? Of all of his accomplishments—and he had a lifetime batting average of 290, and 288 career home runs—in the end, he can only recall, in total detail, his most embarrassing moment: an error he'd made in 1947.

He saw our faces and realized it wasn't the kind of story we'd wanted to hear, but it was one he needed to tell. I stared at him and wondered what he was going through. I felt the booze had taken him into a place he hadn't wanted to go.

He smiled into the empty glass, then took out a handkerchief and wiped his forehead. A fleeting moment of self-reproach sat on his tight-lipped expression, when he looked up and saw us differently. Since the third inning of the tale, we'd been as far away as people in the stands. But now, he'd refocused and we were on him again, staring him in the eye, waiting in anticipation, like ashes ready to fall off of cigars.

"Hey, guys," he pleaded, needing to reassure us it really wasn't his fault. "Listen to me, I'm tellin' the truth. Musial hit that ball so hard, if it had hit me in the chest, it would have gone right through me."

Like the other guys at the table that night, I was stunned by the story that Ennis had told us. Here was a guy who was a star in the major leagues, was loved in Philadelphia, and the thing he remembers is the error he made thirty years earlier.

Only the Earth Will Abide (written in 1984)

Only the earth will abide,
That we have learned before;
Yet man has programmed his destiny,
To be like that of the dinosaur.
Eager to throw his fate into the hurling wind,
He continues to make the same mistakes over and over again.

Marching to the drum beats of war;
Building bigger weapons and arms like never before;
When will we learn what's important?
What are we trying to prove?

We must secure the future;
We must learn from the past;
For if we do not mend our ways,
We simply will not last.

Take a look around;
Breathe in the autumn air.
Feel the snow in winter;
Dance without a care.
Fall in love in the springtime;
Bask in the warmth of the sun....

Aaron the Young spit five times into the fire,
and danced on one leg as the flames grew higher,
and tossed five shells and two stones in the air,
so that all would know and hear him in prayer.
"Oh, great Munta, who rides in the sky,
for you I shall kill, twenty will die.
For you, great Munta, who sees over all;

For you, oh great one, twenty shall fall."
And he held his great war club over his head,
and repeated again what he had just said;
and the people around him began to chant;
"Munta," they murmured; "Munta," they cried;
And their cries turned bitter and louder, and into a scream,
and that's … when I woke from this terrible dream.
And I sat there shivering in the warmth of the sun;
what have we wrought, what have we done?
For at that precise moment, I wasn't quite sure,
if I'd dreamed of the future or what occurred long before.

Oh, I wish this were a happier song,
or a tale of holiday cheer,
one that would inspire our hearts to be strong,
where the message is instantly clear.

The Gnome Man

Dick Humphreys, the Gnome Man, was tired and fed up. He just couldn't take it anymore. He'd fought it for many years, and it had cost him. It tore at his gut that he now needed people like he'd never needed them before. Now, as he stood on his deck and stared out into the woods, all he could see was fuzz. He angrily gripped the rail of his deck. Shit. It was so hard not to be able to see the things he loved. He cherished his twenty-seven acres.

And friends. He'd never see their faces when he played his April Fool tricks on them. He had many friends. At his eightieth birthday party, just last week, they'd thrown a party for him. Over a hundred people had shown up. But that didn't matter.

The sun was beginning to set.

But that didn't matter, either.

He didn't need the sun to get where he was planning to go; he knew every inch of ground that would take him there. He worked his way back into the house and fetched his coat and hat. The weather was starting to change; he might as well be warm before he took the plunge.

He left the house and walked down the trail that led to the bridge he'd built forty years before, to cross the stream that divided his land. Like him, it was old and sometimes cranky. His dog had followed him out of the house and was with him when he'd reached the other side of the span. Together, they trudged up the small incline. The dog seemed to know where they were going; they'd made this little journey together many times before.

As he walked, he spoke to the little gnome statues that he himself had placed along the trail. Humphreys had, many years before, created Gnome Land and made his living taking elementary school kids through his woods, telling them stories about nature and the little people who inhabited his hills. He instructed them to keep an eye out for the gnomes, and every time a kid saw one, Dick would tell them a story about the gnome they'd spotted. Just thinking about it put a smile on his face.

The trail wandered for about twenty minutes and led to his favorite spot in the whole world: a collected pool of water created by the Gnome Stream he'd crossed. He sat on a rock he'd known was there, the dog beside him. He stroked the dog's head and gazed out on the setting he couldn't clearly see. When he closed his eyes, though, he saw it perfectly.

The water was now black and reflected the light of the fast-setting sun. He used to skip stones across the pond. On the other side, was a stand of trees, and in his mind he could see them swaying gently in the breeze. They'd just changed color and their leaves were starting to fall. How many times over the last forty-five years had he sat in this very spot and watched them flutter to the ground?

This would be the last.

He patted his pockets to make sure he wasn't taking anything of importance with him. He'd left his wallet, his phone, and his insulin on the kitchen table. He didn't need anything where he was going.

He stood up, and as he did, he saw his mother. He loved her with all his heart. He remembered how she looked when the doctor had told them he had Type 1 diabetes. He would, at that early age, have to learn how to take care of himself, learn how to adjust his blood glucose levels in order to survive.

Back then, there were no instruments to gauge what his levels were, so for the first thirty years, he had to gauge his sugar levels by how he felt. He gauged himself four times a day. Then, for the next twenty years or so, he pricked his finger, two to three times a day, so he could inject himself with the appropriate amount of insulin. Not once, not twice, but every day! Every fucking day.

And for the rest of his life, that's what he did: he'd gauge himself, inject himself. That ordeal he could cope with, and he did so for nearly sixty-six years. Time had taught him how to cope, how to withstand the emotional pain, until the disease wasn't satisfied and had begun to take something more: his sight. And that, he couldn't handle.

Jesus Christ, he couldn't bear not seeing his kids, his grandchildren, the forest he treasured, the meandering stream he loved. And that's why he planned to kill himself.

He would fill his pockets with stones and jump into the pond. A noble way to go—cold, efficient, deadly. He walked to the edge of the pool. The water was a good foot and a half below the ledge upon which he stood. He planned to leap out as far as he could, let the weight of the stones that filled his pockets pull him down.

He walked to the edge of the pool and readied himself to jump.

On the count of three, he thought.

"One..." He crouched down. "Two..."

And then he heard: "Dad? Dad, are you down there?"

It was his daughter. He blew out a deep breath and stood up. "Yes," he called back. He saw the light of her flashlight flickering along the path.

"What are you doing?" she asked.

"Come down here and I'll tell you." He moved back onto the rock, and she joined him there, and when she sat next to him, he took her hand. "How did you know I was here?" he said.

"I brought some dinner over for you and saw that you left your cell phone on the kitchen table, so I figured you were down here."

He heard her sigh, and he could tell it was a sigh of wonder. He could picture her looking up at the skies just the way she had when she was a little girl.

"What a beautiful night," she whispered.

"I wouldn't know."

"Dad, what's going on? You don't seem like yourself."

"Well, baby girl, the truth is, I'm not myself." He hesitated, took a breath, then said, "You know, all my life I've done things. I traveled around the world when I was thirty. I taught school in Alaska. I rode my Schwinn Super Sport bike across the country to bring awareness to the public about diabetes."

"I know you're in pain, Dad," his daughter said.

In the pause, only the dog murmured.

"Tell me," she finally whispered.

"Kourtney, you know I've always been an energetic person, adventurous, a person who never had to depend on anyone…"

"Ye … yes…." Concern sat in her voice.

"Well, that's who I was. I can't be that person anymore. I can't see, which means I can't drive, or find my phone, or work the land, or guide the kids who come to Gnome Land. It's over for me. You came here as … as I was getting ready to kill myself. I was going to jump into the pond to drown myself."

He heard her sob. "Try to understand," he said. "Just let me die. I don't want to be dependent on anyone."

"You said you were going to live to be one hundred and four. I can take care of you."

"No. You have a husband and three kids, my grandkids. It's their future you should be concerned about, not mine."

They talked for another fifteen minutes. He knew she was crying silently. He knew she loved him. She started to leave, took about ten steps, then turned around. "I have your phone with me," she said. "You should call your sons. They love you as much as I do." And she handed him the phone.

"Okay … okay, I promise I will. You head back now. I'll call them in a couple of minutes."

He heard her walking away, and for a couple of minutes, his mind was blank. Then images of an old friend came into his head. Joseph Homan was Amish, bearded, with long white hair. He was a master carpenter who had recently been near death. Ten years before, when Dick's house had burned down to the ground, Homan had built the new one. And he'd done a magnificent job. Everything was fitted—the beams, twelve by twelve; the rafters, four by twelves, all held together with wooden pegs.

Three days before he'd passed, Dick had paid him a visit. It was a Spring day. Homan had been on the porch, lying in a hammock, and Dick could tell the end was very near for his old friend. Still, he asked, "How you feelin', Joseph?"

"As well as can be expected. Sometimes the pain is unbearable, but I get by."

Dick's head dropped and he stared at the plank floor.

"Don't be so sad, Richard," Joseph said. "Everybody's time comes ridin' in, you know. Isn't that what you told those kids at that diabetes camp you once directed? What was the name of it?"

"Camp Ho Mita Koda. It means 'Welcome, my friend' in Lenape."

"Yes, that is it. Didn't you tell them, and teach them, to live their lives?"

"What's left?"

Joseph closed his eyes, gritted his teeth, and groaned from a flash of pain that seemed to run through his entire body.

"Make me laugh, Richard. You can do it. You are a gnome, a trickster. Open the shade so I can see you and the sun. The sun, and the warmth of the sun, is worth its weight in gold."

Dick had not lifted his head. He wasn't quite sure what the old man was getting at. They were outside. There were no shades.

"You know, Richard, every time I laugh, every time I see the sun, or a beautiful flower, or feel my kitten snuggle up close, it makes the pain go away."

Dick raised his head. "Why do you fight it so, Joseph? Why?" This was a question he'd asked himself many times.

"Why?" The old man had laughed. "I'm surprised you don't know … you, of all people. You, who has been fighting it for so long. Why? Because, Richard, life is short and death is forever."

Now, sitting on the rock, Dick picked up his phone and started to call his oldest boy, Luke, who was now forty-one. He knew the number by heart. After several rings, the phone was answered.

"Hey, Dad. What's going on?" Luke said. It always made Dick laugh when he dialed a number and the person on the other end knew who it was.

"Luke," he said, "I want you to know something, and please try to understand." There was a long pause. "I … I'm planning to kill myself, and I wanted to say goodbye." There was another long silence.

"Listen, Dad," Luke said, "I love you, but I could never really know what you're going through. I know its heavy, tough, and I love you with all my heart, you know that, but I could never put my feet in your shoes, so … so … if this is something you have to do, I understand. I won't love you any less for doing it."

They talked for another couple of minutes, then hung up. Then he called his youngest son, Kase, and they basically had the same kind of conversation. When he finished the call, he put the phone down onto the rock and walked back to the pool. He took a deep breath and started the count, and once again, he never reached three. Once again, the stupid phone he'd left on the rock had started to ring.

Who the hell wanted him now?

He walked back to the rock, answered the phone.

"Hello?"

"Dick! It's Jeremy." Jeremy's farm abutted Dick's land. Jeremy, who had a high voice, always had a piece of straw in his mouth, and wore nothing but farm overalls.

"Hey, Jeremy," Dick said. "What's up?"

"Have you had dinner?

"No," he said flatly.

"Well, that's great, 'cause I just made my special chili, you know the one. The one you love. I made it hot, man—hot!"

"Chili?"

"Yeah, the kind you like: hot! Where are you?"

"I'm down by the pond."

"Okay. I'll jump in the car, and you head back to the house. Do you have any beer? No? Okay, I'll bring some. See you then."

"Chili!"

"Can you taste it? Can you taste it?"

Dick Humphreys could no longer see and he still had diabetes. But on the other hand, he had not had Jeremy's chili in over a year.

Dying would have to wait.

*** You can see Dick Humphreys on YouTube. He plays John Tuttle in my YouTube video, Lost in the Ooze. A lot of it was filmed at Gnome Land.

Born and raised in Philadelphia, ***Ted Fink*** started writing poetry when he was five, stories when he was twelve, and music when he was eighteen. Throughout his young adult life, he was a restaurateur, entrepreneur, and educator. His unique businesses and life experiences helped set the stage for the tales and novels he has created to date.

From 1977 to 1981 he was co-owner of Superior Fish Company, the largest exporter of Anquilla Rostrata (the American eel), shipping millions of pounds to Europe and Japan. This adventurous business was the catalyst for Ted's first published novel, In Search of Joel Gomez.

He has written five additional books:

The Tales I've Told, a compelling collection of original stories.

Game of the Gods, an action-packed adventure novel about a journey into "maybe."

The Incident at Parkside, a gripping crime drama of a 77 year-old hero who returns to the transformed inner-city neighborhood of his youth.

Pebbles in the Fire, a mesmerizing tale that takes place in Nicaragua and is a story of hope.

Descent into Darkness, a thriller about a militant group's plot to destroy America.

His original songs and music enhance his intense, humorous, and poignant monologues. He is the ultimate performance artist.

Many things may change, but one constant will always remain: Ted Fink will push the boundaries of traditional storytelling.

Visit his websites at:

https://www.tedfink.com
https://twitter.com/TedFinkAuthor
https://www.facebook.com/tedfinkstoryteller

Made in the USA
Middletown, DE
23 March 2024

51615219R00275